CompTIA® Linux+™ Portable Command Guide

All the commands for the CompTIA XK0-004
exam in one compact, portable resource

William "Bo" Rothwell

Pearson

CompTIA® Linux+™ Portable Command Guide

All the commands for the CompTIA XK0-004 exam in one compact, portable resource

William "Bo" Rothwell

Copyright © 2020 Pearson

Published by:
Pearson IT Certification
221 River Street
Hoboken, NJ 07030 USA

1 2019

Library of Congress Control Number: 2019908202

ISBN-13: 978-0-13-559184-0

ISBN-10: 0-13-559184-8

Warning and Disclaimer

This book is designed to provide information about the CompTIA Linux+ exam. Every effort has been made to make this book as complete and as accurate as possible, but no warranty or fitness is implied.

The information is provided on an "as is" basis. The authors and Pearson shall have neither liability nor responsibility to any person or entity with respect to any loss or damages arising from the information contained in this book or from the use of the discs or programs that may accompany it.

The opinions expressed in this book belong to the author and are not necessarily those of Pearson.

Trademark Acknowledgments

All terms mentioned in this book that are known to be trademarks or service marks have been appropriately capitalized. Pearson cannot attest to the accuracy of this information. Use of a term in this book should not be regarded as affecting the validity of any trademark or service mark.

Special Sales

For information about buying this title in bulk quantities, or for special sales opportunities (which may include electronic versions; custom cover designs; and content particular to your business, training goals, marketing focus, or branding interests), please contact our corporate sales department at corpsales@pearsoned.com or (800) 382-3419.

For government sales inquiries, please contact governmentsales@pearsoned.com.

For questions about sales outside the U.S., please contact intlcs@pearson.com.

Editor-in-Chief
Mark Taub

Product Line Manager
Brett Bartow

Executive Editor
Mary Beth Ray

Acquisitions Editor
Paul Carlstroem

Development Editor
Christopher Cleveland

Managing Editor
Sandra Schroeder

Project Editor
Mandie Frank

Copy Editor
Bart Reed

Technical Editor
Casey Boyles

Editorial Assistant
Cindy Teeters

Designer
Chuti Prasertsith

Composition
codeMantra

Indexer
Ken Johnson

Proofreader
Karen Davis

Credits

Figure 1-2   Screenshot of GNU GRUB © 2010-2018 Free Software Foundation, Inc.

Figure 1-3   Screenshot of GNU GRUB © 2010-2018 Free Software Foundation, Inc.

Figure 3-1   Screenshot of NMTUI interface © 2005–2014 The GNOME Project

Figure 3-2   Screenshot of NMTUI interface © 2005–2014 The GNOME Project

Figure 7-1   Screenshot of Aptitude Utility © The Distro Tracker Developers

Figure 9-1   Screenshot of GNU nano © Chris Allegretta

Figure 9-2   Screenshot of vi Editor © Bill Joy

Figure 21-1   Screenshot of Iftop © Paul Warren

Figure 21-2   Screenshot of Wireshark © Wireshark Foundation

Figure 21-3   Screenshot of mtr © BitWizard

Figure 22-1   Screenshot of Top © William LeFebvre

Cover   Pressmaster/Shutterstock

Contents at a Glance

Table of Contents

Part II: Systems Operation and Maintenance

About the Author

At the impressionable age of 14, **William "Bo" Rothwell** crossed paths with a TRS-80 Micro Computer System (affectionately known as a "Trash 80"). Soon after the adults responsible for Bo made the mistake of leaving him alone with the TSR-80, he immediately dismantled it and held his first computer class, showing his friends what made this "computer thing" work.

Since this experience, Bo's passion for understanding how computers work and sharing this knowledge with others has resulted in a rewarding career in IT training. His experience includes Linux, Unix, IT Security, DevOps, and programming languages such as Perl, Python, Tcl, and BASH. He is the founder and lead instructor of One Course Source, an IT training organization.

About the Technical Reviewer

Casey Boyles started working in the IT field more than 27 years ago and quickly moved on to distributed application and database development. Casey later moved on to technical training and course development, where he specializes in full stack Internet application development, database architecture, and systems security. Casey typically spends his time smoking cigars while "reading stuff and writing stuff."

Dedications

As always, I owe more gratitude than I could ever provide to those in my life who support me the most: Sarah, Julia, Mom, and Dad.

Acknowledgments

To everyone at Pearson who helped make this book come to life, I thank you. I know that this is a team effort, and I appreciate everyone's hard work.

Special thanks go to Mary Beth Ray. I'm very sad that this will be our last book together. I have enjoyed working with you the last few years. Good fortune in your new journey in life. :)

We Want to Hear from You!

As the reader of this book, you are our most important critic and commentator. We value your opinion and want to know what we're doing right, what we could do better, what areas you'd like to see us publish in, and any other words of wisdom you're willing to pass our way.

We welcome your comments. You can email or write to let us know what you did or didn't like about this book—as well as what we can do to make our books better.

Please note that we cannot help you with technical problems related to the topic of this book.

When you write, please be sure to include this book's title and author as well as your name and email address. We will carefully review your comments and share them with the author and editors who worked on the book.

Email: community@informit.com

Reader Services

Register your copy of *CompTIA Linux+ Portable Command Guide* at www.pearsonitcertification.com for convenient access to downloads, updates, and corrections as they become available. To start the registration process, go to www.pearsonitcertification.com/register and log in or create an account.* Enter the product ISBN 9780135591840 and click Submit. When the process is complete, you will find any available bonus content under Registered Products.

*Be sure to check the box that you would like to hear from us to receive exclusive discounts on future editions of this product.

Introduction

In 2019, COMPTIA released a new version of the Linux+ certification exam. This new exam isn't just an update from the last certification, but really a completely new exam.

The previous Linux+ certification was titled "CompTIA Linux+ powered by LPI." However, the new certification no longer involves LPI (the Linux Professional Institute). As a result, the format and topics are significantly different.

For example, the new certification only requires passing one exam, not two. Additionally, the exam objectives have undergone a major rewrite, and you will see several DevOps-based topics not included in the previous certification.

Additionally, you should be prepared for a handful of scenario questions that you will be asked to answer based on a situation described to you. However, most of the exam will be multiple choice, much like the previous exams.

Use this book as a reference to all the key exam-testable topics. This book makes for an excellent roadmap on your journey to learning Linux and passing the Linux+ certification exam.

Good luck!

—William "Bo" Rothwell
May 18, 2019

Who Should Read This Book

This book is for those people preparing for the CompTIA Linux+ certification exam, whether through self-study, on-the-job training and practice, or study via a training program. The book provides you with the depth of knowledge to help you pass the exam as well as introduces valuable features of the Linux operating system.

Command Syntax Conventions

The conventions used to present command syntax in this book are as follows:

- **Boldface** indicates commands and keywords that are entered literally as shown. In actual configuration examples and output (not general command syntax), boldface indicates commands that are manually input by the user (such as a **show** command).
- *Italic* indicates arguments for which you supply actual values.
- Vertical bars (|) separate alternative, mutually exclusive elements.
- Square brackets ([ ]) indicate an optional element.
- Braces ({ }) indicate a required choice.
- Braces within brackets ([{ }]) indicate a required choice within an optional element.

Organization of This Book

Because this book is designed to help you prepare for the CompTIA Linux+ certification exam, I have opted to match the organization of the book to align with the exam objective topics. There are 27 topics for the exam, and those topics match with each of the 27 chapters in this book. This organization should help aid you in your preparation for the exam.

Here is the layout for each section of this book:

Part I: Hardware and System Configuration

- **Chapter 1, "Explain Linux boot process concepts"**—You will learn the process of how the system behaves during the boot process and how the administrator can modify this behavior in this chapter.

- **Chapter 2, "Given a scenario, install, configure, and monitor kernel modules"**—In this chapter, you will explore kernel modules, which are small programs that add to the functionality of the kernel.

- **Chapter 3, "Given a scenario, configure and verify network connection parameters"**—You will learn how to set up network interfaces in this chapter.

- **Chapter 4, "Given a scenario, manage storage in a Linux environment"**—In this chapter, you learn how to create partitions and filesystems using utilities like fdisk and mkfs.

- **Chapter 5, "Compare and contrast cloud and virtualization concepts and technologies"**—The focus of this chapter is the core concepts of virtual OS instances, both on a local system and in the cloud.

- **Chapter 6, "Given a scenario, configure localization options"**—In this chapter, you will discover how to modify the system to behave differently in different locations throughout the world.

Part II: Systems Operation and Maintenance

- **Chapter 7, "Given a scenario, conduct software installations, configurations, updates, and removals"**—You will learn in this chapter how to manage software packages.

- **Chapter 8, "Given a scenario, manage users and groups"**—This chapter focuses on utilities that allow you to add, modify, and delete user and group accounts.

- **Chapter 9, "Given a scenario, create, modify, and redirect files"**—Learn how to create files using commonly used Linux editors as well as sending the output of commands into files.

- **Chapter 10, "Given a scenario, manage services"**—The focus of this chapter is services, which are programs that run on the local system and provide some sort of feature or function to either the local system or remote systems.

- **Chapter 11, "Summarize and explain server roles**—The understanding of servers and the role they play on Linux systems are explored in this chapter.

- **Chapter 12, "Given a scenario, automate and schedule jobs"**—Learn the process of scheduling programs and applications to run at future times.

- **Chapter 13, "Explain the use and operation of Linux devices"**—Learn how to manage devices, such as USB devices, memory, and physical storage devices.

- **Chapter 14, "Compare and contrast Linux graphical user interfaces"**—Explore the wide variety of graphical user interfaces (GUIs) in this chapter.

Part III: Security

- **Chapter 15, "Given a scenario, apply or acquire the appropriate user and/or group permissions and ownership"**—Building on the concepts you learned in Chapter 8, this chapter will focus on how to manage permissions that provide access to files and directories.

- **Chapter 16, "Given a scenario, configure and implement appropriate access and authentication methods"**—This chapter explores the different authentication methods, a feature that allows users to gain access to the system.

- **Chapter 17, "Summarize security best practices in a Linux environment"**— This chapter provides a high-level overview of important security best practices to implement on Linux systems.

- **Chapter 18, "Given a scenario, implement logging services"**—Learn how system logging is configured in this chapter.

- **Chapter 19, "Given a scenario, implement and configure Linux firewalls"**— The focus of this chapter is the concept and configuration of firewalls on Linux systems.

- **Chapter 20, "Given a scenario, backup, restore, and compress files"**—Protect against data loss by learning how to create backups in this chapter.

Part IV: Linux Troubleshooting and Diagnostics

- **Chapter 21, "Given a scenario, analyze system properties and remediate accordingly"**—This chapter explores the essentials of troubleshooting common problems on Linux systems.

- **Chapter 22, "Given a scenario, analyze system processes in order to optimize performance"**—The focus of this chapter is tools and concepts related to determining if a Linux system is performing at an optimal level.

- **Chapter 23, "Given a scenario, analyze and troubleshoot user issues"**—Learn how to troubleshoot common problems related to user accounts in this chapter.

- **Chapter 24, "Given a scenario, analyze and troubleshoot application and hardware issues"**—This chapter provides you with the concepts and tools needed to discover and resolve issues related to system hardware and applications.

Part V: Automation and Scripting

- **Chapter 25, "Given a scenario, deploy and execute basic BASH scripts"**—Shell scripts, a collection of shell commands, are covered in this chapter.

- **Chapter 26, "Given a scenario, carry out version control using Git"**—In this chapter, you will learn how to manage a Git repository.

- **Chapter 27, "Summarize orchestration processes and concepts"**—In this chapter, you will explore orchestration, which includes the process of quickly and effectively installing and configuring systems.

Did I Miss Anything?

I am always interested to hear how my students, and now readers of my books, do on both certification exams and future studies. If you would like to contact me and let me know how this book helped you in your certification goals, please do so. Did I miss anything? Let me know. Contact me at bo@OneCourseSource.com or through the Pearson IT Certification website, http://www.pearsonitcertification.com/.

## CHAPTER 1

Explain Linux boot process concepts

This chapter provides information and commands concerning the following topics:

Boot loaders

- GRUB
- GRUB2

Boot options

- UEFI/EFI
- PXE
- NFS
- Boot from ISO
- Boot from HTTP/FTP

File locations

- /etc/default/grub
- /etc/grub2.cfg
- /boot
- /boot/grub
- /boot/grub2
- /boot/efi

Boot modules and files

- Commands (mkinitrd, dracut, grub2-install, grub2-mkconfig)
- initramfs
- vmlinuz
- vmlinux

Kernel panic

Boot Loaders

A boot loader is a software piece that is designed to handle the initial booting of the operating system (OS). Figure 1.1 provides an overview of the boot process and the Bootloader's place in this process.

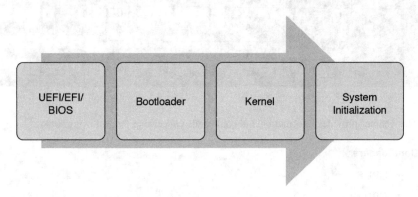

Figure 1.1   Overview of the Boot Process

UEFI/EFI/BIOS performs sanity checks and then loads the bootloader. See the "UEFI/EFI" subsection in this chapter for more details.

The standard Linux bootloader is the GRand Unified Bootloader (GRUB or GRUB2). It is responsible for loading the kernel and associated kernel modules (or *libraries*) stored in a file referred to as the **initramfs** (see the "initramfs" subsection of this chapter for more details).

The kernel is loaded from the hard disk, performs some critical boot tasks, and then passes control of the boot process to the system initialization software.

The three different system initialization systems in Linux are SysVinit (the oldest), Upstart, and Systemd (currently the most widely used). The system initialization is responsible for starting system services.

GRUB

The GRand Unified Bootloader, also called Legacy GRUB, is an older bootloader that is rarely used on modern Linux systems. Most of the configuration files and commands on the exam focus on GRUB2, an improved version of GRUB. See the "GRUB2" subsection next for more details.

GRUB2

GRUB2 is designed as a replacement for Legacy GRUB. There are several changes between the two, including the following:

- Different configuration files.
- GRUB2 supports more devices to boot from, including LVM (Logical Volume Management) and software RAID devices.
- GRUB2 supports UEFI and EFI. See the "UEFI/EFI" subsection in this chapter for more details.

Expect exam questions to focus on GRUB2, as Legacy GRUB is rarely used in modern Linux distributions.

Boot Options

GRUB2 allows you to boot from different media. This section focuses on which media you can boot from as well as how to boot from the different media sources.

During the boot process, you can interact with the boot loader. This is normally useful for one of the following reasons:

- To boot to an alternative stanza
- To modify the existing boot parameters

This interaction starts with the boot menu screen, as demonstrated in Figure 1.2.

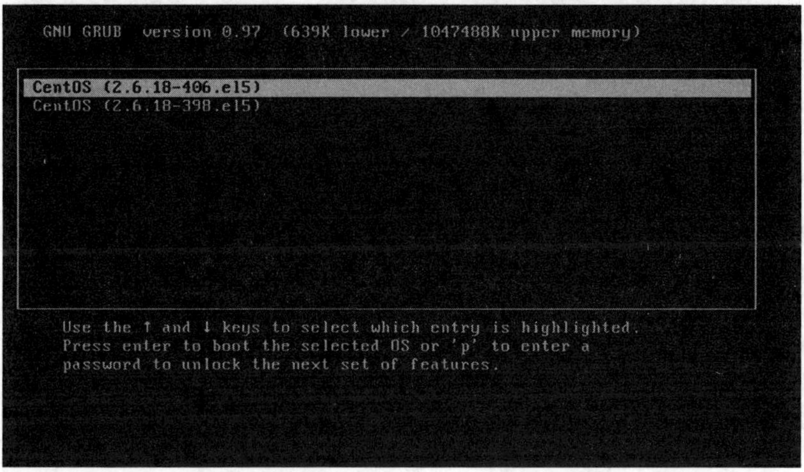

Figure 1.2   The GRUB Boot Menu Screen

The following table describes the commands available at the GRUB boot menu screen:

Command	Description
Arrow keys	Used to select a stanza.
e	Edit the currently selected stanza.
c	Enter a GRUB command prompt.
p	Only visible when a password is required to edit a stanza; use **p** to enter the required password.

If you edit a stanza, a new screen with different menu options will be provided. See Figure 1.3 for a demonstration.

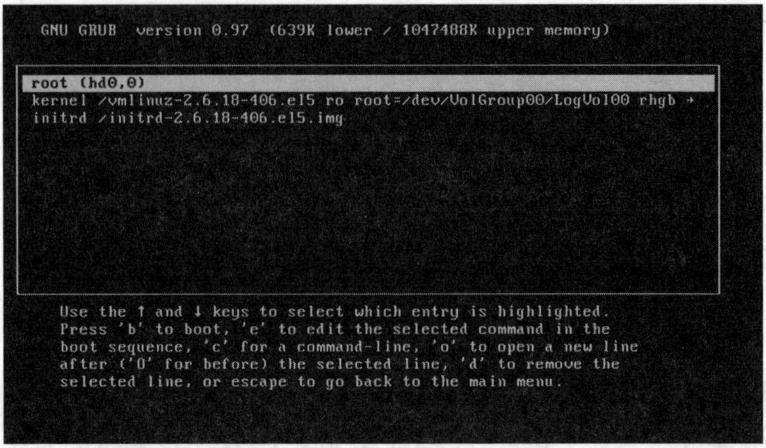

Figure 1.3   The GRUB Stanza-Editing Screen

The following table describes the commands available at the GRUB stanza-editing screen:

Command	Description
Arrow keys	Used to select a stanza.
e	Edit the currently selected line.
c	Enter a GRUB command prompt.
o	Open (create) a new line below the current line.
O	Open (create) a new line above the current line.
d	Remove the selected line.
b	Boot the current stanza.
[ESC]	The Escape key returns you to the main menu.

UEFI/EFI

Basic Input/Output System (BIOS), Unified Extensible Firmware Interface (UEFI), and Extensible Firmware Interface (EFI) are all similar in that they are used to provide a connection between a system's firmware and the operating system. These programs are provided by the system's manufacturer and are able to start the boot process.

BIOS is only mentioned here in passing. It is an older software piece that officially will no longer be supported after 2020. However, many UEFI and EFI systems are often referred to as "BIOS," hence the purpose of mentioning the term here.

UEFI is the successor to EFI and considered the standard in most modern systems.

In regard to the exam, you should be aware that UEFI/EFI is the software piece that starts the boot process. It is the component that starts the bootloader. Additionally, it is configurable; for example, you can specify which devices (hard disk, CD/DVD, and so on) to boot from and in which order to attempt to find a bootload on these devices.

PXE

Preboot Execution Environment (PXE) allows you to boot a system across the network, assuming that a boot server has been created on the network. PXE uses a Dynamic Host Configuration Protocol (DHCP) server to obtain network configuration information, such as an IP address and subnet address.

The boot server listens for PXE boot requests and then provides an operating system to the client system. Typically this operating system will call the client machine to perform an installation so further PXE boots are not required.

Note that PXE boots are initiated from BIOS/UEFI/EFI software.

NFS

A Network File System (NFS) boot is similar to a PXE boot; however, there are a few differences:

- The bootloader, not BIOS/UEFI/EFI, normally initiates the boot from the NFS server process.
- Client network information normally comes from a DHCP server, but it can be statically assigned.
- NFS could be used for the root filesystem, requiring only a small **/boot** filesystem that holds the kernel files.

Boot from ISO

There are several Live Linux distributions that allow you to boot directly from a CD or DVD. This technique is referred to as "booting from an ISO" because the file format used to store the operating system on this media is called an ISO image.

Here are several advantages to and reasons for booting from an ISO:

- The system may be a thin client with no hard drive.
- Booting from a security-based ISO image can be helpful in resolving issues (virus, worms, or other security compromises) on the host OS.
- Some Live Linux distributions can fix problems with booting the host OS.
- A ISO can also be used to install a new distribution on the system.

In most cases, booting from an ISO image requires instructing BIOS/UEFI/EFI to boot from the drive that contains the ISO media. However, it is possible to configure GRUB to boot from ISO media as well (although this tends to be rarely done).

Boot from HTTP/FTP

Booting from HTTP or FTP is almost exclusively done to perform an installation from an install server. This sort of media is normally "read-only," meaning it doesn't offer a good method of providing a live filesystem in which one can both read and write data.

File Locations

This section focuses on the file and directories where legacy GRUB and GRUB2 configuration data is stored.

/etc/default/grub

GRUB 2 is configured by editing either the **/etc/default/grub** file or the files in the **/etc/grub.d** directory. The files in the **/etc/grub.d** directory are "advanced files" and beyond the scope of this book. These files are typically created by software developers and inserted into this directory as part of the installation of a software package.

Here's an example of a typical **/etc/default/grub** file:

```
[root@localhost ~]$ cat /boot/grub/grub.conf
GRUB_TIMEOUT=5
GRUB_DEFAULT=saved
GRUB_TERMINAL_OUTPUT="console"
GRUB_CMDLINE_LINUX="crashkernel=auto rhgb quiet"
```

Figure 1.4 describes the typical settings of the **/etc/default/grub** file.

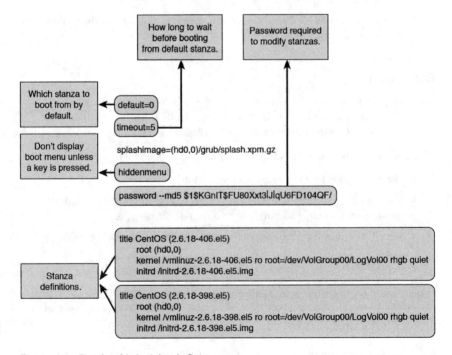

Figure 1.4   The **/etc/default/grub** Components

/etc/grub2.cfg

The primary configuration file for GRUB2 is the **/boot/grub2/grub.cfg** file. This file should never be edited directly, as it is created by the **grub2-mkconfig** command (see the "grub2-mkconfig" subsection in this chapter for more details).

The **/etc/grub2.cfg** file is just a symbolic link to the **/boot/grub2/grub.cfg** file.

/boot

The **/boot** directory is the location where boot files are found. This includes the following:

- The kernel files (for example, **vmlinuz-4.17.8-200.fc32.x86_64**)
- The **initramfs** files (for example, **initramfs-4.17.8-200.fc32.x86_64.img**)
- The **grub2** directory, which holds GRUB2 configuration files.

/boot/grub

The **/boot/grub** directory is the location for traditional GRUB configuration files.

/boot/grub2

The **/boot/grub2** directory is the location for GRUB2 configuration files.

/boot/efi

On systems that utilize UEFI, the **/boot/efi** directory is the location for GRUB configuration files.

Boot Modules and Files

Kernel modules are small pieces of code that provide more functionality to the kernel. See Chapter 2, "Given a scenario, install, configure, and monitor kernel modules," for more details regarding kernel modules and how to use them on a system that has already been booted.

Often these kernel modules are needed during the boot process. For example, the kernel doesn't know how to read LVM (Logical Volume Management) volumes by default, so a kernel module that provides that capability may be needed to boot the system correctly if a key filesystem resides on an LVM volume.

This section focuses on how to provide the kernel with the necessary modules during the boot process.

Commands

This subsection focuses on the commands you need to know to manage the kernel modules needed during the boot process.

mkinitrd

This **initramfs** file is created by the **mkinitrd** command, which in turn calls the **dracut** utility:

```
[root@localhost ~]# mkinitrd /boot/initramfs-2.6.32.68.x86_64.img
  2.6.32.68
```

The first argument to the **mkinitrd** command is the **initramfs** filename that you want to create. The second is the version of the kernel.

Note that you rarely use the **dracut** utility directly; however, it is listed as an exam objective, so be aware that **mkinitrd** executes the **dracut** command behind the scenes.

Note that if you are working on a Debian-based system, the **mkinitramfs** command is used in place of the **mkinitrd** command.

dracut

See the "mkinitrd" subsection in this chapter.

grub2-install

Typically the bootloader is installed during the boot process, but it is possible that the bootloader could become corrupt and need to be reinstalled. To install the bootloader, execute the **grub-install** command and provide the device where you want to install GRUB. For example, the following installs GRUB on the first SATA hard drive:

```
[root@localhost ~]# grub2-install /dev/sda
```

grub2-mkconfig

Only used for GRUB2, **grub2-mkconfig** will generate GRUB2 configuration files from the user-editable files located in the **/etc** directory structure. This command converts data from the **/etc/default/grub** file and the files in the **/etc/grub.d** directory into the GRUB2 configuration file (either **/boot/grub/grub.cfg** or **/boot/grub/menu.lst**).

Figure 1.5 provides a visual example.

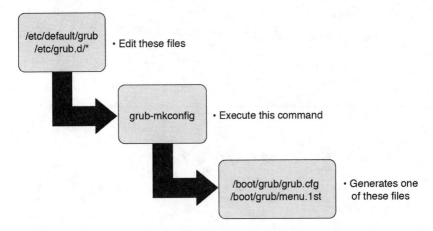

Figure 1.5   The **grub-mkconfig** Command

> **NOTE:**   On some systems, the command name is **grub-mkconfig**.

initramfs

This file contains a mini-root filesystem that has the kernel modules necessary when the system is booting. It is located in the **/boot** filesystem, and there is a unique **initramfs** file for each kernel. The **initramfs** file is created by the **mkinitrd** command (see the subsection in this chapter for more information).

vmlinuz

The **vmlinuz** file is stored in the **/boot** directory. Each version of the kernel will have a different **vmlinuz** file, typically with a name that includes the version of the kernel. Here is an example:

```
vmlinuz-4.17.8-200.fc32.x86_64
```

Unlike the **vmlinux** file, the **vmlinuz** file is a compressed version of the kernel.

vmlinux

The **vmlinux** file refers to the kernel itself in a "statically linked executable file format." This file is not typically one that an administrator views or modifies directly. Normally this file is used to build the **vmlinuz** file, a compressed version of the **vmlinux** file.

Kernel Panic

A kernel panic occurs when something goes wrong with the kernel and the system crashes. Typically when this happens, data is stored using a feature called **kdump**. An kernel expert can view this data to determine the cause of the crash.

## CHAPTER 2

Given a scenario, install, configure, and monitor kernel modules

This chapter provides information and commands concerning the following topics:

Commands

- lsmod
- insmod
- modprobe
- modinfo
- dmesg
- rmmod
- depmod

Locations

- /usr/lib/modules/[kernelversion]
- /usr/lib/modules
- /etc/modprobe.conf
- /etc/modprobe.d/

Commands

This section covers the commands related to managing modules on a Linux system. A module is code stored in a file that allows the kernel to perform specific tasks. A module may provide features like networking functions or the ability to handle specific types of filesystems.

lsmod

The **lsmod** command displays the kernel modules that are loaded into memory.

Syntax:

`lsmod`

Output of the **lsmod** Command:

Each line describes one module. There are three columns of information for each line:

- The module name.
- The size of the module in bytes.

- The "things" that are using the module. A "thing" could be a filesystem, a process, or another module. In the event that another module is using this module, the dependent module name is listed. Otherwise, a numeric value that indicates how many "things" use this module is provided.

Example:

```
[root@OCS ~]# lsmod | head
Module                    Size      Used by
tcp_lp                    12663     0
bnep                      19704     2
bluetooth                 372944    5     bnep
rfkill                    26536     3     bluetooth
fuse                      87741     3
xt_CHECKSUM               12549     1
ipt_MASQUERADE            12678     3
nf_nat_masquerade_ipv4    13412     1     ipt_MASQUERADE
tun                       27141     1
```

insmod

The **insmod** command is used to add modules to the currently running kernel.

Syntax:

```
insmod [module_name]
```

The exact location of the module needs to be specified. For example:

```
[root@OCS ~]# lsmod | grep fat
[root@OCS ~]# insmod /usr/lib/modules/3.19.8-100.fc20.x86_64/kernel/fs/
   fat.ko
[root@OCS ~]# lsmod | grep fat
fat                65107   0
```

There are no options to the **insmod** command; however, each module might have modules that can be passed into the module using the following syntax:

```
insmod module options
```

The **insmod** command has two disadvantages:

- You have to know the exact location of the module.
- If the module has any dependencies (a module that needs another module), it will fail to load.

modprobe

The **modprobe** command is used to add and remove modules from the currently running kernel. Note that it also attempts to load module dependencies.

Syntax:

```
modprobe [options] [module_name]
```

When used to remove modules (the **-r** option), the **modprobe** command will also remove dependency modules unless they are in use by another part of the subsystem (such as by the kernel or a process).

Key Options for the **modprobe** Command:

- **-c** displays the current **modprobe** configuration.
- **-q** causes **modprobe** to run in quiet mode.
- **-R** displays all modules that match an alias to assist you in debugging issues.
- **-r** removes the specified module from memory.
- **-v** displays verbose messages; this is useful for determining how **modprobe** is performing a task.

modinfo

The **modinfo** command is used to provide details about a module.

Syntax:

```
modinfo [module_name]
```

Example:

```
[root@OCS ~]# modinfo xen_wdt
filename:       /lib/modules/3.19.8-100.fc20.x86_64/kernel/drivers/
watchdog/xen_wdt.ko
license:        GPL
version:        0.01
description:    Xen WatchDog Timer Driver
author:         Jan Beulich <jbeulich@novell.com>
srcversion:     D13298694740A00FF311BD0
depends:
intree:         Y
vermagic:       3.19.8-100.fc20.x86_64 SMP mod_unload
signer:         Fedora kernel signing key
sig_key:        06:AF:36:EB:7B:28:A5:AD:E9:0B:02:1E:17:E6:AA:B2:B6:52:
63:AA
sig_hashalgo:   sha256
parm:           timeout:Watchdog timeout in seconds (default=60)(uint)
parm:           nowayout:Watchdog cannot be stopped once
started (default=0) (bool)
```

One of the most important parts of the output of the **modinfo** command is the "parm" values, which describe parameters that can be passed to this module to affect its behavior. See the subsection of this chapter for more details.

dmesg

The **dmesg** command displays the in-memory copy of the kernel ring buffer. It is often used to display bootup messages for debugging purposes.

Syntax:

dmesg

Example:

```
[root@OCS ~]# dmesg | head
Initializing cgroup subsys cpuset
Initializing cgroup subsys cpu
Linux version 2.6.32-573.7.1.el6.x86_64
   (mockbuild@c6b8.bsys.dev.centos.org) (gcc version 4.4.7
     20120313
   (Red Hat 4.4.7-16) (GCC) ) #1 SMP Tue Sep 22 22:00:00
     UTC 2015
Command line: ro root=/dev/mapper/VolGroup-lv_root
rd_NO_LUKS LANG=en_US.UTF-8 rd_NO_MD rd_LVM_LV=VolGroup/lv_swap

SYSFONT=latarcyrheb-sun16 crashkernel=auto rd_LVM_LV=VolGroup/
lv_root KEYBOARDTYPE=pc KEYTABLE=us rd_NO_DM rhgb quiet
KERNEL supported cpus:
      Intel GenuineIntel
      AMD AuthenticAMD
      Centaur CentaurHauls
BIOS-provided physical RAM map:
   BIOS-e820: 0000000000000000 - 000000000009fc00 (usable)
```

rmmod

The **rmmod** command is used to remove modules from the currently running kernel.

Syntax:

rmmod [*options*] [*module_name*]

Example:

```
[root@OCS ~]# lsmod | grep fat
fat                    65107  0
[root@OCS ~]# rmsmod fat
[root@OCS ~]# lsmod | grep fat
```

Modules that are currently in use will not be removed by this command by default.

Key Options for the **rm** Command:

- **-f** attempts to force removal of modules that are in use (very dangerous).
- **-w** will wait for a module to be no longer used and then remove it.
- **-v** displays verbose messages.

depmod

The **depmod** command builds the **modules.dep** file.

Syntax:

```
depmod
```

The **modules.dep** file contains module dependencies and is used by the **modprobe** command to determine which modules need to be loaded. For example:

```
[root@OCS ~]# grep fat /usr/lib/modules/3.19.8-100.fc20.x86_64/
  modules.dep
kernel/fs/fat/fat.ko:
kernel/fs/fat/vfat.ko: kernel/fs/fat/fat.ko
kernel/fs/fat/msdos.ko: kernel/fs/fat/fat.ko
```

In the preceding example, the **vfat.ko** and **msdos.ko** modules require the **fat.ko** module, but the **fat.ko** module has no dependencies.

The **depmod** command is typically executed when new modules are placed on the system. This normally happens as part of the installation of a software package, but it can be executed manually. When the **depmod** command does have a few options, they are not typically used.

Files

Modules and module-related information are stored in specific locations. This section reviews these locations, which you should be familiar with for the exam.

/usr/lib/modules/[kernelversion]

Each kernel that is installed on the system will have a directory under the /usr/lib/modules directory for its specific modules:

```
[root@OCS ~]# ls /usr/lib/modules
3.17.8-200.fc20.x86_64   3.18.7-100.fc20.x86_64   3.19.8-100.fc20.x86_64
```

In the preceding sample output, three kernel directories are displayed. This means that three kernels are stored on this system. Typically the most recent version is the one currently being used, but you can verify this by running the **uname** command:

```
[root@OCS ~]# uname -r
3.19.8-100.fc20.x86_64
```

The important part of these directories is that if you manually add new kernel modules to the system, you should place them in the currently used kernel directory under **/usr/lib/modules** prior to running the **depmod** command.

/usr/lib/modules

See the preceding "/usr/lib/modules/[kernelversion]" section in this chapter.

/etc/modprobe.conf

On some distributions, the **/etc/modprobe.conf** file is used to modify how modules are loaded and unloaded. While this file was commonly used in previous releases of Linux distributions, most distributions now make use of configuration settings in the **/etc/modprobe.d** directory.

See the next section, "/etc/modprobe.d/," for more details.

/etc/modprobe.d/

The contents of the **/etc/modprobe.d** directory are files that modify how modules are loaded and unloaded. Note that on some systems you might also file these files in the **/lib/modprobe.d** and **/run/modprobe.d** directories.

Settings in these files include the following:

- **alias**: A nickname for a module.
- **install**: A command or commands to run instead of loading a module (typically a script that will also load the specific module after other conditions have been met).
- **options**: Parameters to pass to a module when it is loaded to modify the module's behavior. Note that these parameters are displayed by the **modinfo** command (see the section in this chapter for more details).
- **remove**: A command or commands to run instead of unloading a module (typically a script that will also unload the specific module after other conditions have been met).

Example of the **install** setting:

```
[root@OCS ~]# cat /lib/modprobe.d/dist-alsa.conf
# ALSA Sound Support
#
# We want to ensure that snd-seq is always loaded for those
    who want to use
# the sequencer interface, but we can't do this
    automatically through udev
# at the moment...so we have this rule.
#
# Remove the following line if you don't want the sequencer.
install snd-pcm /sbin/modprobe --ignore-install snd-pcm && /sbin/
    modprobe snd-seq
```

## CHAPTER 3

Given a scenario, configure and verify network connection parameters

This chapter provides information and commands concerning the following topics:

Diagnostic tools

- **ping**
- **netstat**
- **nslookup**
- **dig**
- **host**
- **route**
- **ip**
- **ethtool**
- **ss**
- **iwconfig**
- **nmcli**
- **brctl**
- **nmtui**

Configuration files

- **/etc/sysconfig/network-scripts/**
- **/etc/sysconfig/network**
- **/etc/hosts**
- **/etc/network**
- **/etc/nsswitch.conf**
- **/etc/resolv.conf**
- **/etc/netplan**
- **/etc/sysctl.conf**
- **/etc/dhcpd.conf**

Bonding

- Aggregation
- Active/passive
- Load balancing

Diagnostic Tools

ping

The **ping** command is used to verify that a remote host can respond to a network connection:

```
[root@OCS ~]# ping -c 4 google.com
PING google.com (172.217.5.206) 56(84) bytes of data.
64 bytes from lax28s10-in-f14.1e100.net (172.217.5.206):
  icmp_seq=1 ttl=55 time=49.0 ms
64 bytes from lax28s10-in-f206.1e100.net (172.217.5.206):
  icmp_seq=2 ttl=55 time=30.2 ms
64 bytes from lax28s10-in-f14.1e100.net (172.217.5.206):
  icmp_seq=3 ttl=55 time=30.0 ms
64 bytes from lax28s10-in-f206.1e100.net (172.217.5.206):
  icmp_seq=4 ttl=55 time=29.5 ms

--- google.com ping statistics ---
4 packets transmitted, 4 received, 0% packet loss, time 3008ms
rtt min/avg/max/mdev = 29.595/34.726/49.027/8.261 ms
```

By default, the **ping** command will continuously send "pings" to the remote system until the user cancels the command (Ctrl-C). The **-c** option specifies a count of how many ping requests to send.

netstat

The **netstat** command is useful for displaying a variety of network information. It is a key utility when troubleshooting network issues. The following table describes common options for the **netstat** command:

Option	Description
-t or **--tcp**	Display TCP information.
-u or **--udp**	Display UDP information.
-r or **--route**	Display the routing table.
-v or **--verbose**	Verbose; display additional information.
-i or **--interfaces**	Display information based on a specific interface.
-a or **--all**	Apply to all.
-s or **--statistics**	Display statistics for the output.

For example, the following command will display all active TCP connections:

```
[root@OCS ~]# netstat -ta
Active Internet connections (servers and established)
Proto   Recv-Q   Send-Q   Local Address        Foreign Address State
tcp     0        0        192.168.122.1:domain 0.0.0.0:* LISTEN
```

```
tcp     0      0      0.0.0.0:ssh           0.0.0.0:* LISTEN
tcp     0      0      localhost:ipp         0.0.0.0:* LISTEN
tcp     0      0      localhost:smtp        0.0.0.0:* LISTEN
tcp6    0      0      [::]:ssh              [::]:* LISTEN
tcp6    0      0      localhost:ipp         [::]:* LISTEN
tcp6    0      0      localhost:smtp        [::]:* LISTEN
```

nslookup

The **nslookup** command is designed to perform simple queries on DNS servers.

Syntax:

nslookup *hostname*

Example:

```
[root@OCS ~]# nslookup google.com
Server:        8.8.8.8
Address:       8.8.8.8#53

Non-authoritative answer:
Name:    google.com
Address: 216.58.219.238
```

While this command has often been referred to as obsolete, it is still often used on modern distributions. The **nslookup** command is normally run without options.

dig

The **dig** command is useful for performing DNS queries on specific DNS servers. The format of the command is demonstrated here:

```
[root@OCS ~]# dig google.com

; <<>> DiG 9.9.4-RedHat-9.9.4-38.el7_3 <<>> google.com
;; global options: +cmd
;; Got answer:
;; ->>HEADER<<- opcode: QUERY, status: NOERROR, id: 56840
;; flags: qr rd ra; QUERY: 1, ANSWER: 1, AUTHORITY: 0, ADDITIONAL: 1

;; OPT PSEUDOSECTION:
; EDNS: version: 0, flags:; udp: 512
;; QUESTION SECTION:
;google.com.                    IN      A

;; ANSWER SECTION:
google.com.           268       IN      A       216.58.217.206
```

```
;; Query time: 36 msec
;; SERVER: 192.168.1.1#53(192.168.1.1)
;; WHEN: Sun Mar 05 17:01:08 PST 2017
;; MSG SIZE rcvd: 55
```

To query a specific DNS server, rather than the default DNS servers for your host, use the following syntax:

```
dig @server host_to_lookup
```

The following table describes common options for the **dig** command:

Option	Description
-f *file*	Use the content of *file* to perform multiple lookups; the file should contain one hostname per line.
-4	Only perform IPv4 queries.
-6	Only perform IPv6 queries.
-x *address*	Perform a reverse lookup (return the hostname when provided an IP address).

host

The **host** command is normally used to perform simple hostname-to-IP-address translation operations (also called *DNS queries*). Here is an example:

```
[root@OCS ~]# host google.com
google.com has address 172.217.4.142
google.com has IPv6 address 2607:f8b0:4007:800::200e
google.com mail is handled by 30 alt2.aspmx.l.google.com.
google.com mail is handled by 50 alt4.aspmx.l.google.com.
google.com mail is handled by 20 alt1.aspmx.l.google.com.
google.com mail is handled by 10 aspmx.l.google.com.
google.com mail is handled by 40 alt3.aspmx.l.google.com.
```

The following table describes common options for the **host** command:

Option	Description
-t	Specify a type of query that you want to display; for example, **host -t ns google.com** will display Google's name servers.
-4	Only perform IPv4 queries.
-6	Only perform IPv6 queries.
-v	Verbose; output is like that of the **dig** command.

route

The **route** command can be used to display the routing table:

```
[root@OCS ~]# route
Kernel IP routing table
Destination Gateway     Genmask       Flags Metric Ref Use Iface
default       192.168.1.1 0.0.0.0       UG    100    0   0   enp0s3
192.168.0.0 0.0.0.0     255.255.0.0   U     100    0   0   enp0s3
192.168.1.0 0.0.0.0     255.255.0.0   U     100    0   0   enp0s3
```

This information can also be displayed with the **ip** command:

```
[root@OCS ~]# ip route show
default via 192.168.1.1 dev enp0s3 proto static metric 100
192.168.0.0/16 dev enp0s3 proto kernel scope link
   src 192.168.1.24 metric 100
192.168.1.0/24 dev enp0s3 proto kernel scope link
   src 192.168.1.26 metric 100
192.168.122.0/24 dev virbr0 proto kernel scope link
   src 192.168.122.1
```

The **route** command can also be used to modify the default router:

```
route add default gw 192.168.1.10
```

To add a new router, execute the following command:

```
route add -net 192.168.3.0 netmask 255.255.255.0 gw 192.168.3.100
```

This command will send all network packets destined for the 192.168.3.0/24 network to the 192.168.3.100 router.

> **NOTE:** These changes are temporary and will only survive until the next time the system is booted. Permanent changes are made within your system's configuration files, which vary from one distribution to another.

ip

The **ip** command is a newer command that is designed to replace a collection of commands related to network interfaces.

Syntax:

```
ip [options] object command
```

The following table describes some of the more important objects:

Object	Refers to
addr	IPv4 or IPv6 address
link	Network device
route	Routing table entry

The following table describes some of the more important commands that can be executed:

Command	Description
add	Add an object.
delete	Delete an object.
show (or **list**)	Display information about an object.

The following example displays network information for devices, much like the **ifconfig** command:

```
[root@OCS ~]# ip addr show
1: lo: <LOOPBACK,UP,LOWER_UP> mtu 65536 qdisc noqueue state UNKNOWN
      link/loopback 00:00:00:00:00:00 brd 00:00:00:00:00:00
      inet 127.0.0.1/8 scope host lo
      valid_lft forever preferred_lft forever
      inet6 ::1/128 scope host
      valid_lft forever preferred_lft forever
2: enp0s3: <BROADCAST,MULTICAST,UP,LOWER_UP> mtu 1500 qdisc pfifo_fast
   state UP qlen 1000
      link/ether 08:00:27:b0:dd:dc brd ff:ff:ff:ff:ff:ff
      inet 192.168.1.26/24 brd 192.168.1.255 scope global
   dynamic enp0s3
      valid_lft 2384sec preferred_lft 2384sec
      inet 192.168.1.24/16 brd 192.168.255.255 scope global enp0s3
      valid_lft forever preferred_lft forever
      inet6 fe80::a00:27ff:feb0:dddc/64 scope link
      valid_lft forever preferred_lft forever
```

ethtool

The **ethtool** command is used to display and configure network device settings, such as the transmission speed and duplex value. Typically these settings are automatically configured through a process called auto-negotiation. With auto-negotiation, two network devices determine the best speed and duplex value and use that value automatically; however, these settings can also be manually set. The **ethtool** command also displays or modifies other useful network device settings.

Syntax:

```
ethtool [option] device
```

For example, to display a summary of information, use the following command:

```
[root@OCS ~]# ethtool eth0
Settings for eth0:
        Supported ports: [ TP ]
        Supported link modes:    10baseT/Half 10baseT/Full
                                 100baseT/Half 100baseT/Full
                                 1000baseT/Full
        Supported pause frame use: No
        Supports auto-negotiation: Yes
        Advertised link modes:   10baseT/Half 10baseT/Full
                                 100baseT/Half 100baseT/Full
                                 1000baseT/Full
        Advertised pause frame use: No
        Advertised auto-negotiation: Yes
        Speed: 1000Mb/s
        Duplex: Full
        Port: Twisted Pair
        PHYAD: 0
        Transceiver: internal
        Auto-negotiation: on
        MDI-X: off (auto)
        Supports Wake-on: umbg
        Wake-on: d
        Current message level: 0x00000007 (7)
                                 drv probe link
        Link detected: yes
```

The **ethtool** command provides a lot of output. The following table describes some of the more useful data:

Output	Description
Supported link modes	The speed and duplex values that this device is able to use.
Supports auto-negotiation	If this device and the connected-to device both support auto-negotiation, the speed and duplex settings don't need to be manually set.
Advertised link modes	The speed and duplex values that this device is telling other devices it can use.
Speed	The current speed setting the device is using.
Duplex	The duplex value the device is currently using.
Link detected	If this item is set to "yes," the device is currently connected via the network to another device.

Useful options for the **ethtool** command include the following:

Option	Description
-i	Provide driver information for this device.
-S	Display statistics for this device.
-p	Identify this device by causing its link light to blink. Very useful when the system has multiple network interface cards.
speed *value*	Manually set the speed value of the device; *value* is the speed value to set the device to.
duplex *value*	Manually set the duplex value of the device; *value* should be full or half.
autoneg *value*	Enable auto-negotiation; value should be either yes or no.

ss

The **ss** command is used to display socket information.

Syntax:

```
ss [options]
```

Without any options, it lists all open sockets. For example:

```
[root@OCS ~]# ss | wc -l
160
[root@OCS ~]# ss | head
Netid   State      Recv-Q Send-Q    Local Address:Port Peer Address:Port
u_str   ESTAB      0      0         /var/run/dovecot/anvil 23454966
   * 23454965
u_str   ESTAB      0      0         /var/run/dovecot/anvil 23887673
   * 23887672
u_str   ESTAB      0      0         /run/systemd/journal/stdout
   13569                * 13568
u_str   ESTAB      0      0                           * 13893 * 13894
u_str   ESTAB      0      0                           * 13854 * 13855
u_str   ESTAB      0      0                           * 13850 * 13849
u_str   ESTAB      0      0                           * 68924 * 68925
u_str   ESTAB      0      0                           * 17996 * 17997
u_str   ESTAB      0      0         /var/run/dovecot/config 9163531
   * 9163871
```

Useful options for the **ss** command include:

Option	Description
-lt	List listening TCP sockets.
-lu	List listening UDP sockets.
-lp	List the process ID that owns each socket.
-n	Don't resolve IP addresses to hostnames or port numbers to port names.
-a	Display all information.
-s	Display a summary.

iwconfig

The **iwconfig** command is used to display or set information about wireless network interfaces.

Syntax:

```
iwconfig [interface] [parameters]
```

If no arguments are provided, this command displays all network interfaces:

```
[root@OCS ~]# iwconfig
lo          no wireless extensions.
eth0        no wireless extensions.
wlan0       IEEE 802.11bgn  ESSID:"test1"
            Mode:Managed  Frequency:2.412 GHz  Access Point:
              Not-Associated
            Tx-Power=20 dBm
            Retry min limit:7    RTS thr:off    Fragment thr=2352 B
            Power Management:off
            Link Quality:0  Signal level:0  Noise level:0
            Rx invalid nwid:0  Rx invalid crypt:0 Rx invalid frag:0
            Tx excessive retries:0  Invalid misc:0 Missed beacon:0
```

Parameters can be used to configure the wireless interface. For example, to change the device mode to Ad-Hoc, execute the following command:

```
[root@OCS ~]# iwconfig wlan0 mode Ad-Hoc
```

Useful parameters for the **iwconfig** command include the following:

Parameter	Description
essid *value*	Set the ESSID name (aka, network name).
nwid *value*	Set the network ID.
mode *value*	Set the mode (*value* is Ad-Hoc, Managed, Master, and so on).
ap *value*	Force the network card to use the specified access point.

nmcli

The **nmcli** command is used to configure NetworkManager, a tool designed to detect and configure network connections.

Syntax:

```
nmcli [options] object [command]
```

Example:

```
[root@OCS ~]# nmcli device status
DEVICE       TYPE       STATE        CONNECTION
virbr0       bridge     connected    virbr0
enp0s3       ethernet   connected    enp0s3
lo           loopback   unmanaged    --
virbr0-nic   tun        unmanaged    --
```

The object is one of the following keywords:

Keyword	Description
connection	To manage network connections
device	To manage a specific device
general	For NetworkManager status information
networking	To enable or disable networking or display the current status
radio	For radio (wireless) networking information and configuration

Common **nmcli** commands include the following:

Command	Description
status	Display the current setting.
on|off	Turn on (or off) a setting.
up|down	Bring an interface up (or down).
add|delete	Add a new device or delete an existing one.

brctl

The **brctl** command is used to create, modify, or view an Ethernet bridge. An Ethernet bridge connects separate networks into a single network from the perspective of users.

Syntax:

```
brctl [command]
```

Start by creating the bridge:

```
[root@OCS ~]# brctl addbr bridge1
```

Next, add the interface or interfaces that will be a part of the bridge:

```
[root@OCS ~]# brctl addif bridge1 eth1
```

Common **brctl** commands include the following:

Command	Description
delbr	Delete a bridge as long as no interfaces are part of the bridge.
delif	Delete an interface from a bridge.
show	List all bridges on this system.
show *brname*	Display information about a specific bridge.

nmtui

The **nmtui** command provides a text-based interface to configure NetworkManager. When executed, it provides an interface like the one shown in Figure 3.1.

Figure 3.1   The **nmtui** Interface

Configuration Files

Specifying network information each time you bring up an interface isn't effective. Configuration files are used to store network-based information for the system to automatically use when activating an interface.

This is one area where different distributions have different solutions. This section will focus on the configuration files that you will typically see on different Linux distributions.

/etc/sysconfig/network-scripts/

This directory is found on Red Hat–based distributions, such as Red Hat Enterprise Linux, CentOS, and Fedora. It contains a collection of files that are used to configure network devices:

```
[root@OCS ~]# ls /etc/sysconfig/network-scripts/
ifcfg-eth0      ifdown-Team       ifup-plusb
ifcfg-lo        ifdown-TeamPort   ifup-post
ifdown          ifdown-tunnel     ifup-ppp
ifdown-bnep     ifup              ifup-routes
ifdown-eth      ifup-aliases      ifup-sit
ifdown-ippp     ifup-bnep         ifup-Team
ifdown-ipv6     ifup-eth          ifup-TeamPort
ifdown-isdn     ifup-ippp         ifup-tunnel
ifdown-post     ifup-ipv6         ifup-wireless
ifdown-ppp      ifup-ipx          init.ipv6-global
ifdown-routes   ifup-isdn         network-functions
ifdown-sit      ifup-plip         network-functions-ipv6
```

In most cases you can probably guess what a configuration file is used for by its name. For example, the **ifup-wireless** file is used to configure wireless networks. Many of these files also have comments that are used to describe the purpose and use of the file.

The most common file edited is **ifcfg-***interface*, where *interface* is the name of your network interface. For example, **ifcfg-eth0** is used to configure the eth0 device:

```
[root@OCS ~]# more /etc/sysconfig/network-scripts/ifcfg-eth0
DEVICE=eth0
BOOTPROTO=static
ONBOOT=yes
IPADDR=192.168.0.100
NETMASK=255.255.255.0
GATEWAY=192.168.0.1
```

The following table lists some common **ifcfg-***interface* configuration settings:

Setting	Description
DEVICE	The name of the interface.
BOOTPROTO	Set to **static** if you manually provide network information, such as IP address, netmask, and gateway. Set to **dhcp** to have these values dynamically assigned from a DHCP server.
ONBOOT	Normally set to "yes" to activate this device during the boot process.
IPADDR	The IP address that should be assigned to the device.
NETMASK	The device's netmask.
GATEWAY	The default router for this interface.

/etc/sysconfig/network

This file is found on Red Hat–based distributions, such as Red Hat Enterprise Linux, CentOS, and Fedora. It contains basic networking information:

```
[root@OCS ~]# more /etc/sysconfig/network
HOSTNAME=ocs.onecoursesource.com
NETWORKING=yes
```

The following table lists some common **/etc/sysconfig/network** configuration settings:

Setting	Description
HOSTNAME	The hostname of this system.
NETWORKING	When set to **yes**, networking is enabled when the system boots. When set to **no**, no networking is configured when the system boots.

/etc/hosts

The **/etc/hosts** file is where hostname-to-IP-address translation is defined:

```
[root@OCS ~]# more /etc/hosts
192.168.1.24  server.sample999.com
127.0.0.1     OCS
::1           OCS
```

Each line describes one translation. The first field is the IP address, the second field is the hostname, and the optional third field shows the alias addresses.

In most cases, this file is only used for the local host itself or hosts on the local network. Normally hostname-to-IP-address translation is handled by a DNS server.

/etc/network

The **/etc/network** directory is the traditional location where Debian-based network files are stored. This include the Debian, Ubuntu, and MintOS distributions.

The primary configuration file is **/etc/network/interfaces**. In the following example, the loopback device is defined by the first two lines of the file, and a statically assigned eth0 device is defined by the rest of the file:

```
[root@OCS ~]# /etc/network/interfaces
auto lo
iface lo inet loopback
iface eth0 inet static
 address 192.168.11.100
 netmask 255.255.255.0
 gateway 192.168.11.1
 dns-domain example.com
 dns-nameservers 192.168.11.1
```

A DHCP client configuration for eth0 could look like the following:

```
auto eth0
iface eth0 inet dhcp
```

Note that on some systems, such as Ubuntu, **/etc/network/interfaces** has been replaced by configuration files in the **/etc/netplan** directory. See the "/etc/netplan" section in this chapter for more details.

/etc/nsswitch.conf

The Name Service Switch (NSS) configuration file, **/etc/nsswitch.conf**, is used by applications to determine the sources from which to obtain name service information, as well as in what order. For example, for networking, this file contains the location of the name server resolver, the utility that provides hostname-to-IP-address translation:

```
[root@OCS ~]# grep hosts /etc/nsswitch.conf
#hosts:     db files nisplus nis dns
hosts:      files dns
```

The value of **files dns** means "look at the local **/etc/hosts** file first, and then look at the DNS server if the required translation isn't in the local file."

The following table describes common hostname-to-IP-address translation utilities:

Utility	Description
files	The local **/etc/hosts** file
dns	A DNS server
NIS	A Network Information Service server

/etc/resolv.conf

The **/etc/resolv.conf** file contains a list of the DNS servers for the system. A typical file looks like the following:

```
[root@OCS ~]# cat /etc/resolv.conf
search sample999.com
nameserver 192.168.1
```

If you are using a utility such as NetworkManager to configure your network settings or are using a DHCP client, then this file is normally populated by those utilities. For servers, this file is typically manually defined.

The following table describes common settings for the **/etc/resolv.conf** file:

Setting	Description
nameserver	The IP address of the DNS server; there can be up to three **nameserver** lines in the file.
domain	Used to specify the local domain, which allows for the use of short names for DNS queries.
search	A list of optional domains to perform DNS queries when using short names.

/etc/netplan

The **/etc/netplan** directory is the new location where network configuration files are stored on Ubuntu and some other Debian-based distributions. The format of these files is YAML (YAML Ain't Markup Language), a file format that is similar to JSON.

Here is an example of a statically assigned ens33 device:

```
[root@OCS ~]# cat /etc/netplan/01-netcfg.yaml
network:
 version: 2
 renderer: networkd
 ethernets:
   ens33:
     dhcp4: no
     dhcp6: no
     addresses: [192.168.1.2/24]
     gateway4: 192.168.1.1
     nameservers:
       addresses: [8.8.8.8,8.8.4.4]
```

To configure the ens33 device as a DHCP client, use the following syntax:

```
[root@OCS ~]# cat /etc/netplan/01-netcfg.yaml
network:
 version: 2
 renderer: networkd
 ethernets:
   ens33:
     dhcp4: yes
     dhcp6: yes
```

NOTE: After changing a file in the **/etc/netplan** directory, run the **netplan apply** command to have the changes take effect.

/etc/sysctl.conf

The **/etc/sysctl.conf** file is used to specify which kernel settings to enable at boot.

Example:

```
[root@OCS ~]# cat /etc/sysctl.conf
# System default settings live in/usr/lib/sysctl.d/00-system.conf.
# To override those settings, enter new settings here, or
# in an /etc/sysctl.d/<name>.conf file.
#
# For more information, see sysctl.conf(5) and sysctl.d(5).
net.ipv4.ip_forward=1
```

In the previous example, the kernel parameter of **ip_forward** is turned on, which means this machine will act as a router between two networks.

There are thousands of possible kernel settings, including dozens of settings that affect networking. The **ip_forward** setting is one of the most common network settings.

/etc/dhcpd.conf

The **/etc/dhcpd.conf** file is used to configure a DHCP server. After the DHCP server packages have been installed, a sample **dhcpd.conf** file will be placed in the **/usr/share/ doc** directory structure (the **/usr/share/doc/dhcp*/dhcpd.conf.sample** file). Usually the administrator who configures the DHCP server copies this sample file to the **/etc** directory and modifies it to fit the local network.

The following table describes common settings for the **/etc/dhcpd.conf** file:

Setting	Description
option domain-name	The default domain name to provide to DHCP clients. This can be overridden by subnet settings (see subnet later in this table).
option domain-name-servers	The default DNS server names to provide to DHCP clients. This can be overridden by subnet settings (see subnet later in this table).
default-lease-time	How long of a lease to provide by default to DHCP clients. This can be overridden by subnet settings (see subnet later in this table).
max-lease-time	The maximum lease period allowed for a DHCP client. This can be overridden by subnet settings (see subnet next in this table).
subnet	The definition of a collection of IP address and other network information to provide to DHCP clients. See the next table for more information.

The following table describes common subnet settings for the **/etc/dhcpd.conf** file:

Setting	Description
range	The range of IP addresses to provide to DHCP clients.
option domain-name-servers	The DNS server names to provide to DHCP clients associated with this subnet. This overrides any default setting.
option domain-name	The domain name to provide to DHCP clients associated with this subnet. This overrides any default setting.
option routers	The gateway address.
default-lease-time	How long of a lease to provide by default to DHCP clients for this subnet. This overrides any default setting.
max-lease-time	The maximum lease period allowed for a DHCP client for this subnet. This overrides any default setting.

Here is a simple example taken from the sample file:

```
option domain-name "example.org";
option domain-name-servers ns1.example.org, ns2.example.org;
default-lease-time 600;
log-facility local7;
subnet 10.254.239.0 netmask 255.255.255.224 {
  range 10.254.239.10 10.254.239.20;
    option routers rtr-239-0-1.example.org, rtr-239-0-2.example.org;
}
```

Bonding

The purpose of bonding is to have the system treat multiple network interfaces as if they were a single network interface. This provides much greater bandwidth than a single network interface can manage. This section discusses the concept of bonding.

Aggregation

Aggregation is the core concept of bonding. To create a network bond, you need to put together two or more network interfaces into a single cluster. This is the very definition of aggregation.

Aggregation can be managed manually, by first creating a network bond and then adding devices to the bond:

```
[root@OCS ~]#  ip link add bond0 type bond
[root@OCS ~]#  ip link set eth0 master bond0
[root@OCS ~]#  ip link set eth1 master bond0
```

To have this bond created automatically, you need to modify a configuration file. For example, in traditional Debian-based distributions, the following code would be added to the **/etc/network/interfaces** file:

```
iface bond0 inet static
        address 192.168.1.100
        netmask 255.255.255.0
        gateway 192.168.1.1
        dns-nameservers 192.168.1.1
        dns-search domain.local
                slaves eth0 eth1
                bond_mode 0
                bond-miimon 100
                bond_downdelay 200
                bound_updelay 200
```

Note that you can also create a network bond using NetworkManager, as shown in Figure 3.2.

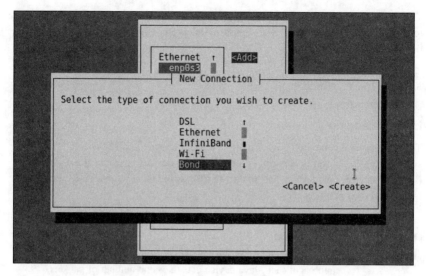

Figure 3.2   Creating a Network Bond Using NetworkManager

In order for bonding to work correctly, you first need to load the bonding kernel module. This can be done manually:

```
[root@OCS ~]# modprobe bonding
```

NOTE: This module should automatically be loaded during system boot if bonding is configured in a configuration file.

Active/Passive

Network bonding supports several modes. One mode is referred to as "active-backup," in which only one device is active and the other devices are backups in the event the active device goes down.

To set this mode, use the following syntax:

```
[root@OCS ~]# ip link add bond0 type bond mode 1
```

```
iface bond0 inet static
        address 192.168.1.100
        netmask 255.255.255.0
        gateway 192.168.1.1
        dns-nameservers 192.168.1.1
        dns-search domain.local
                slaves eth0 eth1
                bond_mode 1
                bond-miimon 100
                bond_downdelay 200
                bound_updelay 200
```

This can also be passed into the bonding kernel parameter by adding the following to the
/etc/sysctl.conf file (note that most administrators prefer editing the network configuration files over this method):

```
alias bond0 bonding
options bond0 miimon=80 mode=5
```

Load Balancing

There are several bonding modes that affect load balancing. Load balancing allows the system to share the traffic between different network devices based on some criteria (speed of device, round robin, and so on). The following table provides a list of all the modes and their purpose:

Setting	Description
mode=0	Balanced round robin: Packets are transmitted in a round-robin approach; each slave device gets the same number of packets.
mode=1	See the "Active/Passive" subsection in this chapter.
mode=2	XOR: Transmit interface is based on an XOR operation using source and destination MAC addresses.
mode=3	Broadcast: All packets are broadcast on all salve devices.
mode=4	802.3ad: Creates network bonds for devices that share the same speed and duplex settings. Requires **ethtool** be installed to perform a probe of network devices.
mode=5	Adaptive transmit load balancing: Load balancing based on criteria such as the speed of the network slave devices.
mode=6	Adaptive load balancing: Similar to mode=5, but also performs MAC address rewriting in the network packets.

## CHAPTER 4

Given a scenario, manage storage in a Linux environment

This chapter provides information and commands concerning the following topics:

Basic partitions

- Raw devices
- GPT
- MBR

Filesystem hierarchy

- Real filesystems
- Virtual filesystems
- Relative paths
- Absolute paths

Device mapper

- LVM
- mdadm
- Multipath

Tools

- XFS tools
- LVM tools
- EXT tools
- Commands:
  - **mdadm**
  - **fdisk**
  - **parted**
  - **mkfs**
  - **iostat**
  - **df**
  - **du**
  - **mount**
  - **umount**
  - **lsblk**

- **blkid**
- **dumpe2fs**
- **resize2fs**
- **fsck**
- **tune2fs**
- **e2label**

Location

- **/etc/fstab**
- **/etc/cryptab**
- **/dev/**
- **/dev/mapper**
- **/dev/disk/by-**
  - **id**
  - **uuid**
  - **path**
  - **multipath**
- **/etc/mtab**
- **/sys/block**
- **/proc/partitions**
- **/proc/mounts**

Filesystem types

- ext3
- ext4
- xfs
- nfs
- smb
- cifs
- ntfs

Basic Partitions

Partitions are used to separate a hard disk into smaller components. Each component can then be treated as a different storage device. On each partition, a separate filesystem (btrfs, xfs, etx4, and so on) can be created.

Traditional PC-based partitions have limitations regarding the number of them you can create. Originally only four partitions were permitted. These are referred to as *primary partitions*. As more partitions were needed, a technique was created that allowed you to convert one of the primary partitions into an extended partition. Within an extended partition, you could create additional partitions called *logical partitions*.

In Figure 4.1, **/dev/sda1**, **/dev/sda2**, and **/dev/sda3** are primary partitions. The **/dev/sda4** partition is an extended partition that is used as a container for the **/dev/sda5**, **/dev/sda6**, and **/dev/sda7** logical partitions.

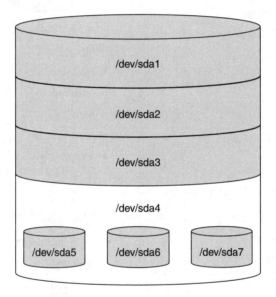

Figure 4.1   Traditional Partition Structure

On most distributions that use traditional partitions, you will be limited to a total of 15 partitions (a kernel tweak can increase this number to 63).

Traditional partition tables are stored on the master boot record (MBR). A newer partition table, called the GUID partition table (GPT), does not have the same limitations or layout that an MBR partition table has.

Several different tools can be used to create or view partitions, including **fdisk**, **parted**, and the GUI-based tool provided by the installation program. The GUI-based tool can vary based on the distribution.

Both **fdisk** and **parted** support command-line options, and both can be executed as an interactive tool.

Raw Devices

A raw device is a device file that is associated with a block device file (partition, hard disk, and so on). When you create this association, direct access to the block device is available. To create a raw device, use the **raw** command:

```
# raw /dev/raw/raw1 /dev/vda
/dev/raw/raw1:  bound to major 252, minor 0
```

Once a raw device is created, you can use commands like the **dd** command to perform actions on the corresponding block file. The **dd** command is often used to create a copy of an entire hard disk.

GPT

GUID partition table (GTP) is a partitioning scheme that is designed to overcome the limitations of MBR (see the "MBR" section in this chapter). Unlike MBR, GPT doesn't have the limitation of four primary partitions. There also isn't a need for extended or logical partitions. GPT supports up to 128 partitions per hard disk device.

MBR

MBR partition tables are often referred to as "traditional" partitions, as opposed to newer partition tables such as the GUID partition table. An MBR partition table has the restriction of only permitting four partitions by default. This is an extremely limiting factor for operating systems such as Linux.

However, one of the primary partitions in an MBR partition table can be converted into an extended partition. Within this extended partition, additional partitions can be added. These additional partitions are called *logical* partitions. See Figure 4.2 for a visual example.

See the "fdisk" and "parted" sections in this chapter for details on creating MBR partitions.

A note regarding hard disk device names: Hard disks are referred to via device names in the **/dev** directory. IDE-based devices have names that start with **/dev/hd**, whereas SATA, SCSI, and USB devices have names that start with **/dev/sd**. The first drive on the system is named **a**, so the first SATA device would be **/dev/sda**. The second SETA would be **/dev/sdb**, and so on. Partitions are numbered sequentially, starting from 1, such as **/dev/sda1**, **/dev/sda2**, and **/dev/sda3**.

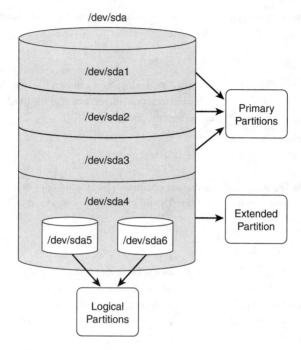

Figure 4.2   Partitions

Filesystem Hierarchy

The term *filesystem* is often a confusing term because it can refer to two different things: real filesystems and virtual filesystems. This section explores the difference between these two types as well as the difference between relative and absolute paths.

Real Filesystems

A real filesystem is a filesystem that is placed on a physical storage device, such as a partition, software RAID device, or LVM logical volume. Typical real filesystems include ext3, ext4, and xfs. See the "Filesystem Types" section later in this chapter for more information about these real filesystems.

Virtual Filesystems

Once a real filesystem has been placed on a physical device, it needs to be grafted onto the virtual filesystem. The virtual filesystem starts from the root directory (the / directory) and contains a collection of physical filesystems. The root directory itself is one of the real filesystems. Others are found under directories called "mount points."

Common mount points include the **/usr**, **/var**, and **/home** directories; however, these directories may also contain data from the root filesystem. This depends on how the partitioning scheme was laid out during the installation process.

See the "lsblk" and "/proc/partitions" sections later in this chapter to learn how to display partitions that contain real filesystems. See the "df" section to learn how to view space usage on the real filesystems. Viewing this information provides you with a good idea of how the virtual filesystem structure is laid out on the distribution.

Relative Paths

A path is how you refer to a file or directory. If you use a path name that is relative to the current directory, it is called a *relative path*. Here are some examples:

- **cd test**: Move to the **test** directory under the current directory.

- **ls abc/xyz**: List files in the **xyz** directory, which is under the **abc** directory, which is under the current directory.

- **cd ..**: Move one level up from the current directory (the **..** characters represents the directory above the current directory).

- **cp data/abc.txt .**: Copy the **abc.txt** file, which is under the **data** directory, which is under the current directory into the current directory (a single **.** represents the current directory).

Also see the next section, "Absolute Paths."

Absolute Paths

A path is how you refer to a file or directory. If you use a path name that is relative to the root directory (**/**), it is called a relative path. Here are some examples:

- **cd /etc/skel**
- **ls /usr/bin**
- **cp /etc/hosts /tmp**

Note that an absolute path always begins with the **/** character, and relative paths never begin with the **/** character.

Also see the previous "Relative Paths" section in this chapter.

Device Mapper

Regular partitions are assigned device names that are predictable and automatically assigned. The first disk on the system is assigned to **/dev/sda** (unless it is an older IDE device, in which case it is assigned the device file of **/dev/hda**). The second disk on the system is assigned to **/dev/sdb**.

Other device types, such as the Logical Volume Manager (LVM), don't have predictable, automatically assigned device names. Instead, they use a feature called the device mapper.

See the next section, "LVM," for an example of the device mapper in action.

LVM

LVM is designed to address a few issues with regular partitions, including the following:

- Regular partitions are not "resizable." LVM provides the means to change the size of partition-like structures called *logical volumes*.

- The size of a regular partition cannot exceed the overall size of the hard disk on which the partition is placed. With LVM, several physical devices can be merged together to create a much larger logical volume.

- Active filesystems pose a challenge when you're backing up data because changes to the filesystem during the backup process could result in a corrupt backup. LVM provides a feature called a "snapshot" that makes it easy to correctly back up a live filesystem.

LVM consists of one or more physical devices merged into a single container of space that can be used to create partition-like devices. The physical devices can be entire hard disks, partitions on a hard disk, removable media devices (USB drives), software RAID devices, or any other storage device.

The first step in creating an LVM is to take existing physical devices and convert them into physical volumes (PVs). This is accomplished by executing the **pvcreate** command. For example, if you have three hard drives, as shown in Figure 4.3, and you want to make them all PVs, you can execute the following command:

```
pvcreate /dev/sdb /dev/sdc /dev/sdd
```

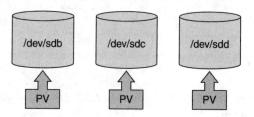

Figure 4.3   Physical Volumes

Next, place these PVs into a volume group (VG) by executing the following command:

```
# vgcreate vol0 /dev/sdb /dev/sdc /dev/sdd
```

Consider a VG to be a collection of storage devices that you want to use to create partition-like structures called logical volumes. So, if **/dev/sdb** is a 60GB hard drive, **/dev/sdc** is a 30GB hard drive, and **/dev/sdd** is a 20GB hard drive, then the VG created by the previous command has 110GB of space available to create the logical volumes (LVs). You could create a single LV using all 110GB or many smaller LVs. See Figure 4.4 for a visual demonstration of volume groups.

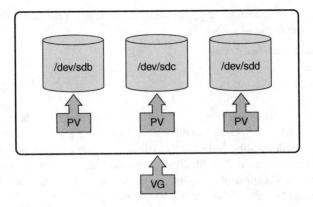

Figure 4.4   Volume Groups

The space within the PVs is broken into small chunks called *extents*. Each extent is 4MB by default (this can be modified when creating the VG by using the **-s** option to the **vgcreate** command). To create an LV, execute the **lvcreate** command and either specify how many extents to assign to the LV or provide a size (which will be rounded up to an extent size):

```
lvcreate -n lv0 -L 400MB vol0
```

The result will be a device file named **/dev/vol0/lv0** that will have 400MB of raw space available. See Figure 4.5 for a visual example.

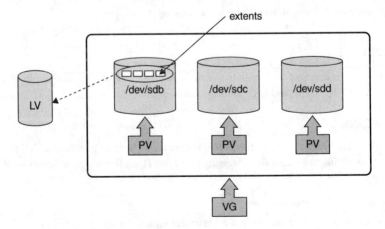

Figure 4.5   Logical Volumes

You can treat **/dev/vol0/lv0** like a regular partition, including creating a filesystem on the device and mounting it, like so:

```
mkfs -t ext4 /dev/vol0/lv0
mkdir /data
mount /dev/vol0/lv0 /data
```

You can use this device name to refer to the new LV device name (the **/dev/vol0/lv0** file). However, you will discover that this isn't really a device name but rather a symbolic link to the **/dev/mapper/vol0_lv0** file. The device mapper is a component of the kernel that generates new devices files (technically block devices files). It creates these files under the **/dev/mapper** directory and, in the case of LVM, creates symbolic links that are backward compatible with older LVM technologies.

Multipath

Some storage devices will be available only through the network. This creates a point-of-failure: the network itself. If you lose network access to a remote storage device, perhaps because a router went down or a new firewall rule was implemented, then applications on your system may fail to function properly.

The concept of Multipath is to create different network paths to a remote storage device. This requires additional network setup, including configuring different routes to the network storage device.

Details regarding *configuring* Multipath are beyond the scope of the Linux+ exam and will not be covered in this book. The concept of Multipath is an exam objective, so be prepared to answer questions regarding the *purpose* of Multipath.

Tools

There are several sets of tools used to manage filesystems and storage devices. In this section, the XFS, LVM, and EXT tools are covered.

XFS Tools

The **xfs_metadump** command dumps (copies) metadata from an unmounted XFS filesystem into a file to be used for debugging purposes. The following table details some important options for XFS tools:

Option	Description
-e	Stop the dump if a filesystem error is found.
-g	Show the progress of the dump.
-w	Display error messages if filesystem errors are found.

The **xfs_info** command is used to display the geometry of an XFS filesystem, similar to the **dumpe2fs** command for ext2/ext3/ext4 filesystems. There are no special options for the **xfs_info** command.

LVM Tools

Review the following list for a summary of the more important LVM tools:

- **vgremove**: Deletes a VG. The VG must not have any LVs.

- **vgreduce**: Deletes a PV from a VG.

- **vgextend**: Adds a PV to an existing VG.

- **vgdisplay**: Displays information about a VG.

- **pvdisplay**: Displays information about a PV.

- **lvdisplay**: Displays information about an LV.

- **lvextend**: Extends the size of an LV. Note that this only resizes the LV, not the filesystem that resides within the LV. See the "resize2fs" section in this chapter to learn how to resize the filesystem.

See the "LVM" section in this chapter for additional details regarding configuring LVM.

EXT Tools

See the "mkfs," "dumpe2fs," "resize2fs," and "tune2fs" sections in this chapter for additional details.

Commands

Many commands may appear on the Linux+ exam related to managing storage devices. This section covers these commands.

mdadm

To create a software RAID device, execute a command like the following:

```
# mdadm -C /dev/md0 -1 1 -n 2 /dev/sdb /dev/sdc
mdadm: array /dev/md0 started.
```

The preceding command uses the following options:

- **-C**: Used to specify the device name for the RAID device

- **-l**: Used to specify the RAID level

- **-n**: Used to specify the number of physical storage devices in the RAID

After creating the RAID device, you can see information about the device by viewing the contents of the **/proc/mdstat** file:

```
# more /proc/mdstat
Personalities : [raid1]
md0 : active raid1 sdc[1] sdb[0]
      987840 blocks [2/2] [UU]
unused devices: <none>
```

The **mdadm --detail** command can also be useful to display information about a software RAID device.

fdisk

The **fdisk** utility is an interactive tool that allows you to display and modify traditional (non-GUID) partition tables. To display a partition table, use the **-l** option (as the root user), like so:

```
# fdisk -l /dev/sda

Disk /dev/sda: 42.9 GB, 42949672960 bytes
4 heads, 32 sectors/track, 655360 cylinders, total 83886080 sectors
Units = sectors of 1 * 512 = 512 bytes
Sector size (logical/physical): 512 bytes / 512 bytes
I/O size (minimum/optimal): 512 bytes / 512 bytes
Disk identifier: 0x000c566f

    Device Boot Start    End       Blocks    Id     System
   /dev/sda1   *  2048   83886079  41942016  83     Linux
```

To modify the partition table of a drive, run the **fdisk** command without the **-l** option:

```
# fdisk /dev/sda
Command (m for help):
```

There are several useful commands you can type at the "Command" prompt, including the following:

Command	Description
d	Delete a partition.
l	List partition types.
m	Print a menu of possible commands.
n	Create a new partition.
p	Print the current partition table.
q	Quit without saving any changes.
t	Change a partition table type.
w	Write (save) changes to the partition table on the hard drive.

parted

The **parted** utility is an interactive tool that allows you to display and modify both traditional and GUID partition tables. It can also create a filesystem on a partition.

To display a partition table, use the **-l** option (run this command as the root user):

```
# parted -l /dev/sda
Model: ATA VBOX HARDDISK (scsi)
```

```
Disk /dev/sda: 42.9GB
Sector size (logical/physical): 512B/512B
Partition Table: msdos

Number   Start    End      Size     Type      File system   Flags
 1       1049kB   42.9GB   primary  ext4                     boot


Model: Linux device-mapper (thin) (dm)
Disk /dev/mapper/docker-8:1-264916-
f9bd50927a44b83330c036684911b54e494e4e48efbc2329262b6f0e909e3d7d: 107GB
Sector size (logical/physical): 512B/512B
Partition Table: loop

Number   Start    End      Size     File system   Flags
 1       0.00B    107GB    ext4


Model: Linux device-mapper (thin) (dm)
Disk /dev/mapper/docker-8:1-264916-
77a4c5c2f607aa6b31a37280ac39a657bfd7ece1d940e50507fb0c128c220f7a: 107GB
Sector size (logical/physical): 512B/512B
Partition Table: loop

Number   Start    End      Size     File system Flags
 1       0.00B    107GB    ext4
```

To modify the partition table of a drive, run the **parted** command without the **-l** option:

```
# parted /dev/sda
GNU Parted 2.3
Using /dev/sda
Welcome to GNU Parted! Type 'help' to view a list of commands.
(parted)
```

The following table shows several useful commands you can type at the "parted" prompt:

Command	Description
rm	Delete a partition.
? or help	Print a menu of possible commands.
mkpart	Create a new partition.
mkpartfs	Create a new partition and filesystem.
print	Print the current partition table.
quit	Quit without saving any changes.
w	Write (save) changes to the partition table on the hard drive.

mkfs

The **mkfs** command will create a filesystem on a partition. The basic syntax of the command is **mkfs -t** *fstype partition*. The *fstype* can be one of the following:

Type	Description
ext2	Create an ext2 filesystem (the default on most distributions).
ext3	Create an ext3 filesystem.
ext4	Create an ext4 filesystem.
bfs	Create a btrfs filesystem.
vfat	Create a VFAT (DOS) filesystem.
ntfs	Create an NTFS (Windows) filesystem.
xfs	Create an XFS filesystem.

Note that the **mkfs** command is a front-end utility to other commands. For example, executing the command **mkfs -t ext4 /dev/sdb7** will result in the **mkfs.ext4 /dev/sdb7** command being executed.

Each specific filesystem-creation utility has dozens of possible options that affect how the filesystem is created. These options are passed from the **mkfs** command to the specific filesystem-creation command that **mkfs** launches.

iostat

The **iostat** command provides input/output statistics on devices, including partitions. When executed with the **-d** option, it provides a variety of information:

```
#iostat -d egrep "Device|sd"
Device          tps     kB_read/s     kB_wrtn/s     kB_read     kB_wrtn
sda            1.62        17.05         12.08        969749      686696
sdb            0.02         3.76          0.00        213643          88
sdc            0.01         0.11          3.59          6239      203860
```

Here are the values of this output:

- **Device**: Device filename of the storage device
- **tps**: Transactions per second
- **kB_read/s**: Kilobytes of data read from the device per second
- **kB_wrtn/s**: Kilobytes of data written to the device per second
- **kB_read**: Total kilobytes of data read from the device
- **kB_wrtn**: Total kilobytes of data written to the device

This data can be useful when trying to determine if the read/write actions on the device are too great of a load. This requires you to monitor this information over time, as it is difficult to determine if there are issues by reading this output once. Output must be compared to data from other points in time to determine if there is an issue.

NOTE: There are other options to the **iostat** command, but the focus on the exam is using the **iostat** command to display storage device information. As a result, the **-d** option is the one you should be familiar with.

df

The **df** command displays usage of partitions and logical devices:

```
# df
Filesystem    1K-blocks  Used      Available  Use%  Mounted on
udev          2019204    12        2019192    1%    /dev
tmpfs         404832     412       404420     1%    /run
/dev/sda1     41251136   6992272   32522952   18%   /
none          4          0         4          0%    /sys/fs/cgroup
none          5120       0         5120       0%    /run/lock
none          2024144    0         2024144    0%    /run/shm
none          102400     0         102400     0%    /run/user
```

The following table details important options for the **df** command:

Option	Description
-h	Display values in human-readable size.
-i	Display inode information.

du

The **du** command provides an estimated amount of disk space usage in a directory structure. For example, the following command displays the amount of space used in the **/usr/lib** directory:

```
# du -sh /usr/lib
791M    /usr/lib
```

The following table details important options for the **du** command:

Option	Description
-h	Display values in a human-readable size (instead of always displaying in bytes, it will display in more understandable values, such as megabytes or kilobytes, depending on the overall size of the file).
-s	Display a summary rather than the size of each subdirectory.

mount

The **mount** command can display the currently mounted filesystems:

```
# mount
/dev/sda1 on / type ext4 (rw)
proc on /proc type proc (rw,noexec,nosuid,nodev)
sysfs on /sys type sysfs (rw,noexec,nosuid,nodev)
```

```
none on /sys/fs/cgroup type tmpfs (rw)
none on /sys/fs/fuse/connections type fusectl (rw)
none on /sys/kernel/debug type debugfs (rw)
none on /sys/kernel/security type securityfs (rw)
udev on /dev type devtmpfs (rw,mode=0755)
devpts on /dev/pts type devpts (rw,noexec,nosuid,gid=5,mode=0620)
tmpfs on /run type tmpfs (rw,noexec,nosuid,size=10%,mode=0755)
none on /run/lock type tmpfs
   (rw,noexec,nosuid,nodev,size=5242880)
none on /run/shm type tmpfs (rw,nosuid,nodev)
none on /run/user type tmpfs
   (rw,noexec,nosuid,nodev,size=104857600, mode=0755)
none on /sys/fs/pstore type pstore (rw)
rpc_pipefs on /run/rpc_pipefs type rpc_pipefs (rw)
systemd on /sys/fs/cgroup/systemd type cgroup
   (rw,noexec,nosuid,nodev, none,name=systemd)
```

The **mount** command can also be used to manually mount a filesystem. Provide the device to mount as the first argument and the mount point (mount directory) as the second argument (execute the following commands as the root user):

```
# mkdir /data
# mount /dev/sdb1 /data
```

The following table details important options for the **mount** command:

Option	Description
-a	Mount all filesystems listed in the **/etc/fstab** file that have a mount option of "auto."
-o	Specify a mount option (for example, **mount -o acl /dev/sdb1 /data**).
-t	Specify the filesystem type to mount. This is typically not necessary because the **mount** command can determine the filesystem type by probing the partition.

umount

Use the **umount** command to manually unmount a filesystem:

```
# mount | grep /data
/dev/sdb1 on /data type ext3 (rw)
# umount /data
```

The following table details important options for the **umount** command:

Option	Description
-r	Attempt to mount the filesystem as read-only if the unmount operation fails.
-f	Force the unmount. This is typically used on NFS mounts when the NFS server is nonresponsive.

lsblk

If you have just created the filesystem, it will likely be easy to remember which device file was used to access the filesystem. However, if you forget which device files are available, you can execute the **lsblk** command (the following command was performed on a native virtual machine—hence the device names of **vda**, **vda1**, and **vda2**):

```
# lsblk
NAME    MAJ:MIN RM  SIZE RO TYPE MOUNTPOINT
vda     252:0    0  254G  0 disk
├─vda1 252:1    0  250G  0 part /
└─vda2 252:2    0    4G  0 part [SWAP]
```

blkid

You can see your label and UUIDs with the **blkid** command:

```
# blkid
/dev/sda1: UUID="4d2b8b91-9666-49cc-a23a-1a183ccd2150" TYPE="ext4"
/dev/sda3: LABEL="mars" UUID="bab04315-389d-42bf-
   9efa-b25c2f39b7a0" TYPE="ext4"
/dev/sda4: UUID="18d6e8bc-14a0-44a0-b82b-e69b4469b0ad" TYPE="ext4"
```

dumpe2fs

The **dumpe2fs** command will display filesystem metadata, as described in the following command:

```
# dumpe2fs /dev/sdb1 | head
dumpe2fs 1.42.9 (4-Feb-2014)
Filesystem volume name:       <none>
Last mounted on:              <not available>
Filesystem UUID:              dbc79125-2d95-47c7-
                              8799-2ef7842c79cc
Filesystem magic number:      0xEF53
Filesystem revision #:         1 (dynamic)
Filesystem features:          has_journal ext_attr resize_inode
                              dir_index filetype sparse_super
Filesystem flags:             signed_directory_hash
Default mount options:        user_xattr acl
```

```
Filesystem state:              clean
Errors behavior:         Continue
```

> **NOTE:** The previous command should be executed as the root user. Because the output of this command could be over 100 lines long, the **head** command was used to limit the output.

Although the **dump2efs** command has a few options, they are typically only employed in specific use cases.

resize2fs

The **resize2fs** command is commonly used in conjunction with resizing a logical volume. Once the LV has been resized, the underlying ext3 or ext4 filesystem also must be resized.

If the plan is to make the LV larger, the **lvextend** command should be executed first, followed by the **resize2fs** command. No size value is needed for the **resize2fs** command, as it will increase to the size of the LV. Here is an example:

```
lvextend -L+1G /dev/vol0/lv0
resize2fs /dev/vol0/lv0
```

If the plan is to make the LV smaller, you first have to resize the filesystem and then use the **lvreduce** command to decrease the size of the LV. This is because if you reduced the LV first, the system would not be able to access the filesystem beyond the new LV size:

```
resize2fs /dev/vol0/lv0 2G
lvreduce -L2G /dev/vol0/lv0
```

fsck

The **fsck** utility is designed to find filesystem problems on unmounted filesystems (run this command as the root user):

```
# fsck /dev/sdb1
fsck from util-linux 2.20.1
e2fsck 1.42.9 (4-Feb-2014)
Pass 1: Checking inodes, blocks, and sizes
Pass 2: Checking directory structure
Pass 3: Checking directory connectivity
Pass 4: Checking reference counts
Pass 5: Checking group summary information
/dev/sdb1: 11/12544 files (0.0% non-contiguous), 6498/50176 blocks
```

This utility is fairly straightforward. It calls the correct filesystem check utility based on a probe of the filesystem and then prompts the user when errors are found. To fix an error, answer "y" or "yes" to the prompts.

Since "yes" is almost always the appropriate answer, the **fsck** utility supports a **-y** option, which automatically answers "yes" to each prompt.

The **fsck** command executes filesystem-specific utilities. In the case of ext2/ext3/ext4 filesystems, the **fsck** command executes the **e2fsck** utility. See the "fsck" section earlier in this chapter for details regarding the **fsck** command.

tune2fs

The **tune2fs** command is used to display or modify specific metadata for an ext2/ext3/ext4 filesystem. For example, by default, 5% of an ext2/ext3/ext4 filesystem is reserved for the system administrator (run the following command as the root user):

```
# tune2fs -l /dev/sdb1 | grep block
Inode count:              12544
Block count:              50176
Reserved block count:      2508
Mount count:                  0
Maximum mount count:         -1
```

Note that the reserved block count (2508) is 5% of the block count (50176). Use the following command to change this to a different percentage:

```
# tune2fs -m 20 /dev/sdb1
tune2fs 1.42.9 (4-Feb-2014)
Setting reserved blocks percentage to 20% (10035 blocks)
```

The following table details important options for the **tune2fs** command:

Option	Description
-J	Modify journal options.
-o	Modify mount options.
-L	Modify the filesystem label.
-l	List filesystem metadata.
-m	Modify the percentage of the filesystem reserved for the root user.

e2label

To change the label of a filesystem, use the **e2label** command:

```
# e2label /dev/sda3 pluto
# blkid
/dev/sda1: UUID="4d2b8b91-9666-49cc-a23a-1a183ccd2150" TYPE="ext4"
/dev/sda3: LABEL="pluto" UUID="bab04315-389d-42bf-
   9efa-b25c2f39b7a0" TYPE="ext4"
/dev/sda4: UUID="18d6e8bc-14a0-44a0-b82b-e69b4469b0ad" TYPE="ext4"
```

Location

Many files and directories related to storage device management may appear on the Linux+ exam. This section covered these files and directories.

/etc/fstab

The **/etc/fstab** file is used to specify which filesystems to mount, where to mount the filesystems, and what options to use during the mount process. This file is used during the boot process to configure filesystems to mount on bootup.

Each line describes one mount process. The following is an example of one of these lines:

```
/dev/sda1 / ext4 defaults 1 1
```

Each line is broken into six fields of data, separated by whitespace:

- The device to mount (**/dev/sda1**).
- The mount point (**/**).
- The filesystem type (**ext4**).
- The mount options (**defaults**).
- Dump level (**1**). This field is related to the **dump** command and is rarely used.
- The **fsck** pass field (**1**). A value of 0 means "do not run **fsck** on this filesystem during system boot," whereas a value of 1 or higher means "run **fsck** on this filesystem during system boot."

/dev/

The **/dev** filesystem contains device files. Device files are used to access physical devices (such as hard drives, keyboards, and CPUs) and virtual devices (such as LVM devices, pseudo-terminals, and software RAID devices). The **/dev** filesystem is memory based, not stored on the hard drive.

The following table details the key files in **/dev**:

File	Description
/dev/sd*	Devices that begin with "sd" in the **/dev** directory are either SATA, SCSI, or USB devices. The device name **/dev/sda** refers to the first device, **/dev/sdb** refers to the second device, and so on. If a device has partitions, they are numbered starting with the value of 1.
/dev/sda1	Example: the first partition of the first SATA, SCSI, or USB device.
/dev/hd*	Devices that begin with "hd" in the **/dev** directory are IDE-based devices. The device name **/dev/hda** refers to the first device, **/dev/hdb** refers to the second device, and so on. If a device has partitions, they are numbered starting with the value of 1.

File	Description
/dev/hda1	Example: the first partition of the first IDE-based device.
/dev/cdrom	Symbolic link that points to the first CD-ROM on the system.
/dev/dm*	Devices that begin with "dm" in the **/dev** directory are either software RAID or LVM devices. The device name **/dev/dm-0** refers to the first device, **/dev/dm-1** refers to the second device, and so on.
/dev/tty*	Devices that begin with "tty" in the **/dev** directory are terminal devices. The device name **/dev/tty0** refers to the first device, **/dev/tty1** refers to the second device, and so on.

/dev/mapper

See the "Device Mapper" section in this chapter.

/dev/disk/by-

You may also find it useful to use the contents of the **/dev/disk** directory to see devices by UUID, label, and so on:

```
# ls /dev/disk
by-label  by-uuid
# ls -l /dev/disk/by-uuid
total 0
lrwxrwxrwx 1 root root 10 Oct 25 22:06
   14872d7d-bd78-49a2-a179-8d5c168310ca -> ../../vda1
lrwxrwxrwx 1 root root 10 Oct 25 22:06
   a1345ce8-384a-4a25-8170-a066a147c53c -> ../../vda2
```

Common subdirectories under the **/dev/disk** directory include the following:

- **id**: Symbolic links to device files using filenames that are based on the serial number of the hardware

- **uuid**: Symbolic links to device files using filenames that are based on the UUID of the device

- **path**: Symbolic links to device files using filenames that are based on the hardware path to the device (the hardware path from the CPU to the device)

- **multipath**: Symbolic links to device files using filenames that are based on the multipath assigned to the device

- **uuid**: Symbolic links to device files using filenames that are based on the UUID of the device

id

See the "/dev/disk/by-" section earlier in this chapter.

uuid

See the "/dev/disk/by-" section earlier in this chapter.

path

See the "/dev/disk/by-" section earlier in this chapter.

multipath

See the "/dev/disk/by-" section earlier in this chapter.

/etc/mtab

A list of all mounted filesystems is stored in **/etc/mtab** automatically by the system. Here is an example:

```
# cat /etc/mtab
/dev/sda1 / ext4 rw,errors=remount-ro 0 0
proc /proc proc rw,noexec,nosuid,nodev 0 0
sysfs /sys sysfs rw,noexec,nosuid,nodev 0 0
udev /dev devtmpfs rw,mode=0755 0 0
devpts /dev/pts devpts rw,noexec,nosuid,gid=5,mode=0620 0 0
tmpfs /run tmpfs rw,noexec,nosuid,size=10%,mode=0755 0 0
/dev/sda3 /mnt/data ext4 rw 0 0
/dev/sda4 /mnt/timemachine ext4 rw 0 0
```

The contents of this file are similar to the contents of the **/proc/mounts** file. See the "/proc/mounts" section later in this chapter for more information.

/sys/block

The **/sys** filesystem is designed to provide important information regarding devices and buses that the kernel is aware of. The **/sys** filesystem is memory based, not stored on the hard drive.

The following table details key files and directories in **/sys**:

File/Directory	Description
/sys/block	Describes block devices, such as hard drives, CD-ROMs, DVDs, and RAID and LVM devices. Examples: sda (first SATA or USB drive), dm-0 (first LVM device), and sr0 (first CD-ROM or DVD).
/sys/bus	Describes devices that are attached to the system bus.
/sys/bus/cpu	Describes the CPUs attached to the system. Look under "/sys/bus/cpu/devices" to see details about each CPU.
/sys/bus/cpu /devices	Describes the USB devices attached to the system.

/proc/partitions

The **/proc** filesystem provides information regarding processes, kernel features, and system hardware. The **/proc** filesystem is memory based, not stored on the hard drive.

The following table details key files and directories in **/proc**:

File/Directory	Description
/proc/cmdline	The kernel parameters used to boot the system.
/proc/cpuinfo	Information about the CPUs.
/proc/devices	A list of each character and block device file that the kernel has recognized.
/proc/mdstat	Information about RAID devices.
/proc/meminfo	Information about system memory.
/proc/modules	A list of all kernel modules currently loaded into memory.
/proc/partitions	The kernel's partition table. Note that this may be different from what is in the hard disk's partition table.
/proc/swaps	A list of all swap space recognized by the kernel.
/proc/vmstat	Virtual memory information.
/proc/sys	A directory that contains tunable kernel parameters.

/proc/mounts

A list of all mounted filesystems is stored in **/proc/mounts** automatically by the system. Here is an example:

```
$ cat /proc/mounts
rootfs / rootfs rw 0 0
sysfs /sys sysfs rw,nosuid,nodev,noexec,relatime 0 0
proc /proc rw,nosuid,nodev,noexec,relatime 0 0
udev /dev devtmpfs rw,relatime,size=1980172k,nr_inodes=495043,
  mode=755 0 0
devpts /dev/pts devpts rw,nosuid,noexec,relatime,gid=5,
  mode=620,ptmxmode=000 0 0
tmpfs /run tmpfs rw,nosuid,noexec,relatime,size=404804k,
  mode=755 0 0
/dev/disk/by-uuid/309b3416-5a59-4954-b4a6-f2c105d9aac5
  / ext4 rw,relatime,errors=remount-ro,data=ordered 0 0
/dev/sda3 /mnt/data ext4 rw,relatime,data=ordered 0 0
/dev/sda4 /mnt/timemachine ext4 rw,relatime,data=ordered 0 0
```

The major difference between the contents of the **/etc/mtab** file and the **/proc/mounts** file is that the **/proc/mounts** file contains more information, including mount options.

See the "/etc/mtab" section in this chapter for more information.

Filesystem Types

While taking the Linux+ exam, you may be asked questions about filesystem types. You should be aware of some of the basic features and functions of each of the following filesystems.

ext3

This filesystem is an extension of the ext2 filesystem and designed to be placed on disk-based devices (partitions). While there are several differences, the big change in ext3 was the introduction of journaling. Journaling helps to prevent filesystem corruption by creating a log (journal) of changes made to files. In the event of a system crash, the recovery time of an ext3 filesystem should be relatively quick, as the journal can be used to quickly fix corrupted file metadata.

ext4

The ext4 filesystem is a replacement for the ext3 filesystem. It has support for larger file-system and individual file sizes. Performance was improved in this version as well.

xfs

Another disk-based filesystem that is known for high performance and handling larger file sizes.

nfs

This is a network-based filesystem that originated on Unix systems. While it is an older filesystem, it has been a standard way of sharing directory structures between Unix and Linux systems. Newer versions of this filesystem include modern securing features and performance improvements.

smb

This filesystem is also known as the Samba filesystem. It is based on cifs and designed to provide network-based sharing.

cifs

This filesystem is used on Microsoft Windows systems to share folders across the net-work. Samba utilities on Linux are used to connect to cifs shares.

ntfs

This filesystem is found on disk-based systems on the Microsoft Windows platform. It is important to remember that Linux distributions cannot recognize ntfs filesystems.

## CHAPTER 5

Compare and contrast cloud and virtualization concepts and technologies

This chapter provides information and commands concerning the following topics:

Templates

- VM
- OVA
- OVF
- JSON
- YAML
- Container images

Bootstrapping

- Cloud-init
- Anaconda
- Kickstart

Storage

- Thin vs. thick provisioning
- Persistent volumes
- Blob
- Block

Network considerations

- Bridging
- Overlay networks
- NAT
- Local
- Dual-homed

Types of hypervisors

Tools

- libvirt

- virsh

- vmm

> **NOTE:** It is important to realize for the exam that this objective asks you to "**compare and contrast** cloud and virtualization concepts and technologies." For the Linux+ exam, you should not be asked any questions on configuration or administration of these technologies. Cloud and virtualization are very large topics themselves, and there are several certification exams that focus just on these technologies. An individual who is Linux+ certified should understand the concepts behinds these technologies but not necessarily be an expert.

The focus of this chapter is the cloud and virtualization concepts and technologies in order to be in line with the exam requirements.

Templates

A virtual machine (VM) is an operating system that shares a physical system with one or more other operating systems. Access to the system's hardware is managed through special software called a hypervisor (see the "Types of Hypervisors" section in this chapter for more details).

One advantage of a VM is the ability to move a VM from one physical system to another. Another advantage is the ability to clone or duplicate a VM. In order to perform either of these tasks, a VM template is used. A template is a definition of a VM that contains information about the VM.

This section focuses on different template format types. In most cases, you won't need to modify the templates directly because there are tools to create and modify these files. However, it is important to understand some of the differences between the template types so you know when you can use the types.

VM

See the "Templates" section in this chapter for a description of virtual machines (VMs).

OVA

An OVA is a VM template that is saved using the Open Virtualization Format and has been stored in TAR format. Besides that it has been stored in TAR format, it is essentially the same as OVF. Some hypervisor software supports OVA format, while others only support OVF format. See the "OVF" subsection in this chapter.

OVAs are typically used to distribute a VM solution, while OVFs are typically used natively by hypervisors to define and clone VMs. OVA file formats should end with an **.ova** extension.

OVF

Open Virtualization Format (OVF) is a standard developed by the Distributed Management Task Force (DMTF). The standard defines a template package, including the following files:

- A descriptor file (in XML format) that describes the components (metadata) and settings for the VM
- Disk images (optional)
- Additional resources (such as ISO files)

OVF file formats should end with an **.ovf** extension.

JSON

Some virtualization and cloud-based technologies make use of JavaScript Object Notation (JSON) file format to store or transfer data. JSON is a simple structure that makes use of the following primary data formats: object (a key-value pair), array (also called list), string, and number. There are also three keyword values: true, false, and null.

Here is a sample JSON file:

```
{
        "name": "Sue Smith",
        "phone": ["555-555-5555", "555-555-5556"],
        "address": {
                "street": "123 Main St.",
                "city": "Anytown",
                "state": "CA"
        }
}
```

YAML

YAML is similar to JSON, as some virtualization and cloud-based technologies make use of YAML file format to store data. It has a similar data structure to JSON, but there are some noticeable difference. JSON uses characters such as "{ }" and "[ ]" to define data structures like objects and arrays, while YAML uses indention to create these structures.

Here is a sample YAML file (note: contrast this with the example in the "JSON" section of this chapter to see how the two file formats differ):

```
---
name: Sue Smith
phone:
- 555-555-5555
- 555-555-5556
```

```
address:
  street: 123 Main St.
  city: Anytown
  state: CA
```

NOTE: YAML originally was an acronym that stood for "Yet Another Markup Language." XML and HTML are other examples of makeup languages. Over time, the goal of YAML changed to being a "human-friendly data serialization standard," so YAML was converted into a backronym that now stands for "YAML Ain't Markup Language."

Container Images

Containers are similar to VMs in that they can appear to act like a separate operating system (OS). However, VMs typically need more hardware resources, whereas containers are more lightweight and run as applications on the host OS. As a result, a system can support many more containers than VMs.

A container is similar to a VM in that they both use images to create a running instance. This image and the running container are managed by a software program, similar to the hypervisor software that manages VMs. Popular container software includes:

- Docker
- Container Linux
- cgroups

Bootstrapping

In general, bootstrapping refers to any process that self-starts without the need for any external assistance. For example, all operating systems use bootstrapping to boot the system. When you power on the system, it starts executing code that comes from either the BIOS or UEFI. That code finds and starts the boot loader software (GRUB or GRUB2 on Linux systems), and the boot loader in turn starts the kernel. The kernel itself is responsible for starting the rest of the operating system.

However, bootstrapping isn't just a term for starting operating systems. The term is also applied to automating the process of installing an OS. This is a critical component of cloud and virtualization technologies, and this section focuses on some of the bootstrapping tools used for these technologies.

Cloud-init

As its name implies, cloud-init is a tool that can be configured to provide the initialization of a cloud instance. This tool makes use of pre-provisioned images, and it is flexible enough to use with different solutions. Typical operations you may include with cloud-init are to add SSH keys, perform networking configurations, execute scripts that will run "post-install," and other similar tasks.

Anaconda

Anaconda is a very popular open source installer program. Many distributions use this program as the default installer, including the following:

- Red Hat Enterprise Linux
- Fedora
- CentOS
- Scientific Linux
- Oracle Linux

Anaconda has a feature that can automate the installation process called "kickstart." See the "Kickstart" subsection in this chapter next for details.

Kickstart

To automate installations that are performed by the Anaconda installer, you can use a kickstart file. This file essentially contains all the answers to the questions Anaconda asks during installation.

The advantage to using this file is that installations can be automated, so no human interaction is required. A kickstart file can also be configured to perform post-installation tasks, such as installing additional software, creating additional user accounts, and similar tasks. However, providing customized values (such as custom network settings) is a feature the kickstart file lacks.

A kickstart file can be created by hand, but you can also install a program called the kickstart configurator (often the system-config-kickstart package) to provide a GUI-based tool that allows you to easily create a kickstart file. Additionally, if you perform a manual installation on an Anaconda-based system (see the "Anaconda" section in this chapter), then the Anaconda installer program will create a file named **/root/ anaconda-ks.cfg** that contains a properly configured kickstart file with the answers you provided during the installation.

Storage

There are several choices for storage for cloud and virtualization technology. This section explores the essential concepts for these storage devices.

Thin vs. Thick Provisioning

A thick provisioning storage solution is one in which all the requested storage space is provisioned (made available) when the storage device is created. This process is also called "pre-allocation." The problem with this technique is that a large volume of storage may be allocated, and much of that storage space may never be used. This means other VMs that could use this space are not allowed to because the space is *reserved* for this VM.

A thin provisioning storage solution is when volume space is requested, but only a portion of that space is initially allocated. For example, a VM may have a thin-provisioned storage space of 100GB created, but only needs 15GB of space currently. Typically a little more space than the minimum is provided (for example, 20GB in this scenario). The rest of the space is provided only when the VM requires more storage space. In other words, less space is reserved for each VM.

The advantage of thin provisioning is more effective use of storage space. This is a benefit that is commonly desired on cloud solutions or when many VMs exist on a single system. One disadvantage is that the speed at which the additional needed space is provided may be too slow, causing errors on the VM. Additionally, it is possible to run out of space if too many VMs request space too quickly.

Persistent Volumes

A persistent volume (PV) is storage space that can be utilized by an OS. This PV "points to" a physical storage device (called a "block" device), which can be a traditional SATA hard disk, solid state drive (SSD), or other storage media.

The reason this system is considered "persistent" is that the underlying physical storage device could change, but the OS would not be aware of or impacted by this change. The OS would always use the PV, but it could just be mapped to a different block device than it originally was.

The advantage of this system is that older block devices can be seamlessly upgraded without any impact on the operation of the OS.

See the "Block" section in this chapter for details about block devices.

Blob

A binary large object (or blob) is data that is stored as a single object within a database system. This object is a combination of binary data that has been merged into a single object for storage.

Block

A block storage device is a physical storage device and is typically the back-end storage for cloud-based storage systems. Examples include the following:

- Traditional SATA drives
- SSD
- RAID drives
- Storage area networks (SANs), which can include Fibre Control Protocol (FCP), Internet Small Computer System Interface (iSCSI), ATA over Ethernet (AoE), and Fibre Channel over Ethernet (FCoE)

There are additional block storage devices, such as optical discs, but most of these are not suitable for VM or cloud solutions.

Network Considerations

This section focuses on networking components you should consider implementing when working with cloud or VM technologies.

Bridging

In cloud computing, it is common to end up with multiple network segments. One way of establishing a connection between these different segments is by using a router. A router would forward network traffic between the different network segments.

Bridging is an alternative that provides a different solution than routing. A bridge device merges different network segments into a single segment. There are different types of bridges:

- **Simple**: Connects two network segments.
- **Multiport**: Connects multiple networks.
- **Transparent**: Also known as a learning bridge; builds routing tables dynamically.
- **Source route**: Routing is built by the source of the traffic.

There are several advantages of network bridges. They can be used to merge dissimilar network transmissions (think of a physical network merged with a wireless network to form a single network). They can also be used to maximize bandwidth.

Overlay Networks

An overlay network is one that is built on top of another network. This may be necessary in situations where two different network protocols are used. For example, there may be an optical network that uses optical protocols, but there is a need to have IP-based (Internet Protocol) communications on this network. The optical protocols don't support IP, so an overlay network is used.

With an overlay network, network packets are encapsulated within other network packets. So, the data being transported on that optical network could include encapsulated IP packets.

Many overlay network technologies are commonly used on the Internet, including peer-to-peer protocols, Tor, VPN, and VoIP.

NAT

Network Address Translation (NAT) is a technology in which the network packets from a private IP network are translated so they can be routed to a public network. This topic is covered in more detail in the "Netfilter" section of Chapter 19, "Given a scenario, implement and configure Linux firewalls."

Local

A local network (or local area network [LAN]) is a collection of systems that communicate directly with each other. Typically the network sends data as broadcasts, and any device can listen to all network traffic on a LAN. This is one reason to segment a network, especially one in the cloud, as you wouldn't want someone to directly access a system on a network that has sensitive data being broadcast.

Dual-Homed

Consider a situation in which a critical server is attached to the network via a router and that router goes down. Now access to that system has been disrupted.

One way to limit this possibility is to configure the server as a dual-homed system. A dual-homed system is a system that has more than one network interface, typically set up for redundancy purposes. Additional network cards are added to the system, each of which will communicate with a different router. If one router goes down, the server is still reachable via other routers.

Types of Hypervisors

There are primarily two types of hypervisors:

- **Native hypervisors:** Also called bare-metal or Type-1 hypervisors. These hypervisors directly interact with the system hardware. This type of hypervisor has been in existence since the 1960s when IBM created the first hypervisors. Modern native hypervisors include the following:

  - Hyper-V KVM

  - Red Hat Enterprise Virtualization

  - VMware vSphere vCloud

  - VMware Infrastructure Xen

  - Oracle VM Server for x86 XenClient

- **Hosted hypervisors**: Also called Type-2 hypervisors. These hypervisors run as software programs on a host operating system. Modern hosted hypervisors include the following:

  - Microsoft Virtual Server

  - Parallels

  - QEMU

  - VirtualBox

  - VMware Fusion

  - VMware Player

  - Workstation Windows

  - Virtual PC

Tools

This section focuses on a few tools that are used in conjunction with virtual machines. It is important to remember that the objective for this section is "**compare and contrast** cloud and virtualization concepts and technologies." For the exam, you should understand what these tools are used for, but details for these tools should not be examtestable.

libvirt

In order for hypervisors to perform tasks related to hardware, they need to interact with the kernel. The libvirt library is used to provide an interface between hypervisors and the kernel.

Several hypervisors are libvirt compatible, including the following:

- Xen
- VirtualBox
- VMware (Workstation, Player, ESXI, and GSX)
- Parrallels

virsh

A component of the libvert software, **virsh** is a command-line tool that allows you to manage virtual machines (which are called "guest domains" in libvirt documentation). For example, the command **virsh list** would provide a list of all the guest domains.

Here are some other **virsh** commands:

- **autostart**: Have a guest domain start automatically when the host OS starts.
- **console:** Connect to the console of a guest domain.
- **create**: Create a guest domain using data from an XML file.
- **destroy**: Terminate a guest domain immediately. This is not a graceful shutdown but rather like disconnecting a system from its power source.
- **cpu-stats:** Display the CPU statistics of a guest domain.
- **reboot:** Reboot a guest domain.
- **restore:** Restore a guest domain from a saved state.
- **save:** Save the current state of a guest domain.
- **shutdown:** Shut down a guest domain gracefully.

vmm

A vmm is a virtual machine manager. For example, **virt-manager** is a GUI-based tool that can be used to manage KVM VMs.

## CHAPTER 6

Given a scenario, configure localization options

This chapter provides information and commands concerning the following topics:

File locations

- /etc/timezone
- /usr/share/zoneinfo

Commands

- localectl
- timedatectl
- date
- hwclock

Environment variables

- LC_*
- LC_ALL
- LANG
- TZ

Character sets

- UTF-8
- ASCII
- Unicode

File Locations

When the system boots, it needs to know how to adjust the time to reflect the correct time zone. This time zone information is stored in files that are defined in this section.

/etc/timezone

This is the location of the system time zone on Debian-based systems:

```
[root@OCS ~]# more /etc/timezone
America/Los_Angeles
```

This file should be set to values specified in the **/usr/share/zoneinfo** directory. For example, **America/Los_Angeles** refers to the **/usr/share/zoneinfo/America/Los_Angeles** file.

/usr/share/zoneinfo

This directory contains a list of all zone files, either directly in the directory or within subdirectories:

```
[root@OCS ~]# ls /usr/share/zoneinfo
Africa       EET        Greenwich    Mexico       right
America      Egypt      Hongkong     MST          ROC
Antarctica   Eire       HST          MST7MDT      ROK
Arctic       EST        Iceland      Navajo       Singapore
Asia         EST5EDT    Indian       NZ           Turkey
Atlantic     Etc        Iran         NZ-CHAT      UCT
Australia    Europe     iso3166.tab  Pacific      Universal
Brazil       GB         Israel       Poland       US
Canada       GB-Eire    Jamaica      Portugal     UTC
CET          GMT        Japan        posix        WET
Chile        GMT0       Kwajalein    posixrules   W-SU
CST6CDT      GMT-0      Libya        PRC          zone.tab
Cuba         GMT+0      MET          PST8PDT      Zulu
```

The files within this directory are used to specify the system time zone. See the "/etc/timezone" subsection in this chapter for more details.

Commands

Several commands can be used to display or modify the date and time on the system, as well as the locale of the system. This section explores these commands.

localectl

The **localectl** command can display and change both locale values and keyboard layouts.

Syntax:

```
localectl [options] command
```

To display values, use the **status** "command":

```
[root@OCS ~]# localectl status
   System Locale: LANG=en_US.utf8
       VC Keymap: us
      X11 Layout: us
       X11 Model: pc105+inet
     X11 Options: terminate:ctrl_alt_bksp
```

Set the locale and keyboard by using the following syntax:

```
[root@OCS ~]#  localectl set-locale "LANG=de_DE.utf8"set-keymap "de"
```

There are a handful of options to the **localectl** command, but none of them are commonly used.

See the "Environment Variables" section in this chapter for more details regarding locale.

timedatectl

Use the **timedatectl** command to display the system clock.

Syntax:

```
timedatectl [option] [value]
```

Example:

```
[root@OCS ~]# timedatectl
        Local time:  Wed 2018-10-10 14:41:41 PDT
    Universal time:  Wed 2018-10-10 21:41:41 UTC
          RTC time:  Wed 2018-10-10 09:51:09
          Timezone:  America/Los_Angeles (PDT, -0700)
       NTP enabled:  yes
  NTP synchronized:  yes
   RTC in local TZ:  no
        DST active:  yes
   Last DST change:  DST began at
                     Sun 2018-03-11 01:59:59 PST
                     Sun 2018-03-11 03:00:00 PDT
   Next DST change:  DST ends (the clock jumps one hour backwards) at
                     Sun 2018-11-04 01:59:59 PDT
                     Sun 2018-11-04 01:00:00 PST
```

As the root user, you can use this command to set the system clock. The following table demonstrates the more commonly used methods of changing the system clock:

Method	Description
set-time [*time*]	Sets the system clock to the specified *time*
set-timezone [*zone*]	Sets the system time zone to the specified *zone*
set-ntp [0|1]	Enables (**1**) or disables (**0**) the Network Time Protocol

date

Use the **date** command to display the system clock:

Syntax:

```
date [option] [format] [value]
```

Example:

```
[root@OCS ~]# date
Wed Oct 10 14:42:28 PDT 2018
```

The output of the **date** command is commonly used to generate unique filenames because the command has a very flexible output format. Here's an example:

```
[root@OCS ~]# date "+%F"
2018-10-10
[root@OCS ~]# touch data-$(date "+%F")
[root@OCS ~]# ls data*
data-2018-10-10
```

The following table details some of the more commonly used date formats:

Format	Description
%a	Abbreviated weekday name (Sun)
%A	Full weekday name (Sunday)
%b	Abbreviated month (Jan)
%B	Full month (January)
%d	Day of the month
%D	Same as **%m/%d/%y**
%F	Same as **%Y-%m-%d**
%m	Month
%n	A newline character
%y	Two-digit year
%Y	Four-digit year

As the root user, you can use the **date** command to set the system clock using the following syntax:

```
[root@OCS ~]# date Wed Oct 10 14:42:28 PDT 2018
```

hwclock

The **hwclock** command is used to display the real-time clock (RTC).

Syntax:

```
hwclock [option] [value]
```

To view the RTC, execute the **hwclock** command with no arguments:

```
[root@OCS ~]# hwclock
Wed 10 Oct 2018 02:37:52 AM PDT  -0.669647 seconds
```

Important options for the **hwclock** command include the following:

Option	Description
--date	Used with the **--set** option to set the RTC
--set	Sets the RTC based on the argument provided to the **--date** option
-s or **--hctosys**	Sets the system time based on the current RTC time
--systz	Resets the RTC based on the current time zone
-w or **--systohc**	Sets the RTC time based on the current system time

Environment Variables

The BASH shell and other processes need customized operations to fit the location of the user. For example, if currency is to be displayed and the user is located in the United States, the $ character should be used. If the user is located in Great Britain, then the £ character should be used.

This section focuses on the variables used to inform programs what settings to use based on a user's locale.

LC_*

LC_* refers to a collection of locale settings used to change the way the shell and other programs handle differences based on the geographic region of the user (or a region the user is familiar with). These values can be viewed by executing the **locale** command:

```
[root@OCS ~]# locale
LANG=en_US.UTF-8
LANGUAGE=en_US
LC_CTYPE="en_US.UTF-8"
LC_NUMERIC="en_US.UTF-8"
LC_TIME="en_US.UTF-8"
LC_COLLATE="en_US.UTF-8"
LC_MONETARY="en_US.UTF-8"
LC_MESSAGES="en_US.UTF-8"
```

```
LC_PAPER="en_US.UTF-8"
LC_NAME="en_US.UTF-8"
LC_ADDRESS="en_US.UTF-8"
LC_TELEPHONE="en_US.UTF-8"
LC_MEASUREMENT="en_US.UTF-8"
LC_IDENTIFICATION="en_US.UTF-8"
LC_ALL=
```

The more important settings are described in the following table:

Setting	Description
LANG	See the "LANG" section in this chapter.
LC_CTYPE	Case conversion.
LC_NUMERIC	Numeric formats.
LC_TIME	Time and date formats.
LC_COLLATE	Collation order.
LC_MONETARY	Currency formats.
LC_MESSAGES	Format of messages.
LC_PAPER	Paper size formats.
LC_NAME	Name formats.
LC_ADDRESS	Address formats.
LC_TELEPHONE	Telephone formats.
LC_ALL	See the "LC_All" section in this chapter.

Use the **locale -a** command to view all available locales.

LC_ALL

When set, **LC_ALL** will override all other locale settings. This provides an easy means to change all locale settings by modifying one environment variable. Typically this is set for a specific command, as shown here:

```
[root@OCS ~]# LC_ALL=es_ES.UTF8 man
```

See the "LC_*" subsection in this chapter for additional details.

LANG

When set, **LANG** will provide a default locale value. This can be overwritten for specific locale features by setting other locale variables. For example, the following would set the default to Spanish but use the date/time formats for English:

```
[root@OCS ~]# LANG=es_ES.UTF8 LC_TIME=en_US.utf8 man
```

See the "LC_*" subsection in this chapter for additional details.

TZ

The **TZ** variable can be used to set a different time zone than the system default:

```
[root@OCS ~]# date
Tue Feb 28 21:58:33 PST 2017
[root@OCS ~]# TZ=America/Goose_Bay date
Wed Mar 1 01:59:02 AST 2017
```

See the "/etc/timezone" and "/usr/share/zoneinfo" sections in this chapter for more details regarding system time zones.

Character Sets

A character set is a collection of characters that have each been assigned a code (typically a number). Using standard character sets makes it easier for different systems to communicate with each other. This section describes common character sets you may encounter on the exam.

UTF-8

See the "Unicode" section in this chapter.

ASCII

American Standard Code for Information Interchange (ASCII) is an English-only encoding format that is limited to 128 characters (a 7-bit code). Extended ASCII can support additional, non-English characters.

Unicode

An encoding standard that includes ASCII within the first 7 bits (128 characters). The additional bits are used for additional, non-English characters. Unicode has gone through several revisions, including UTF-8, UTF-16, and UCS (which is not considered to be obsolete).

## CHAPTER 7

Given a scenario, conduct software installations, configurations, updates, and removals

This chapter provides information and commands concerning the following topics:

Package types

- .rpm
- .deb
- .tar
- .tgz
- .gz

Installation tools

- RPM
- Dpkg
- APT
- YUM
- DNF
- Zypper

Build tools

- Commands (**make, make install**)
- **ldd**
- Compilers
- Shared libraries

Repositories

- Configuration
- Creation
- Syncing
- Locations

Acquisition commands

- **wget**
- **curl**

Package Types

A package type is a file type used to define what kind of content should be stored in the file. The type is indicated by the file extension (**.rpm**, **.deb**, and so on). It is important to know which package types match up with which extensions, as this will determine which tool is used to manage the package file.

.rpm

An **.rpm** extension indicates a Red Hat package file. Red Hat package files are managed with the **rpm** command. See the "RPM" section in this chapter.

.deb

A **.deb** extension indicates a Debian package file. Debian package files are managed with the **dpkg** command. See the "dpkg" section in this chapter.

.tar

A **.tar** extension indicates a file that has been created with the **tar** command. See the "tar" section of Chapter 20, "Given a scenario, backup, restore, and compress files" for more details.

.tgz

A **.tgz** extension indicates a file that has been created with the **tar** command using the option to compress with the **gzip** utility. See the "tar" and "gzip" sections of Chapter 20, for more details.

.gz

A **.gz** extension indicates a file that has been created with the **gzip** command. See the "gzip" section of Chapter 20 for more details.

Installation Tools

This section focuses on the different installation tools used for different package types.

RPM

The **rpm** command is useful for installing, upgrading, and removing packages that are already downloaded on your system. Here are some useful options:

Option	Description
-i	Installs a package.
-U	Updates a package if an older version of the package exists; installs from scratch if the older version does not exist.
-F	Updates a package if an older version of the package exists; does nothing if an older version does not exist.

Option	Description
-e	Removes the package, including the configuration files.
-l	Lists packages that are currently installed.
-q	Performs a package query; additional options can be used to fine-tune the query.
-f	Determines which package a specific file belongs to.

Use the **-q** option to the **rpm** command to perform queries. Here are some additional options to fine-tune a query:

Option	Description
-a	Returns a list of all installed packages
-c	Lists the configuration files installed with the specified package
-d	Lists the documentation files installed with the specified package
-i	Displays information about the specified package
-K	Verifies the integrity of the specified package
-l	Lists all files installed with the specified package
-provides	Lists which capabilities the specified package provides
-R	Lists which capabilities the specified package requires
-s	Displays the state of each file that was installed by the specified package (normal, not installed, or replaced)

Example:

```
$ rpm -qc cups
/etc/cups/classes.conf
/etc/cups/client.conf
/etc/cups/cups-files.conf
/etc/cups/cupsd.conf
/etc/cups/lpoptions
/etc/cups/printers.conf
/etc/cups/snmp.conf
/etc/cups/subscriptions.conf
/etc/dbus-1/system.d/cups.conf
/etc/logrotate.d/cups
/etc/pam.d/cups
```

dpkg

Use the **dpkg** command to manage local Debian packages.

The syntax of the **dpkg** command is as follows:

```
dpkg [option] command
```

Some useful options:

Option	Description
-i	Installs a package
-r	Removes the package, but keeps the configuration files
-P	Removes the package, including the configuration files (purge)
-l	Lists the packages currently installed
-L	Lists files that were installed with a package (for example, **dpkg -L zip**)
-V	Verifies the integrity of the specified package or packages
-s	Displays package status
-C	Checks for broken packages
-S	Lists the package name that was responsible for a specific file being installed on the system (for example, **dpkg -S /usr/bin/zip**)

When a package is installed, it may run a configuration script as part of the installation process. To run this configuration script again at some point in the future, use the **dpkg-reconfigure** command. Although there are some options to this command, they are rarely used.

The syntax of the **dpkg-reconfigure** command is as follows:

```
dpkg-reconfigure [options] source packages
```

The following example will re-run the tzdata configuration scripts:

```
dpkg-reconfigure tzdata
```

APT

Use the **apt-get** command to manage Debian packages that are located on a repository. This command makes use of the **/etc/apt/sources.list** file to determine which repository to use (see more about this file at the end of this section).

Here are some syntax examples of the **apt-get** command:

```
apt-get [options] command
apt-get [options] install|remove pkg1 [pkg2...]
apt-get [options] source pkg1 [pkg2...]
```

To specify what action to take, provide a keyword (command) to the **apt-get** command. Here are some useful commands for **apt-get**:

Command	Description
install	Installs the specified package; if the package is currently installed, use the **--only-upgrade** option to upgrade rather than install from fresh.
update	Updates the package cache of all available packages.
upgrade	Updates all packages and their dependencies.
remove	Removes a package but leaves its configuration files on the system.
purge	Removes a package, including its configuration files.

Use the **apt-cache** command to display package information regarding the package cache.

Here are some syntax examples of the **apt-cache** command:

```
apt-cache [options] command
apt-cache [options] show pkg1 [pkg2...]
```

Example:

```
# apt-cache search xzip
xzip - Interpreter of Infocom-format story-files
```

To specify what action to take, provide a keyword (command) to the **apt-cache** command. Here are some useful commands for **apt-cache**:

Command	Description
search	Displays all packages with the search term listed in the package name or description; the search term can be a regular expression.
showpkg	Displays information about a package; the package name is provided as an argument.
stats	Displays statistics about the package cache (for example, **apt-cache stats**).
showsrc	Displays information about a source package; the package name is provided as an argument.
depends	Displays a package's dependencies.
rdepends	Displays a package's reverse dependencies (that is, packages that rely on this package).

The **aptitude** utility is a menu-driven tool designed to make it easy to display, add, and remove packages. See Figure 7.1 for a demonstration of this tool.

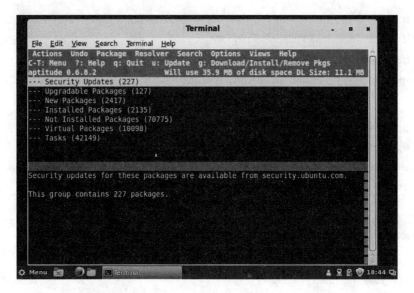

Figure 7.1 The **aptitude** Utility Screen

The **/etc/apt/sources.list** file contains a list of URLs of software repositories. Figure 7.2 provides a description of this file.

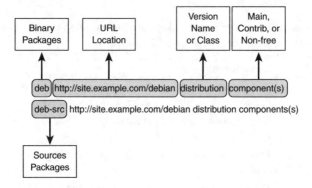

Figure 7.2 The **/etc/apt/sources.list** File

Distribution can be one of the following:

- Release name (for example, wheezy, jessie, stretch, or sid)
- Class name (for example, oldstable, stable, testing, or unstable)

Component can be one of the following:

- **main**: Packages must comply with DFSG (Debian Free Software Guidelines).
- **contrib**: Packages must comply with DFSG, but package dependencies do not.
- **non-free**: Packages do not comply with DFSG.

Example of the default file for the Jessie version of Debian:

```
deb http://httpredir.debian.org/debian jessie main
deb-src http://httpredir.debian.org/debian jessie main

deb http://httpredir.debian.org/debian jessie-updates main
deb-src http://httpredir.debian.org/debian jessie-updates main

deb http://security.debian.org/ jessie/updates main
deb-src http://security.debian.org/ jessie/updates main
```

YUM

The **yum** command is used to install software from repositories. It can also be used to remove software and display information regarding software. The following table highlights the primary **yum** commands and options:

Command/Option	Description
install	Installs a package and any dependency packages from a repository. Example: **yum install zip**.
groupinstall	Installs an entire software group from a repository. Example: **yum groupinstall "Office Suite and Productivity"**.
update	Updates the specified software package.
remove	Removes the specified software package and any dependency packages from the system.
groupremove	Removes the specified software group from the system.
list	Lists information about packages, including which are installed and which are available. Example: **yum list available**.
grouplist	Lists information about software groups, including what packages are part of a group; use **yum grouplist** with no arguments to see a list of available software groups.
info	Provides information about a specific software package. Example: **yum info zip**.
groupinfo	Provides information about a specific software group.
-y	Answers "yes" automatically to any prompts. Example: **yum -y install zip**.

Important options to the **yum list** command:

Option	Description
all	Lists all packages, installed or available.
installed	Lists all packages currently installed.
available	Lists all packages currently not installed but available for installation.
updates	Lists all packages that are currently installed on the system and that also have an available newer version on a repository.

NOTE: Wildcards (or *globs*) may be used with **yum** commands. Here's an example:

```
# yum list installed "*zip*"
Loaded plugins: fastestmirror, langpacks
Repodata is over 2 weeks old. Install yum-cron?
  Or run: yum makecache fast
Loading mirror speeds from cached hostfile
 * base: mirror.supremebytes.com
 * epel: mirror.chpc.utah.edu
 * extras: mirrors.cat.pdx.edu
 * updates: centos.sonn.com
Installed Packages
bzip2.x86_64                      1.0.6-13.el7          @base
bzip2-libs.x86_64                 1.0.6-13.el7          @base
gzip.x86_64                       1.5-8.el7             @base
perl-Compress-Raw-Bzip2.x86_64 2.061-3.el7             anaconda
unzip.x86_64                      6.0-15.el7            @base
zip.x86_64                        3.0-10.el7            @anaconda
```

The **yumdownloader** command is used to download software packages without installing the software. The resulting RPM file could be installed manually or copied to other systems to install.

Here are some important options to the **yumdownloader** command:

Option	Description
--destdir	Used to specify the directory to download RPM files. (The default is the current directory.)
--resolve	Used to download dependency packages for the specified package. (The default is to only download specified packages.)
--source	Used to download the source RPM, not the binary (installable) RPM.

The **/etc/yum.conf** file is the primary configuration file for **yum** commands.

Example:

```
[main]
cachedir=/var/cache/yum/$basearch/$releasever
keepcache=0
debuglevel=2
logfile=/var/log/yum.log
```

```
exactarch=1
obsoletes=1
gpgcheck=1
plugins=1
installonly_limit=5
bugtracker_url=http://bugs.centos.org/set_project.php
  ?project_id=23&ref=http://bugs.centos.org/
  bug_report_page.php?category=yum
distroverpkg=centos-release
```

Here are some key settings of the **/etc/yum.conf** file:

Setting	Description
cachedir	Directory where RPMs will be placed after download.
logfile	Location of the log file that contains **yum** actions.
gpgcheck	A value of 1 means perform a GPG (GNU Privacy Guard) check to ensure the package is valid; 0 means do not perform a GPG check. (This can be overridden by specific settings for each repository configuration file; see the "/etc/yum.repos.d" section in this chapter for more details.)
assumeyes	A value of 1 means always assume "yes" to yes/no prompts; 0 means do not make any assumption (provide a prompt instead).

The **/etc/yum.repos.d** directory contains files that end in ".repo" and are used to specify the location of yum repositories. Each file defines one or more repositories, as described in Figure 7.3.

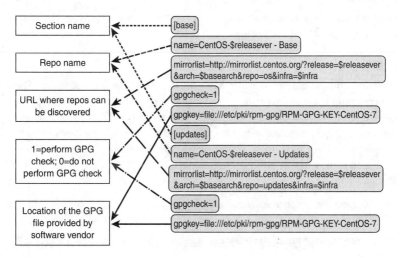

Figure 7.3   The Format of Files in the **/etc/yum.repos.d** Directory

DNF

The DNF tool is designed as an enhancement and replacement for yum. The majority of the changes were made to the "back end" of the software. Most **dnf** commands work just like **yum** commands, only with **dnf** being the command name.

On the back end, the DNF tool handled dependencies better and addressed some additional YUM deficiencies (such as using older versions of Python). YUM hasn't been completely replaced, so knowing that either command may be used is important.

Zypper

The **zypper** command is found on SUSE Linux. It is derived from the RPM software suite and works very similar to **yum**. It has automatic dependence checking and uses repositories. Its command structure and options are almost identical to **yum**. Here's an example:

```
zypper install pkg_name
```

If you know how to use the **yum** command, then in most cases you can replace "yum" with "zypper" and the command will work successfully.

Build Tools

Build tools are used to create software that will be used by others. This section explores some of the more useful build tools.

Commands

Several commands can be used to create software. This section covers the more important and exam-testable of these commands.

make

The **make** command uses a file named **Makefile** to perform specific operations. The **make** command is a utility for building and maintaining programs and other types of files from source code. A primary function of the make utility is to determine which pieces of a large program need to be recompiled and to issue the commands necessary to recompile them. Each **Makefile** is written by the software developer to perform operations related to the software project. Typically this will include the following types of functions:

- An operation to compile the software. See "Compilers" in this chapter for more information on this topic.
- An operation to install the software.
- An operation to "clean" previous versions of the compiled code.

The following is an example of a simple **Makefile** that only has an install operation:

```
# more /usr/lib/firmware/Makefile
# This file implements the GNOME Build API:
# http://people.gnome.org/~walters/docs/build-api.txt

FIRMWAREDIR = /lib/firmware

all:

install:
        mkdir -p $(DESTDIR)$(FIRMWAREDIR)
        cp -r * $(DESTDIR)$(FIRMWAREDIR)
        rm -f $(DESTDIR)/usbdux/*dux $(DESTDIR)/*/*.asm
        rm $(DESTDIR)$(FIRMWAREDIR)/{WHENCE,LICENSE.*,LICENCE.*}
```

make install

The **install** option for the **make** command is designed to install code from source on the system. It may also include a compile process, depending on how the software developer created the **Makefile**. See the "Compilers" and "make" sections in this chapter for more details.

ldd

You can see what shared libraries a specific command uses by using the **ldd** command. Here is the syntax of the **ldd** command:

```
ldd [options] FILE
```

Example:

```
# ldd /bin/cp
        linux-vdso.so.1 =>  (0x00007ffc35df9000)
        libselinux.so.1 => /lib64/libselinux.so.1  (0x00007f93faa09000)
        libacl.so.1 => /lib64/libacl.so.1 (0x00007f93fa800000)
        libattr.so.1 => /lib64/libattr.so.1 (0x00007f93fa5fa000)
        libc.so.6 => /lib64/libc.so.6 (0x00007f93fa239000)
        libpcre.so.1 => /lib64/libpcre.so.1 (0x00007f93f9fd8000)
        liblzma.so.5 => /lib64/liblzma.so.5 (0x00007f93f9db2000)
        libdl.so.2 => /lib64/libdl.so.2 (0x00007f93f9bae000)
        /lib64/ld-linux-x86-64.so.2 (0x00007f93fac42000)
        libpthread.so.0 => /lib64/libpthread.so.0(0x00007f93f9992000)
```

The purpose of using the **ldd** command is to troubleshoot problems with code that you are writing. This command tells you not only what libraries are being called, but specifically which directory each library is being called from. This can be extremely useful when a library is not behaving as you would expect it to behave.

The following table describes useful options for the **ldd** command:

Option	Description
-v	Verbose; print additional information.
-u	Display any unused direct dependencies.

Compilers

A compiler is a utility that takes source code (written in plain-text format) and converts it into executable binary code. There are many different compilers, each designed to work with a specific language. For example, the **gcc** compiler is used to compile code written in the C or C++ programming language.

Although an administrator may need to learn the details about a particular compiler, this would happen on a case-by-case basis. Normally compilers are called automatically during the build process of software. This is performed by the **make** utility. See the "make" section in this chapter for more details.

Shared Libraries

Shared libraries are files used by executable programs. They are designed so developers can rely on established code to perform functions.

These shared libraries follow the naming convention lib*name*.so.*ver*, where *name* is a unique name for the library and *ver* is used to indicate the version number of the library (for example, **libkpathsea.so.6.1.1**).

Normally shared library files are stored in one of the following locations on Linux distributions:

- **/lib** or **/lib64**
- **/usr/lib** or **/usr/lib64**
- **/usr/local/lib** or **/usr/local/lib64**

If your operating system is a 32-bit distribution, expect to see the libraries under **/lib**, **/usr/lib**, and **/usr/local/lib**. On 64-bit platforms, the **/lib64**, **/usr/lib/64**, and **/usr/local/lib64** directories are where you can expect to find libraries.

Repositories

A repository is a central location where information is stored. For software management, a repository is where software packages are stored. Utilities like **apt** and **yum** can connect to a repository, verify package dependencies, and install software packages.

Configuration

See the "yum" and "apt" sections in this chapter for details on how to configure these tools to connect to a repository.

Creation

To create a repository on a **yum**-based system, complete the following steps:

Step 1.   Install the **createrepo** package: **yum install createrepo**.

Step 2.   Create a directory to store the repository: **mkdir** */directory*.

Step 3.   Copy packages to the directory.

Step 4.   Run the **createrepo** command: **createrepo** */directory*.

Step 5.   Share the repository using either an HTTP or an FTP server.

To create a repository on an **apt**-based system, complete the following steps:

Step 1.   Install the **dpkg-dev** package (if necessary): **apt-get install dpkg-dev**.

Step 2.   Create a directory to store repository information: **mkdir** */var/packages*.

Step 3.   Copy packages into the new directory.

Step 4.   Run the following command in the directory: **dpkg-scanpackages .
/dev/null | gzip -9c > Packages.gz**.

Step 5.   Share the repository using either an HTTP or an FTP server.

Syncing

The process of repository syncing is to duplicate an existing repository onto the local system with the intent of making the local system either a standalone repository or a mirror repository. A mirror repository would need to be updated regularly using the syncing method so it contains the same package information as the original.

To sync a YUM repository, use the **reposync** command. To sync an APT repository, use the **apt-mirror** command. Both commands have many configuration options and features that are beyond the scope of the Linux+ exam.

Locations

Most repository systems can be accessible via the local file system using FTP or HTTP.

Acquisition Commands

The **wget** and **curl** commands are designed to acquire data from remote systems. This section covers these commands.

wget

The **wget** command is designed to be a noninteractive tool to download files from remote systems via HTTP, HTTPS, or FTP. It is often used within scripts.

Syntax:

```
wget location
```

Example:

```
# wget http://onecoursesource.com
--2019-01-09 15:18:26--  http://onecoursesource.com/
Resolving onecoursesource.com (onecoursesource.com)...38.89.136.109
Connecting to onecoursesource.com (onecoursesource.com)
   |38.89.136.109|:80... connected.
HTTP request sent, awaiting response... 301 Moved Permanently
Location: http://www.onecoursesource.com/ [following]
--2019-01-09 15:18:26--  http://www.onecoursesource.com/
Resolving www.onecoursesource.com
   (www.onecoursesource.com)... 38.89.136.109
Reusing existing connection to onecoursesource.com:80.
HTTP request sent, awaiting response... 200 OK
Length: unspecified [text/html]
Saving to: 'index.html'

index.html                [ <=>                 ]
   12.25K  --.-KB/s    in 0s


2019-01-09 15:18:26 (259 MB/s) - 'index.html' saved [12539]
```

Here are some useful options:

Option	Description
-h	Display help.
-b	Perform downloads in the background. Useful for large downloads.
-q	Download quietly.
-v	Be verbose.
-nc	Don't clobber existing files.
-c	Continue a partial download. Useful if a download fails due to a disconnect.
-r	Recursive.

curl

The **curl** command allows for noninteractive data transfer from a large number of protocols, including the following:

- FTP
- FTPS
- HTTP
- SCP
- SFTP

- SMB
- SMBS
- Telnet
- TFTP

Although the **curl** command supports more protocols than the **wget** command, the **wget** command can perform recursive downloads and can recover from failed download attempts, making it advantageous in certain situations. The **curl** command also supports wildcard characters. The goal of both of the commands is essentially the same.

Syntax:

curl *location*

Example:

```
# curl http://onecoursesource.com
<!DOCTYPE HTML PUBLIC "-//IETF//DTD HTML 2.0//EN">
<html><head>
<title>301 Moved Permanently</title>
</head><body>
<h1>Moved Permanently</h1>
<p>The document has moved
   <a href="http://www.onecoursesource.com/">here</a>.</p>
</body></html>
```

Note that the data is displayed, not stored in a file like the **wget** command. You can use redirection to put the contents into a file.

## CHAPTER 8

Given a scenario, manage users and groups

This chapter provides information and commands concerning the following topics:

Creation

- useradd
- groupadd

Modification

- usermod
- groupmod
- passwd
- chage

Deletion

- userdel
- groupdel

Queries

- id
- whoami
- who
- w
- last

Quotas

- User quota
- Group quota

Profiles (BASH parameters)

- User entries (**.bashrc**, **.bash_profile**, **.profile**)
- Global entries (**/etc/bashrc**, **/etc/profile.d/**, **/etc/skel**, **/etc/profile**)

Important files and file contents

- **/etc/passwd**
- **/etc/group**
- **/etc/shadow**

Creation

This section focuses on the commands designed to create user and group accounts.

useradd

The **useradd** command is used by the root user to create a user account.

Example:

```
[root@OCS ~]$ useradd julia
```

Here are some important options for the **useradd** command:

Option	Description
-c	Set the comment or GECOS field for the user.
-d	Specify the home directory for the user. This is often used with the -m option, which creates the home directory.
-e	Set the account's Expiration Date value (see the "/etc/shadow" section in this chapter for more details).
-f	Set the account's Inactive value (see the "/etc/shadow" section in this chapter for more details).
-g	Specify the user's primary group.
-G	Specify the user's secondary groups.
-k	Specify the skel directory; this is the directory from where files are copied automatically into the user's home directory.
-s	Specify the user's login shell.
-u	Specify the user's UID.

groupadd

The **groupadd** command is used by the root user to create a group account.

Example:

```
[root@OCS ~]$ groupadd -g 2050 test
```

The **-g** option is used to specify the GID for the new group.

Modification

This section focuses on the commands designed to modify user and group accounts.

usermod

The **usermod** command is used by the root user to modify a user account.

Example:

```
[root@OCS ~]$ usermod -s /bin/tcsh julia
```

The **usermod** command uses many of the same options as the **useradd** command. See the "useradd" section in this chapter for a list of these options.

groupmod

The **groupmod** command is used by the root user to modify a group account.

Example:

```
[root@OCS ~]$ groupmod -n proj test
```

Important options for the **groupmod** command include the following:

Option	Description
-g	Change the GID.
-n	Change the group name.

passwd

The **passwd** command allows a user to change her password. The root user can also use this command to change any user password or change other password-based features for a user account. Here are some important options for the **passwd** command:

Option	Description
-d	Delete the user's password.
-e	Expire the user account immediately.
-l	Lock the account.
-u	Unlock the account.
-m	Change the Min field of the **/etc/shadow** file for the user.
-M	Change the Max field of the **/etc/shadow** file for the user.
-w	Change the Warn field of the **/etc/shadow** file for the user.

chage

The **chage** command is executed by the root user to modify password-aging features for a user account. Here are some important options for the **chage** command:

Option	Description
-d	Change the Last Change field of the **/etc/shadow** file for the user.
-E	Set the Expiration Date field of the **/etc/shadow** file for the user (for example, **chage -E 2025-01-01 bob**).
-m	Change the Min field of the **/etc/shadow** file for the user.
-M	Change the Max field of the **/etc/shadow** file for the user.
-W	Change the Warn field of the **/etc/shadow** file for the user.

See the "/etc/shadow" subsection in this chapter for additional information regarding password-aging settings.

Deletion

This section focuses on the commands designed to delete user and group accounts.

userdel

The **userdel** command is used by the root user to delete a user account.

Example:

```
[root@OCS ~]$ userdel susan
```

An important option for the **userdel** command is the **-r** option, which deletes the user account as well as the user's home directory and mail spool.

groupdel

The **groupdel** command is used by the root user to delete a group account.

Example:

```
[root@OCS ~]$ groupdel test
```

> **IMPORTANT NOTE:**   Be sure to remove all files owned by the group before running this command (or reassign the files to another group).

Queries

This section focuses on the commands designed to query user and group accounts.

id

The **id** command will display basic account information. When run with no arguments, it displays the current user's UID, username, primary GID and name, as well as all secondary group memberships:

```
[root@OCS ~]$ id
uid=0(root) gid=0(root) groups=0(root)
```

When passed a username as an argument, it provides information about the user specified:

```
[root@OCS ~]$ id bo
uid=1001(bo) gid=1001(bo) groups=1001(bo),10(wheel),20001(temprandy)
```

While there are a few options for the **id** command, they are not typically used.

whoami

The **whoami** command displays the effective user ID.

Example:

```
[root@OCS ~]$ whoami
```

While there are a few options for the **whoami** command, they are not typically used.

who

The **who** command shows who is currently logged in:

```
[root@OCS ~]# who
student        :0              2017-02-18 01:52 (:0)
student        pts/0           2017-02-18 01:52 (:0)
student        pts/1           2017-03-05 19:55 (:0)
student        pts/2           2017-03-06 18:24 (:0)
root           pts/3           2017-03-06 18:24 (localhost)
```

The output of the **who** command includes the username, the terminal device the user is using, the login date and time, and where the user logged in from (**:0** means a local login). The following table describes common options for the **who** command:

Option	Description
-b or **--boot**	Time of the last system boot.
-H or **--heading**	Display headings on columns.
-q or **--count**	Display the number of users currently logged in.

w

The **w** command displays who is logged in as well as other useful information:

```
[root@OCS ~]# w
 18:25:08 up 3 days,  1:24,  5 users,  load average: 0.27, 0.08, 0.07
USER     TTY      FROM      LOGIN@   IDLE   JCPU   PCPU  WHAT
student :0       :0        18Feb17 41:48  1.01s  gdm-session-wor
student pts/0    :0        18Feb17 4.00s  0.46s  20.33s /usr/libexec/gn
student pts/1    :0        Sun19   1:32   0.04s  0.00s  less -s
student pts/2    :0        18:24   12.00s 0.05s  0.01s  /usr/bin/sss_ss
root    pts/3    localhost 18:24   12.00s 0.03s  0.03s  -bash
```

The first line of output is the same as the **uptime** command. See the "uptime" section in Chapter 21, "Given a scenario, analyze system properties and remediate accordingly," for more details. The JCPU column stands for "Job CPU" and represents how much CPU time has been used by all processes that were launched from the terminal. The PCPU column stands for "Process CPU" and represents how much CPU time has been used by the current process (which is listed as the last item in the line of output).

The following table describes common options for the **w** command:

Option	Description
-h or **--no-header**	Don't display headings on columns.
-s or **--short**	Short; don't display JCPU or PCPU columns.

last

The **last** command displays information about current and previous logins:

```
[root@OCS ~]# last -10
root       pts/3 localhost Mon Mar 6 18:24   still logged in
student  pts/2 :0          Mon Mar 6 18:24   still logged in
student  pts/1 :0          Sun Mar 5 19:55   still logged in
student  pts/1 :0          Sat Feb 18 01:56 - 01:56 (00:00)
student  pts/0 :0          Sat Feb 18 01:52 still logged in
student  :0      :0        Sat Feb 18 01:52 still logged in
(unknown :0      :0        Sat Feb 18 01:48 - 01:52 (00:03)
reboot    system boot 3.10.0-327.18.2.
   Tue Jan 24 13:43 - 19:15 (41+05:31)
student  pts/1 :0          Sun Jan 22 08:22 - 01:46 (26+17:24)
student  pts/0 :0          Thu Jan 19 12:19 - 01:46 29+13:27)

wtmp begins Sat Jun 11 20:51:56 2016
```

The following table describes common options for the **last** command:

Option	Description
-x	Only show *x* number of logins.
-a	Display the hostname for remote logins.
-d	Display the IP address for logins.
-F	Display the full login and logout times.

Quotas

Quotas allow the administrator the ability to limit how much disk space can be used by individuals or groups. Quotas are per filesystem. This section focuses on how to enable and view quotas.

User Quotas

To enable user quotas, you must mount the filesystem with the **usrquota** mount option. This can be accomplished by adding **usrquota** to the mount option field of the **/etc/fstab** file:

```
/dev/sdb1          /          ext4          usrquota     1          1
```

NOTE: To enable group quotas, use the **grpquota** boot option. Both options can be used together (**usrquota,grpquota**) to enable both user and group quotas on a filesystem.

Then you can remount the filesystem with the following command (executed by the root user):

```
[root@OCS ~]$ mount -o remount /
```

See the "/etc/fstab" and "mount" sections in Chapter 4, "Given a scenario, manage storage in a Linux environment," for additional details regarding these tasks.

After mounting the filesystem with the **usrquota** option enabled, you need to create the initial quota databases by executing the following **quotacheck** command:

```
[root@OCS ~]$ quotacheck -cugm /dev/sdb1
```

This will result in new files in the mount point directory of the filesystem:

```
[root@OCS ~]$ ls /aquota*
/aquota.group /aquota.user
```

Here are some important options for the **quotacheck** command:

Option	Description
-c	Create database file(s).
-g	Only create the **aquota.group** file, which means only group quotas will be enabled unless the **-u** option is also used.
-m	Do not attempt to unmount the filesystem while creating the quota file(s).
-u	Only create the **aquota.user** file, which means only user quotas will be enabled unless the **-g** option is also used.

To create or edit a user's quotas, execute the **edquota** command followed by the username (the following command must be executed by the root user):

```
[root@OCS ~]$ edquota sarah
```

NOTE: Use the **-g** option to the **edquota** command to edit a group quota.

The **edquota** command will enter an editor (vi is typically the default) and display all of the user's quotas. The output will look something like the following:

```
Disk quotas for user sarah (uid 507):
  Filesystem      blocks       soft       hard      inodes       soft       hard
  /dev/sdb1       550060          0          0       29905          0          0
```

The following table describes the fields of the quota:

Key	Description
Filesystem	The partition that contains the filesystem with quotas enabled.
blocks	How many blocks the user currently uses in the filesystem.
soft	A value that represents a soft quota for blocks; if the user creates a file that results in exceeding this block limit, a warning is issued.
hard	A value that represents a hard quota for blocks; if the user creates a file that results in exceeding this block limit, an error is issued and no additional files can be created in the filesystem.
inodes	How many files the user currently has in the filesystem.
soft	A value that represents a soft quota for files; if the user creates a file that results in exceeding this file limit, a warning is issued.
hard	A value that represents a hard quota for files; if the user creates a file that results in exceeding this file limit, an error is issued and no additional files can be created in the filesystem.

NOTE: The grace period can be set by executing the **edquota -t** command. See the "Quotas" section for more details regarding the grace period.

The **quota** command can be executed by a user to display the quotas for the account:

```
[sarah@OCS ~]$ quota
Disk quotas for user sarah (uid 507):
     Filesystem  blocks   quota   limit   grace   files   quota   limit   grace
       /dev/sda1  20480    30000   60000             1       0       0
```

Note the output when a user has exceeded a soft quota; in the following example, the user sarah is above the soft limit for block size:

```
[sarah@OCS ~]$ quota
Disk quotas for user sarah (uid 507):
     Filesystem  blocks   quota   limit   grace   files   quota   limit   grace
       /dev/sda1  40960*   30000   60000   7days    2       0       0
```

Once the user has exceeded a soft quota, a grace period is provided. The user must reduce the space used in the filesystem to be below the soft quota within the grace period or else the current usage converts to a hard quota limit.

NOTE: The grace period can be set by the root user by executing the **edquota -t** command. See the "edquota" section for more details about that command.

Here are some important options for the **quota** command:

Option	Description
-g	Display group quotas instead of specific user quotas.
-s	Display information in human-readable sizes rather than block sizes.
-l	Display quota information only for local filesystems (rather than network-based filesystem quotas).

The **repquota** command is used by the root user to display quotas for an entire filesystem (the following command must be executed by the root user):

```
[root@localhost ~]$ repquota /
*** Report for user quotas on device /dev/sda1
Block grace time: 7days; Inode grace time: 7days
                        Block limits                File limits
User              used    soft    hard   grace    used   soft  hard   grace
---------------------------------------------------------------------------
root       --  4559956       0       0           207396      0     0
daemon     --       64       0       0                4      0     0
man        --     1832       0       0              145      0     0
www-data   --        4       0       0                1      0     0
libuuid    --       40       0       0                6      0     0
syslog     --     3848       0       0               23      0     0
messagebus --        8       0       0                2      0     0
landscape  --        8       0       0                2      0     0
pollinate  --        4       0       0                1      0     0
vagrant    --   550060       0       0            29906      0     0
colord     --        8       0       0                2      0     0
statd      --       12       0       0                3      0     0
puppet     --       44       0       0               11      0     0
ubuntu     --       36       0       0                8      0     0
sarah      +-    40960   30000   60000  6days        2      0     0
```

Here are some important options for the **repquota** command:

Option	Description
-a	Display quotas for all filesystems with quota mount options specified in the **/etc/fstab** file.
-g	Display group quotas instead of specific user quotas.
-s	Display information in human-readable sizes rather than block sizes.

The **quotaon** command is used to turn quotas on for a filesystem. Normally when the system is booted, it will turn on quotas automatically. However, you may turn off quotas by executing the **quotaoff** command followed by the name of the filesystem (the following commands must be executed by the root user):

```
[root@OCS ~]$ quotaoff /dev/sdb1
[root@OCS ~]$ quotaon /dev/sdb1
```

Group Quotas

Group quotas are quotas that apply to every member of a group. The way you create group quotas is very similar to with a few exceptions that are covered in the "User Quotas" subsection in this chapter.

Profiles

When a user logs in to the system, a login shell is started. When a user starts a new shell after login, it is referred to as a *non-login shell*. In each case, initialization files are used to set up the shell environment. Which initialization files are executed depends on whether the shell is a login shell or a non-login shell.

Figure 8.1 demonstrates which initialization files are executed when the user logs in to the system.

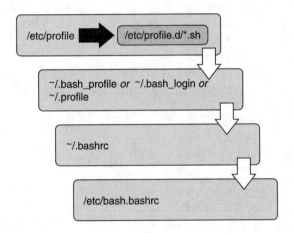

Figure 8.1   Initialization Files Executed When the User Logs In to the System

The following is an explanation of Figure 8.1:

1. The first initialization file that is executed when a user logs in is the **/etc/profile** file. On most Linux platforms, this script includes code that executes all the initialization files in the **/etc/profile.d** directory that end in ".sh". *The purpose of the /etc/profile file is to be a place for system administrators to put code that will execute every time every BASH shell user logs in (typically login messages and environment variable definitions).*

2. After the **/etc/profile** file is executed, the login shell looks in the user's home directory for a file named **~/.bash_profile**. If it's found, the login shell executes the code in this file. Otherwise, the login shell looks for a file named **~/.bash_login**. If it's found, the login shell executes the code in this file. Otherwise, the login shell looks for a file named **~/.profile** and executes the code in this file. *The purpose of these files is to be a place where each user can put code that will execute every time that specific user logs in (typically environment variable definitions).*

3. The next initialization file executed is the **~/.bashrc** script. *The purpose of this file is to be a place where each user can put code that will execute every time the user opens a new shell (typically alias and function definitions).*

4. The next initialization file executed is the **/etc/bash.bashrc** script. *The purpose of this file is to be a place where system administrators can put code that will execute every time the user opens a new shell (typically alias and function definitions).*

Figure 8.2 demonstrates which initialization files are executed when the user opens a new shell.

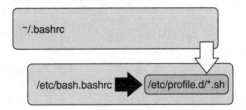

Figure 8.2   Initialization Files Executed When the User Starts a Non-Login Shell

The following is an explanation of Figure 8.2:

1. The first initialization file that is executed when a user opens a non-login shell is the **~/.bashrc** script. *The purpose of this file is to be a place where each user can put code that will execute every time that user opens a new shell (typically alias and function definitions).*

2. The next initialization file executed is the **/etc/bash.bashrc** script. On most Linux platforms, this script includes code that executes all the initialization files in the **/etc/profile.d** directory that end in ".sh". *The purpose of these initialization files is to be a place where system administrators can put code that will execute every time the user opens a new shell (typically alias and function definitions).*

BASH Parameters

Initialization files can be used to modify several bash shell features. For example, shell variables can be set to modify the behavior of the bash shell or other programs. See the "Shell environments and shell variables" section in Chapter 25, "Given a scenario, deploy and execute basic BASH scripts" for more details about shell variables.

This section covers the initialization files where these features are typically set.

User Entries

Users can control their individual environment by modifying initialization files in their home directory. This section covers these files.

.bashrc

When a user opens a new BASH shell, the commands in the ~/.bashrc file are executed. This allows the user to set up the account by placing commands in this file.

See the "Profiles" section in this chapter for further details regarding how initialization files are used.

Note that the .bashrc file often contains BASH scripting code. See Chapter 25 for details regarding BASH scripting.

.bash_profile

When a user logs in to the system and the user's login shell is a BASH shell, the commands in the ~/.bash_profile file are executed if this file exists. This enables the user to set up the account by placing commands in this file.

See the "Profiles" section in this chapter for further details regarding how initialization files are used.

Note that the .bash_profile file often contains BASH scripting code. See Chapter 25 for details regarding BASH scripting.

.profile

When a user logs in to the system and the user's login shell is a BASH shell, the commands in the ~/.profile file are executed if this file exists. This allows the user to set up the account by placing commands in this file.

See the "Profiles" section in this chapter for further details regarding how initialization files are used.

Note that the .profile file often contains BASH scripting code. See Chapter 25 for details regarding BASH scripting.

Global Entries

The administrator can control the BASH environment for all users by modifying initialization files in the /etc directory. This section covers these files.

/etc/bashrc

When a user opens a new BASH shell, the commands in the /etc/bashrc file are executed. Only the root user should be allowed to modify the /etc/bashrc file. This allows the root user to set up all bash user accounts by placing commands in this file.

See the "Profiles" section in this chapter for further details regarding how initialization files are used.

Note that the **/etc/bashrc** file often contains BASH scripting code. See Chapter 25 for details regarding BASH scripting.

/etc/profile.d/

Software developers often have the need to modify the BASH environment of user accounts. For example, consider a software program that uses shell variables as a means to pass the program key information, such as user account information or system information.

Software is normally installed by the root user, so developers could use this elevated privilege to directly modify global initialization files, such as the **/etc/profile** or **/etc/bashrc** file. The danger is that this modification may accidently affect other global settings.

Instead of modifying the primary configuration files, software developers (and sometimes administrators) will place files in the **/etc/profile.d** directory. This directory is also considerd a location for initialization files because of the following code in the **/etc/profile** file:

```
for i in /etc/profile.d/*.sh ; do
    if [ -r "$i" ]; then
        if [ "${-#*i}" != "$-" ]; then
            . "$i"
        else
            . "$i" >/dev/null
        fi
    fi
done
```

This code means "if there is a file that ends in .sh in the **/etc/profile** directory and it is readable, source (run) the contents of this file in the current shell."

NOTE: To learn more about this code, see Chapter 25.

So, when determining what takes place during the BASH initialization process, be sure to look at the contents of the **/etc/profile.d** as well. The following is a common example:

```
[root@OCS ~]$ ls /etc/profile.d
256term.csh      colorls.csh   lang.csh   vim.csh
256term.sh       colorls.sh    lang.sh    vim.sh
colorgrep.csh    cvs.csh       less.csh   which2.csh
colorgrep.sh     cvs.sh        less.sh    which2.sh
```

See the "Profiles" section in this chapter for further details regarding how initialization files are used.

Note that the files in the **/etc/profile.d** directory often contain BASH scripting code. See Chapter 25 for details regarding BASH scripting.

/etc/skel

The **/etc/skel** directory is used when a new user account is created to provide the new account with default files, such as BASH configuration files (**.bashrc**, **.profile**, and so on). See the "useradd" subsection in this chapter for additional details.

/etc/profile

When a user logs in to the system and the user's login shell is a BASH shell, the commands in the **/etc/profile** file are executed. Only the root user should be allowed to modify the **/etc/profile** file. This allows the root user to set up all BASH user accounts by placing commands in this file.

See the "Profiles" section in this chapter for further details regarding how initialization files are used.

Note that the **/etc/profile** file often contains BASH scripting code. See Chapter 25 for details regarding BASH scripting.

Important Files and File Contents

User and group account information is stored in plain-text files. This section covers these files.

/etc/passwd

The **/etc/passwd** file is used to store user account information. It contains most of the user account data, except the password and password-aging policies (see the "/etc/shadow" section in this chapter for details about those settings).

Each line in the **/etc/passwd** file describes one user account.

Example:

```
root:x:0:0:root:/root:/bin/bash
```

Every line is broken into fields of data. The following table describes these fields:

Field	Description
User name	root:x:0:0:root:/root:/bin/bash
	This is the name the user will provide when logging in to the system.
Password placeholder	root:**x**:0:0:root:/root:/bin/bash
	This is the place where the password used to be stored in older versions of Unix.
UID	root:x:**0**:0:root:/root:/bin/bash
	This is the user ID.
GID	root:x:0:**0**:root:/root:/bin/bash
	This is the user's primary group ID.

Field	Description
GECOS	root:x:0:0:**root**:/root:/bin/bash
	GECOS stands for General Electric Comprehensive Operating System; it's typically the user's real name and other identifying data.
Home directory	root:x:0:0:root:**/root**:/bin/bash
	This is the user's home directory.
Login shell	root:x:0:0:root:/root:**/bin/bash**
	This is the user's login shell.

/etc/group

The **/etc/group** file is used to store group account information. Each line in the **/etc/group** file describes one group account.

Example:

```
admin:x:110:bob,sue
```

Every line is broken into fields of data. The following table describes these fields:

Field	Description
Group name	**admin**:x:110:bob,sue
	This is the name of the group.
Password placeholder	admin:**x**:110:bob,sue
	This is the place where the password used to be stored in older versions of Unix.
GID	admin:x:**110**:bob,sue
	This is the group ID.
Member list	admin:x:110:**bob,sue**
	These are the members of the group.

/etc/shadow

The **/etc/shadow** file is used to store user password information (see the "/etc/passwd" section in this chapter for details about other user account data).

Each line in the **/etc/shadow** file describes one user account. Here's an example of an account with a valid password:

```
student:$6$ciPSOxID$E5p6cgsPs2lng7dQjrVMIUBGhd/dqs49d
jnCB1h1oGhryfitzaVGvsODflyNU67uX3uBraVY0GIOO2zaVGeZ/.:
17116:0:99999:7:30:17246:
```

Here's an example of an account with a locked password:

```
bob:*LK*:17116:0:99999:7:30:17246:
```

Every line is broken into fields of data. The following table describes these fields:

Field	Description
User name	**bob**:*LK*:17116:0:99999:7:30:17246: This is the user's name, which is matched up to the entry in the **/etc/passwd** file.
Password	bob:***LK***:17116:0:99999:7:30:17246: This is the user's password or some locked value. Note that passwords are encrypted.
Last change	bob:*LK*:**17116**:0:99999:7:30:17246: This is the number of days since January 1, 1970 and the last time the user's password was changed. It's used by the system for the next three fields.
Min	bob:*LK*:17116:**0**:99999:7:30:17246: It's how many days after a user's password is changed before the user can change his password again.
Max	bob:*LK*:17116:0:**99999**:7:30:17246: This is how many days after a user's password is changed before the user must change his password again. If the user doesn't change his password before this time limit, the account is locked.
Warn	bob:*LK*:17116:0:99999:**7**:30:17246: This is how many days before the account is to be locked to start issuing warnings to the user as the user logs in.
Inactive	bob:*LK*:17116:0:99999:7:**30**:17246: After the account is locked, this is how many "grace days" the user has in which he can log in—but only if a new password is provided at login.
Expiration date	bob:*LK*:17116:0:99999:7:30:**17246**: This is the number of days since January 1, 1970 when the user's account will expire.
Unused	bob:*LK*:17116:0:99999:7:30:17246: This is an unused field that may be used in the future.

## CHAPTER 9

Given a scenario, create, modify, and redirect files

This chapter provides information and commands concerning the following topics:

Text editors

- nano
- vi

File readers

- grep
- cat
- tail
- head
- less
- more

Output redirection

- <
- >
- |
- <<
- >>
- 2>
- &>
- stdin
- stdout
- stderr
- /dev/null
- /dev/tty
- xargs
- tee
- Here documents

Text processing

- grep
- tr

- echo
- sort
- awk
- sed
- cut
- print
- egrep
- wc

File and directory operations

- touch
- mv
- cp
- rm
- scp
- ls
- rsync
- mkdir
- rmdir
- ln (Symbolic (soft); Hard)
- unlink
- inodes
- find
- locate
- grep
- which
- whereis
- diff
- updatedb

Bonus: regex

Text Editors

Most configuration files on Linux systems are in plain text format. This make it critical to know how to edit text files. This section focuses on two common Linux editors: nano and the vi editor.

nano

The **nano** editor is a non-GUI editor that provides a handy "cheat sheet" at the bottom of the screen. See Figure 9.1 for an example.

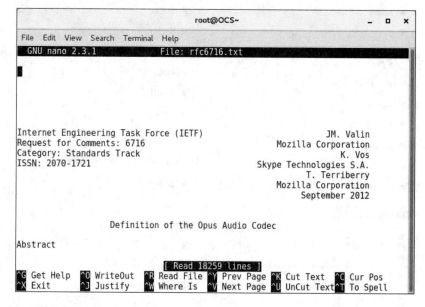

Figure 9.1   The nano Editor

Commands in **nano** are given by holding down the Ctrl button and then pressing another key. For example, **Ctrl-x** will exit the **nano** editor. In the list of commands at the bottom of the screen, the ^ symbol represents the Ctrl key. Also note that **^X** doesn't mean **Ctrl-Shift-x**, but rather just **Ctrl-x**.

You should be aware of the following commonly used **nano** commands:

Command	Description
^G	Display a help document. Note that when the help document appears, different commands are displayed at the bottom of the screen.
^O	Save a file.
^X	Exit the editor.
^K	Cut a line (deletes and places the line into memory). Multiple ^K can be used to cut multiple lines into memory.

Command	Description
^U	Uncut a line. Note that this isn't an "undo" operation, but rather a paste operation.
^^	Begin and end text to mark. Marked text can be copied using **Alt-^**. Use one **^^** to start the mark, use arrow keys to select, and then use a final **^^** to end the mark. Note that the second ^ is an actual ^ character while the first represents the control character.
^W	Search for text in the current document.
^F	Move forward one screen.
^B	Move back one screen.
^*n*	Move to a specific line number. For example, **^5** moves to line #5.
^C	Display the current position in the document.

vi

The vi editor is a standard text editor for both Linux and Unix environments. Although it may not be as user friendly as other editors, it has a few important advantages:

- The vi editor (or vim, an improved version of the vi editor) is on every Linux distribution (and all Unix flavors). This means if you know how to edit files with the vi editor, you can always edit a file regardless of which distribution you are working on.

- Because the vi editor is a command-line only editor, it does not require a graphical user interface (GUI). This is important because many Linux servers do not have a GUI installed, which means you can't use GUI-based text editors.

- Once you understand vi well, you will find it is an efficient editor and you can edit files very quickly using it compared to most other editors. This is because all commands are short and keyboard based, so you don't have to waste time taking your hands off the keyboard to use the mouse.

To edit a new file with the vi editor, you can just type the command with no arguments or type **vi** *filename*.

A note about vim: The vim editor is an improved text editor that has additional features that are not found in the vi editor. Many Linux distributions use the vim editor by default. One advantage of the vim editor is that it includes all the features and commands of the vi editor. So, if you learned the vi editor 30 years ago, your knowledge would still apply when working in the vim editor. All of the commands in this chapter work in both editors.

Because the vi editor was designed to only use a keyboard, this poses a challenge because sometimes a key should execute a command and sometimes a key should represent a character to insert into the document. To allow the keys to perform different tasks, vi has three modes of operation:

- **Command mode:** This mode is the default mode. When you open vi, you are placed in the command mode. Within this mode, you can perform commands that can move around the screen, delete text, and paste text.

- **Insert mode:** While you're in insert mode, any key typed will appear in your document as new text. When you are finished adding new text, you can return to the default mode (the command mode) by pressing the Escape key.

- **Last line mode:** The last line mode, also called the *ex mode*, allows you to perform more complex operations, such as saving a document to a file with a different name. To enter into last line mode from the command mode, press the : key. After you enter your command and press Enter, the command is executed and normally you are returned to the command mode. In some cases, you may need to press the Escape key to return to the command mode.

NOTE: You cannot move from the insert mode to the last line mode, or vice versa. To move to the insert mode or the last line mode, you first must be in the command mode. Pressing the Escape key places you in the command mode.

To search for files while in the vi editor, you can use either the **/** or the **?** character when you are working in the command mode. When you type either the **/** or the **?** character, you will see a prompt appear at the bottom-left side of the screen, as shown in Figure 9.2.

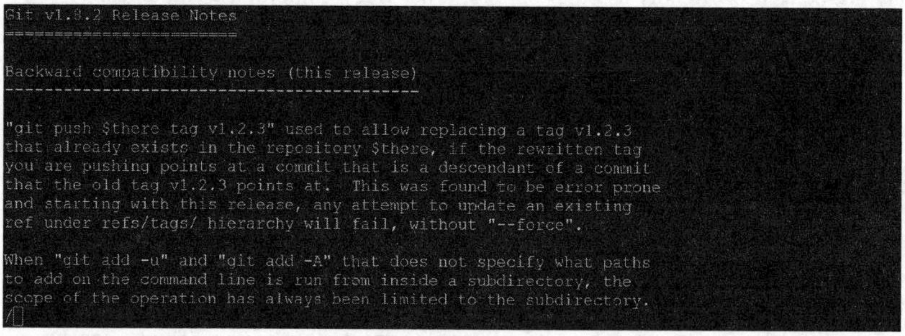

Figure 9.2   Searching for Files in the vi Editor

At the **/** or **?** prompt, type the value you want to search for. You can use regular expressions within this value. For example, if you type **/^the**, then the vi editor will search for the next occurrence of the string "the" that appears at the beginning of a line.

The **/** character performs a forward search, and **?** searches backward in the document. If you don't find what you are searching for, you can use the **n** character to find the next match. When the search is started with a **/** character, the **n** character will continue the search forward in the document. When the search is started with a **?** character, the **n** character will continue the search backward in the document.

To reverse the current search, use the **N** character. For example, suppose you start the search by typing **?^the**. Using the **N** character would result in searching forward in the document.

While in the command mode, you can move around the screen by using the following keys:

Key	Description
h	Move one character to the left.
j	Move one line down.
k	Move one line up.
l	Move one character to the right.

While in the command mode, you can enter the insert mode by using one of the following keys:

Key	Description
i	Enter insert mode before the character the cursor is on; use the **I** key to insert before the beginning of the current line.
o	Open a new line below the current line and enter the insert mode; use the **O** key to open a line above the current line.
a	Enter insert mode after the character the cursor is on; use the **A** key to insert after the end of the current line.

While in the command mode, you can modify text by using the following keys:

Key	Description
c	The **c** key is combined with other keys to change data. For example, **cw** will change the current word and **c$** will change from the cursor position to the end of the line. When finished making your changes, press the Escape key.
d	The **d** key is combined with other keys to delete data. For example, **dw** will delete the current word, and **d$** will delete from the cursor position to the end of the line. All of the deleted data is stored in a buffer and can be pasted back into the document with the **p** or **P** key.
p	After cutting text with the **d** key or copying text with the **y** key, you can paste with the **p** or **P** key. A lowercase **p** will paste after the current cursor, whereas an uppercase **P** will paste before the cursor.
y	The **y** key is combined with other keys to copy data. For example, **yw** will copy the current word and **y$** will copy from the cursor position to the end of the line. All of the copied data is stored in a buffer and can be pasted back into the document with the **p** or **P** key.
dd	The **dd** command will delete the current line.
yy	The **yy** command will copy the current line.

While in the command mode, you can save and/or quit your document by entering the following keys:

Key	Description
ZZ	Saves and quits the document. This is equivalent to **:wq**.
:w!	Forces the vi editor to write changes in the document to the file.
:q!	Forces the vi editor to quit, even if changes in the file have not been saved.
:e!	Opens a new file to edit and forgets all changes in the document since the last write. This requires a filename argument as an option (for example, **:e! myfile.txt**).

File Readers

File readers are commands used to view the contents of a text file. This section focuses on some of the more popular Linux file readers.

grep

Use the **grep** command to search files for lines that contain a specific pattern. By default, the **grep** command will display the entire line when it finds a matching pattern.

Example:

```
[student@OCS ~]$ grep "the" /etc/rsyslog.conf
# To enable high precision timestamps, comment out the following line.
# Set the default permissions for all log files.
```

> **NOTE:**   The pattern used to perform the search uses basic regular expressions. See the "Bonus: regex" section in this chapter for additional details regarding basic regular expressions.

Here are some important options of the **grep** command:

Option	Description
-c	Display a count of the number of matching lines rather than displaying each line that matches.
-color	The text that matches is displayed in a different color than the rest of the text.
-E	Use extended regular expressions in addition to basic regular expressions. See the "Bonus: regex" section in this chapter for additional details regarding extended regular expressions.
-f	Fixed strings; all characters in the pattern will be treated as regular characters, not regular expression characters.
-e	Used to specify multiple patterns in one **grep** command (for example, **grep -e** *pattern1* **-e** *pattern2 file*).
-f *file*	Use patterns found within the specified *file*.

Option	Description
-i	Ignore case.
-l	Display filenames that match the pattern, rather than displaying every line in the file that matches. This is useful when you're searching multiple files (for example, **grep "the" /etc/***).
-n	Display the line number before displaying the line.
-r	Recursively search all the files in a directory structure.
-v	Inverse match; return all lines that don't contain the pattern specified.
-w	Match whole words only; for example, the command **grep "the"** *file* will match the letters "the" even when part of a larger word such as "then" or "there," but the command **grep -w "the"** *file* will only match "the" as a separate word.

cat

The **cat** command displays the contents of text files. Important options include the following:

Option	Description
-A	Same as **-vET**.
-e	Same as **-vE**.
-E	Displays a $ character at the end of each line (used to see trailing whitespace characters).
-n	Numbers all lines of output.
-s	Converts multiple blank lines into a single blank line.
-T	Displays "^I" characters for each tab character (used to see spaces instead of tabs).
-v	Displays "unprintable" characters (such as control characters).

tail

The **tail** command displays the bottom part of text data. By default, the last ten lines are displayed. Use the **-n** option to display a different number of lines:

```
[student@OCS ~]$ cal 12 1999
    December 1999
Su Mo Tu We Th Fr Sa
          1  2  3  4
 5  6  7  8  9 10 11
12 13 14 15 16 17 18
19 20 21 22 23 24 25
26 27 28 29 30 31

[student@OCS ~]$ cal 12 1999 | tail -n 2
26 27 28 29 30 31
```

Here are some important options:

Option	Description
-f	Display the bottom part of a file and "follow" changes, which means to continue to display any changes made to the file as data is written to the file.
-n +x	Display from line number x to the end of the file.

head

The **head** command displays the top part of text data. By default, the top ten lines are displayed. Use the **-n** option to display a different number of lines:

```
[student@OCS ~]$ ls -l | head -3
total 12
drwxrwxr-x. 2 student student 6 Aug 22 16:51 book
drwxrwxr-x. 2 student student 6 Aug 22 16:51 class
```

less

The **less** command is used to display large chunks of text data. Unlike the **cat** command, the **less** command will pause after displaying the first page of information. Keys on the keyboard allow the user to scroll through the document. The following table highlights the more useful movement keys:

Movement Key	Description
h	Display a help screen (summary of the **less** command movement keys).
SPACEBAR	Move forward one page in the current document.
b	Move back one page in the current document.
ENTER	Move down one line in the current document; the down-arrow key can also perform this operation.
UP ARROW	Move up one line in the current document.
/term	Search the document for *term* (this can be a regular expression or just plain text).
q	Quit viewing the document and return to the shell.

more

The **more** command is a slightly less capable version of the **less** command. Essentially everything that the **more** command can do, the **less** command also has as a feature. However, the **less** command has additional features that the **more** command does not have.

See the "less" subsection in this chapter to learn more about these commands (everything listed in that subsection is included as a feature of the **more** command).

Output Redirection

Each command is able to send two streams of output (standard output and standard error) and can accept one stream of data (standard input). In documentation, these terms can also be described using the following:

- Standard output = STDOUT or STDOUT
- Standard error = stderr or STDERR
- Standard input = STDIN or STDIN

By default, STDOUT and stderr are sent to the terminal window, whereas STDIN comes from keyboard input. In some cases you want to change these locations, and this is accomplished by a process called *redirection*.

The following table describes the methods used to perform redirection:

Method	Description
cmd < file	Override STDIN so the input comes from the file specified.
cmd > file	Override STDOUT so the output goes into the file specified.
cmd 2> file	Override stderr so the output goes into the file specified.
cmd &> file	Override both STDOUT and stderr so the output goes into the file specified.
*cmd1	cmd2*	Override STDOUT from *cmd1* so it goes into *cmd2* as STDIN.

In the following example, STDOUT of the **cal** program is sent to a file named **month**:

```
[student@OCS ~]$ cal > month
```

It is common to redirect both STDOUT and stderr into separate files, as demonstrated in the next example:

```
[student@OCS ~]$ find /etc -name "*.cfg" -exec file {} \;
> output 2> error
```

Redirecting STDIN is fairly rare because most commands will accept a filename as a regular argument; however, the **tr** command, which performs character translations, requires redirecting STDIN:

```
[student@OCS ~]$ cat /etc/hostname
localhost
[student@OCS ~]$ tr 'a-z' 'A-Z' < /etc/hostname
LOCALHOST
```

<

See the "Output Redirection" section in this chapter.

>

See the "Output Redirection" section in this chapter.

|

The process of piping (called piping because the | character is referred to as a "pipe") the output of one command to another command results in a more powerful command line. For example, the following takes the standard output of the **ls** command and sends it into the **grep** command to filter files that were changed on April 16:

```
[student@OCS ~]$ ls -l /etc | grep "Apr 16"
-rw-r--r-- 1 root root        321 Apr 16 2014 blkid.conf
drwxr-xr-x 2 root root       4096 Apr 16 2014 fstab.d
```

In the next example, lines 41–50 of the copyright file are displayed (note: some lines were truncated to fit within the margins of this book):

```
[student@OCS ~]$ head -50 copyright | tail
        b) If you have received a modified Vim that was…
           mentioned under a) you are allowed to further…
           unmodified, as mentioned at I). If you make…
           the text under a) applies to those changes.
        c) Provide all the changes, including source code, with every
           copy of the modified Vim you distribute. This…
           the form of a context diff. You can choose what…
           for new code you add. The changes and their license must not
           restrict others from making their own changes…
           version of Vim.
        d) When you have a modified Vim which includes changes as
           mentioned
```

You can add additional commands as demonstrated here:

```
[student@OCS ~]$ head -50 copyright | tail | nl
     1  b) If you have received a modified Vim that was…
     2     mentioned under a) you are allowed to further…
     3     unmodified, as mentioned at I). If you make…
     4     the text under a) applies to those changes.
     5  c) Provide all the changes, including source code…
     6     copy of the modified Vim you distribute. This…
     7     the form of a context diff. You can choose…
     8     for new code you add. The changes and their…
     9     restrict others from making their own changes…
    10     version of Vim.
    11  d) When you have a modified Vim which includes changes as
    12     mentioned
```

Note that the order of execution makes a difference. In the previous example, the first 40 lines of the copyright file are sent to the **tail** command. Then the last ten lines of the first 40 lines are sent to the **nl** command for numbering. Notice the difference in output when the **nl** command is executed first:

```
[student@OCS ~]$ nl copyright | head -50 | tail
    36    b) If you have received a modified Vim that was…
    37       mentioned under a) you are allowed to further…
    38       unmodified, as mentioned at I). If you make…
    39       the text under a) applies to those changes.
    40    c) Provide all the changes, including source code…
    41       copy of the modified Vim you distribute. This…
    42       the form of a context diff. You can choose…
    43       for new code you add. The changes and their…
    44       restrict others from making their own changes…
    45       version of Vim.
    45    d) When you have a modified Vim which includes changes as
    47       mentioned
```

<<

See the "Here Documents" subsection in this chapter.

>>

See the "Output Redirection" section in this chapter.

2>

See the "Output Redirection" section in this chapter.

&>

See the "Output Redirection" section in this chapter.

stdin

See the "Output Redirection" section in this chapter.

stdout

See the "Output Redirection" section in this chapter.

stderr

See the "Output Redirection" section in this chapter.

/dev/null

In some cases, you may not want to see either stdout or stderr of a command. For example, consider the following **find** command:

```
[student@OCS ~]$ find /etc -name "hosts"
find: '/etc/named': Permission denied
find: '/etc/polkit-1/localauthority': Permission denied
find: '/etc/polkit-1/rules.d': Permission denied
find: '/etc/pki/rsyslog': Permission denied
find: '/etc/pki/CA/private': Permission denied
find: '/etc/sudoers.d': Permission denied
find: '/etc/grub.d': Permission denied
find: '/etc/phpMyAdmin': Permission denied
/etc/hosts
find: '/etc/selinux/targeted/modules/active': Permission denied
find: '/etc/webmin/lpadmin': Permission denied
find: '/etc/webmin/iscsi-target': Permission denied
```

Notice the large number of "Permission denied" messages. This is the result of not having permissions to view the contents of specific directories that are located in the search path. You often don't care about these messages and would rather they were not displayed.

You can redirect these messages into the **/dev/null** device file. This file is called the "bit bucket" and acts as a trash can that never needs to be emptied. Anything sent to the **/dev/null** device is immediately discarded.

Because the error messages in the previous **find** command were sent to stderr, they can be discarded by using the following syntax:

```
[student@OCS ~]$ find /etc -name "hosts" 2> /dev/null
/etc/hosts
```

See the "Output Redirection" section in this chapter for details regarding the **2>** symbol.

/dev/tty

Several files in the **/dev** directory are used to send data to display devices. These include virtual terminals:

```
[student@OCS ~]$ ls /dev/tty*
/dev/tty      /dev/tty20   /dev/tty33   /dev/tty46   /dev/tty59
/dev/tty0     /dev/tty21   /dev/tty34   /dev/tty47   /dev/tty6
/dev/tty1     /dev/tty22   /dev/tty35   /dev/tty48   /dev/tty60
/dev/tty10    /dev/tty23   /dev/tty36   /dev/tty49   /dev/tty61
/dev/tty11    /dev/tty24   /dev/tty37   /dev/tty5    /dev/tty62
/dev/tty12    /dev/tty25   /dev/tty38   /dev/tty50   /dev/tty63
/dev/tty13    /dev/tty26   /dev/tty39   /dev/tty51   /dev/tty7
/dev/tty14    /dev/tty27   /dev/tty4    /dev/tty52   /dev/tty8
/dev/tty15    /dev/tty28   /dev/tty40   /dev/tty53   /dev/tty9
/dev/tty16    /dev/tty29   /dev/tty41   /dev/tty54   /dev/ttyS0
/dev/tty17    /dev/tty3    /dev/tty42   /dev/tty55   /dev/ttyS1
```

```
/dev/tty18    /dev/tty30    /dev/tty43    /dev/tty56    /dev/ttyS2
/dev/tty19    /dev/tty31    /dev/tty44    /dev/tty57    /dev/ttyS3
/dev/tty2     /dev/tty32    /dev/tty45    /dev/tty58
/dev/tty17    /dev/tty28    /dev/tty39    /dev/tty5     /dev/tty60
/dev/tty18    /dev/tty29    /dev/tty4     /dev/tty50    /dev/tty61
```

Terminal devices also include pseudo-terminals:

```
[student@OCS ~]$ ls /dev/pts/*
/dev/pts/1    /dev/pts/2    /dev/pts/3    /dev/pts/4
```

Virtual terminals are accessed when you're sitting directly at the system. Using keyboard combinations, you can switch between these virtual terminals. For example, **Ctrl-Alt-F1** brings up the display associated with the **/dev/tty1** file.

Pseudo-terminals are created either by remote login sessions or by GUI-based terminals. The device names for pseudo-terminals are dynamically assigned. In both cases, you can use the **tty** command to determine the terminal device file for the current session:

```
[student@OCS ~]$ tty
/dev/pts/1
```

You can send data directly to a terminal window if you are logged in as the root user or if you own the terminal device file. The user who started the terminal owns the corresponding terminal device file:

```
[student@OCS ~]$ ls -l /dev/pts/1
crw--w---- 1 student tty 136, 1 Oct 12 17:18 /dev/pts/1
```

You can send directly to the device file by using the following syntax (replace the **cal** command with the command you want to execute and the device file with the terminal where you want the output to be displayed):

```
cal > /dev/pts/1
```

xargs

The **xargs** command takes data from STDIN to build and execute commands. Here is the format of the command:

```
input_command | xarg execute_command
```

The *input_command* is designed to provide information for **xargs** to provide as arguments to the *execute_command*. For example, suppose you want to run the **wc -l** command on every file in the **/etc** directory that begins with the letter "e":

```
[student@OCS ~]$ ls -d /etc/e* | xargs wc -l
 1 /etc/ec2_version
 1 /etc/environment
 2 total
```

Here are some important options of the **xargs** command:

Option	Description
-0	Handles whitespace issues. Normally used to handle when filenames have whitespace characters; every character is treated as a literal character.
-d	Used to change the delimiter between arguments (the default is a space character).
-n *max-args*	Indicates the maximum number of arguments per *execute_command*.
-p	Prompts the user before executing the *execute_command*.
-t	Displays the *execute_command* command before executing the command.

tee

If you want STDOUT to be sent both to the terminal and to a file, send the output to the **tee** command and provide an argument that indicates the file in which you want to store the information. Here's an example:

```
[student@OCS ~]$ ls
[student@OCS ~]$ cal | tee cal.txt
      January 2017
Su    Mo  Tu  We  Th  Fr  Sa
 1     2   3   4   5   6   7
 8     9  10  11  12  13  14
15    16  17  18  19  20  21
22    23  24  25  26  27  28
29    30  31

[student@OCS ~]$ ls
cal.txt
```

The **tee** command only has a few options. The most useful is the **-a** option. By default, the **tee** command will completely overwrite the file; the **-a** option tells the **tee** command to append to the file.

Here Documents

A here document is a redirection technique that allows you to send a large chunk of data to a command. For example, suppose you want to send the following text to stdout:

"We choose to go to the moon. We choose to go to the moon in this decade and do the other things, not because they are easy, but because they are hard, because that goal will serve to organize and measure the best of our energies and skills, because that challenge is one that we are willing to accept, one we are unwilling to postpone, and one which we intend to win, and the others, too."

Using a here document, you can use the following syntax:

```
cat <<EOF
We choose to go to the moon. We choose to go to the moon in this
decade and do the other things, not because they are easy, but because
they are hard, because that goal will serve to organize and measure
the best of our energies and skills, because that challenge is one
that we are willing to accept, one we are unwilling to postpone, and
one which we intend to win, and the others, too.
EOF
```

Everything between the two EOF tags is sent to the **cat** command as if it came from stdin. This provides a way to display text using WYSIWYG (What You See Is What You Get). Normally here documents are used in a shell script, but they can be used on the command line as well.

Text Processing

Because Linux is primarily a command-line environment, there is a great deal of text manipulation. Whether it be the output of a command or the contents of a file, there will often be the need to process this data. This section focuses on different text processing tools.

grep

See the previous "grep" subsection in this chapter.

tr

The **tr** command is useful for translating characters from one set to another. The syntax of the command is **tr** *SET1* [*SET2*].

For example, the following will capitalize the output of the **date** command:

```
[student@OCS ~]$ date
Sat Dec 3 20:15:05 PST 2016
[student@OCS ~]$ date | tr 'a-z' 'A-Z'
SAT DEC 3 20:15:18 PST 2016
```

Note that in order to use the **tr** command on a file, you must redirect the file into the **tr** command, like so, because the **tr** command does not accept files as arguments:

```
tr 'a-z' 'A-Z' < file
```

Here are some important options of the **tr** command:

Option	Description
-d	Used when the second set is omitted; it deletes the matching characters. For example, the following deletes all numbers from the output of the **date** command: **date	tr -d '0-9'**.
-s	Repeated matching characters are converted into a single character before being translated. Thus, "aaabc" would be converted into "abc" and then translated to "Abc" if the command **tr -s 'a' 'A'** were executed.

echo

The **echo** command is useful to display information to standard output. For example, suppose you wanted to display the value of the **$PATH** variable:

```
[student@OCS ~]$ echo $PATH
/usr/local/bin:/usr/bin:/usr/local/sbin:/usr/sbin:
  /home/bo/.local/bin:/home/bo/bin
```

Here are some important options of the **echo** command:

Option	Description
-n	Do not include a newline character at the end of the string.
-e	Enable the use of "backslash escapes"; for example, \n would be a newline character and \t would be a tab character.

sort

The **sort** command can be used to sort text data. By default, it will break each line of data into fields, using whitespace as the default delimiter. It also sorts on the first field in the data by default, performing a dictionary sort:

```
[student@OCS ~]$ cat individuals.txt
tom
nick
sue
Tim
[student@OCS ~]$ sort individuals.txt
nick
sue
Tim
tom
```

Here are some important options of the **sort** command:

Option	Description
-f	Fold case (essentially case-insensitive).
-h	Human-based numeric sort (for example, 2K is lower than 1G).
-n	Numeric sort.
-M	Month-based sort.
-r	Used to reverse the sort order.
-t	Used to change the field separator (for example, **sort -t ":" file.txt**).
-u	Used to remove duplicate lines.

To sort on a different field than the default, use the **-k** option. Here's an example:

```
[student@OCS ~]$ more people.txt
1   tom
2   nick
3   sue
4   tim
[student@OCS ~]$ sort -k 2 people.txt
2   nick
3   sue
4   tim
1   tom
```

awk

The **awk** command is used to modify text that is in a simple database format. For example, consider the following data:

```
[student@OCS ~]$ head /etc/passwd
root:x:0:0:root:/root:/bin/bash
bin:x:1:1:bin:/bin:/sbin/nologin
daemon:x:2:2:daemon:/sbin:/sbin/nologin
adm:x:3:4:adm:/var/adm:/sbin/nologin
lp:x:4:7:lp:/var/spool/lpd:/sbin/nologin
sync:x:5:0:sync:/sbin:/bin/sync
shutdown:x:6:0:shutdown:/sbin:/sbin/shutdown
halt:x:7:0:halt:/sbin:/sbin/halt
mail:x:8:12:mail:/var/spool/mail:/sbin/nologin
operator:x:11:0:operator:/root:/sbin/nologin
```

With the **awk** command, you can break apart the data shown in the previous example into different fields and then perform actions on that data:

```
[student@OCS ~]$ head /etc/passwd | awk -F: '{print $1,$7}'
root /bin/bash
bin /sbin/nologin
```

```
daemon /sbin/nologin
adm /sbin/nologin
lp /sbin/nologin
sync /bin/sync
shutdown /sbin/shutdown
halt /sbin/halt
mail /sbin/nologin
operator /sbin/nologin
```

In the previous example, the -F option was used to specify the "field separator." Each field is assigned to a variable. These variables are described in the following table:

Variable	Description
$1, $2, etc	The field variables.
$0	The entire line.
NF	The number of fields on the line. (Do not use the $ character for this variable.)
NR	The current line number.

Here are some important options of the **awk** command:

Option	Description
-F	Used to specify the field separator.
-f	Used to specify a file that contains the **awk** commands to execute.

sed

Use the **sed** utility to make automated modifications to files. The basic format for the **sed** command is **sed** *'s/RE/string/' file*.

The "RE" refers to the term *regular expression*, a feature that uses special characters to match patterns. See the "Bonus: regex" section in this chapter for additional details regarding regular expressions.

Example of the **sed** command:

```
[student@OCS ~]$ head -n 5 /etc/passwd
root:x:0:0:root:/root:/bin/bash
bin:x:1:1:bin:/bin:/sbin/nologin
daemon:x:2:2:daemon:/sbin:/sbin/nologin
adm:x:3:4:adm:/var/adm:/sbin/nologin
lp:x:4:7:lp:/var/spool/lpd:/sbin/nologin
[student@OCS ~]$ head -n 5 /etc/passwd | sed 's/bin/----/'
root:x:0:0:root:/root:/----/bash
----:x:1:1:bin:/bin:/sbin/nologin
daemon:x:2:2:daemon:/s----:/sbin/nologin
```

```
adm:x:3:4:adm:/var/adm:/s----/nologin
lp:x:4:7:lp:/var/spool/lpd:/s----/nologin
```

sed is a very powerful utility with a large number of features. The following table describes some of the more useful **sed** utilities:

Feature	Description
'/RE/d'	Deletes lines that match the RE from the output of the **sed** command.
'/RE/c**_string_'**	Changes lines that match the RE to the value of _string_.
'/RE/a**_string_'**	Add _string_ on a line after all lines that match the RE.
'/RE/i**_string_'**	Add _string_ on a line before all lines that match the RE.

The **sed** command has two important modifiers (characters added to the end of the **sed** operation):

- **g:** Means "global." By default, only the first RE pattern match is replaced. When the **g** modifier is used, all replacements are made. See Figure 9.3 for an example.

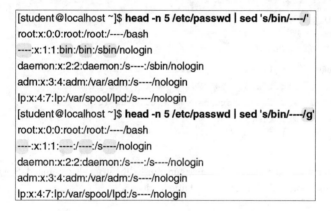

Figure 9.3 The **g** Modifier

- **i:** Means "case-insensitive." This modifier matches an alpha character regardless of its case. So, the command **sed 's/a/-/i'** would match either "a" or "A" and replace it with the "-" character.

The **sed** command can also change the original file (instead of displaying the modified data to the screen). To change the original file, use the **-i** option.

cut

The **cut** command is used to display "sections" of data. Here are some important options of the **cut** command:

Option	Description
-b	Used to define a section to print by bytes.
-c	Used to define a section to print by characters.
-d	Used to specify a delimiter character (used with the **-f** option).
-f	Used to specify which fields to display.

Example using fields:

```
[student@OCS ~]$ head -2 /etc/passwd
root:x:0:0:root:/root:/bin/bash
bin:x:1:1:bin:/bin:/sbin/nologin
[student@OCS ~]$ head -2 /etc/passwd | cut -d: -f1,7
root:/bin/bash
bin:/sbin/nologin
```

Example using characters:

```
[student@OCS ~]$ ls -l /etc/passwd
-rw-r--r--. 1 root root 2607 Nov 3 10:15 /etc/passwd
[student@OCS ~]$ ls -l /etc/passwd | cut -c1-10,42-
-rw-r--r-- /etc/passwd
```

egrep

The **egrep** command performs the same function as the **grep -E** command. See the first "grep" subsection in this chapter for additional details.

wc

Used to display the number of lines, words, or characters of data. By default, all three values are displayed:

```
[student@OCS ~]$ wc sample.txt
 2 4 24 sample.txt
```

Here are some important options of the **wc** command:

Option	Description
-c	Only display the number of bytes. (For text data, a byte is one character.)
-m	Only display the number of characters.
-l	Only display the number of lines.
-w	Only display the number of words.

File and Directory Operations

Any filesystem is bound to have thousands of files and directories that need to be managed. This section focuses on the Linux commands used to manage these filesystem objects.

touch

The **touch** command has two functions: to create an empty file and to update the modification and access timestamps of an existing file. To create a file or update an existing file's timestamps to the current time, use the following syntax:

```
touch filename
```

Here are some important options of the **touch** command:

Option	Description
-a	Modify the access timestamp only, not the modification timestamp.
-d *DATE*	Set the timestamp to the specified *DATE* (for example, **touch -d "2018-01-01 14:00:00"**).
-m	Modify the modification timestamp only, not the access timestamp.
-r *file*	Use the timestamp of *file* as a reference to set the timestamps of the specified file (for example, **touch -r /etc/hosts /etc/passwd**).

mv

The **mv** command will move or rename a file.

Example:

```
mv /tmp/myfile ~
```

Here are some important options of the **mv** command:

Option	Description
-i	Provide an interactive prompt if the move process would result in over-writing an existing file.
-n	Never overwrite an existing file.
-v	Be verbose (describe actions taken when moving files and directories).

cp

The **cp** command is used to copy files or directories. Here's the syntax for this command:

```
cp [options] file|directory destination
```

The *file|directory* is which file or directory to copy. The *destination* is where to copy the file or directory to. The following example copies the **/etc/hosts** file into the current directory:

```
[student@OCS ~]$ cp /etc/hosts .
```

Note that the destination *must* be specified (hence the "." character that represents the current directory in the previous example).

The following table provides some important options for the **cp** command:

Option	Description
-i	Provide an interactive prompt if the copy process results in overwriting an existing file.
-n	Never overwrite an existing file.
-r	Copy the entire directory structure ("r" stands for recursive).
-v	Be verbose (describe actions taken when copying files and directories).

rm

The **rm** command is used to delete files and directories.

Example:

```
rm file.txt
```

Here are some important options of the **rm** command:

Option	Description
-i	Provides an interactive prompt before removing file.
-r	Deletes entire directory structure ("r" stands for recursive).
-v	Is verbose (describes actions taken when deleting files and directories).

scp

The **scp** command is used to copy files to and from remote systems via the Secure Shell service. To copy a file from your local machine to a remote machine, use the following syntax:

```
scp filename user@machine:/directory
```

In this syntax, *user* is an account name on the remote system. The *machine* is the remote system and */directory* represents where you want to store the file.

Here are some important options of the **scp** command:

Option	Description
-P *port*	Specify the port number to connect to. Typically SSH servers use port 22, and that is the default for the **scp** command.
-p	Attempt to preserve the timestamps and permissions of the original file.
-r	Recursive mode (copy entire directories).
-v	Verbose mode.

ls

The **ls** command is used to list files in a directory. Here are some important options of the **ls** command:

Option	Description
-a	List all files, including hidden files.
-d	List the directory name, not the contents of the directory.
-F	Append a character to the end of the file to indicate its type; examples include *=executable file, /=directory, and @=symbolic link file.
-h	When **-h** is used with the **-l** option, file sizes are provided in human-readable format.
-i	Display each file's inode value.
-l	Display a long listing (see the example after this table).
-r	Reverse the output order of the file listing.
-S	Sort by file size.
-t	Sort by modification time (newest files are listed first).

The output of the **ls -l** command includes one line per file, as demonstrated in Figure 9.4.

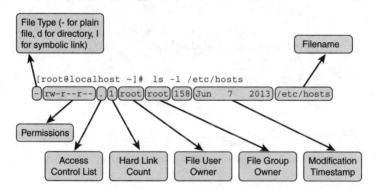

Figure 9.4   The **ls -l** Command

rsync

The **rsync** command is useful in copying files remotely across the network. It is typically used in situations where changes from previous files need to be copied over because it handles this more efficiently than other remote copy methods.

Syntax:

```
rsync [options] source destination
```

Here are some important **rsync** options:

Option	Description
-t	Preserve original modification timestamp.
-v	Verbose.
-r	Recursive (transfer entire directories).
-l	Maintain symbolic links.
-p	Preserve original permissions.

mkdir

The **mkdir** command creates a directory.

Example:

```
mkdir test
```

Here are some important **mkdir** options:

Option	Description
-m *perm*	Sets the permissions for the new directory rather than using the umask value.
-p	Creates parent directories if necessary; for example, **mkdir /home/ bob/data/january** would create all the directories in the path if they don't exist.
-v	Is verbose by printing a message for every directory that is created.

rmdir

The **rmdir** command is used to delete empty directories. This command will fail if the directory is not empty (use **rm -r** to delete a directory and all the files within the directory).

Example:

```
rmdir data
```

ln

There are two different types of link files: hard links and soft (also called symbolic) links. Understanding these link types is important when determining if you should link a file or make a file copy. This subsection covers the purpose of links and how to create them using the **ln** command.

Symbolic (soft)

When you create a soft link, the original file contains the data, whereas the link file "points to" the original file. Any changes made to the original will also appear to be in the linked file because using the linked file always results in following the link to the target file. Deleting the original file results in a broken link, making the link file worthless and resulting in complete data loss.

Figure 9.5 demonstrates soft links.

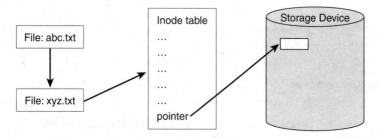

Figure 9.5   Soft Links

In Figure 9.5, the **abc.txt** file is soft-linked to the xyz.txt file. The **abc.txt** file points to the filename **xyz.txt**, not the same inode table (although not shown in this figure, the **abc.txt** file has its own inode table). When the process that is accessing the link file follows the link, the data for the **xyz.txt** file is accessible via the **abc.txt** file.

Copying files results in a complete and separate copy of the data. Changes in the original file have no effect on the data in the copied file. Changes in the copied file have no effect on the data in the original file. Deleting one of these files has no impact on the other file.

To create a link, execute the **ln** command in the following manner: **ln [-s] target_file link_file**. You can create a soft link to any file or directory:

```
[root@OCS ~]$ ln -s /boot/initrd.img-3.16.0-30-generic initrd
```

The **ls** command can be used to view both soft and hard links. Soft links are very easy to see because the target file is displayed when executing the **ls -l** command:

```
[root@OCS ~]$ ls -l /etc/vtrgb
lrwxrwxrwx 1 root root 23 Jul 11 2015
 /etc/vtrgb -> /etc/alternatives/vtrgb
```

Hard

When you create a hard link to a file, there is no way to distinguish the "original" file from the "linked" file. They are just two filenames that point to the same inode (see the "inodes" subsection in this chapter for more details), and hence the same data. If you have ten hard-linked files and you delete any nine of these files, the data is still maintained in the remaining file.

Figure 9.6 demonstrates hard links.

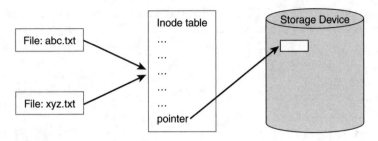

Figure 9.6   Hard Links

In Figure 9.6, the **abc.txt** and **xyz.txt** files are hard-linked together. This means that they share the same inode tables. The "…" in the inode table represents metadata—information about the file such as the user owner and permissions. Included with this metadata are pointers that refer to blocks within the storage device where the file data is stored.

To create a link, execute the **ln** command in the following manner: **ln [-s]** *target_file* *link_file*. For example, to create a hard link from the **/etc/hosts** file to a file in the current directory called **myhosts**, execute the following command:

```
[root@OCS ~]$ ln /etc/hosts myhosts
```

Hard-linked files share the same inode. You can only make a hard link to a file (not a directory) that resides on the same filesystem as the original file. Creating hard links to files on another filesystem or to directories will result in errors:

```
[root@OCS ~]$ ln /boot/initrd.img-3.16.0-30-generic initrd
ln: failed to create hard link 'initrd' =>
  '/boot/initrd.img-3.16. 0-30-generic': Invalid cross-device link
[root@OCS ~]$ ln /etc myetc
ln: '/etc': hard link not allowed for directory
```

The **ls** command can be used to view both soft and hard links. Hard links are more difficult because a hard link file shares an inode with another filename. For example, the value 2 after the permissions in the following output indicates this is a hard link file:

```
[root@OCS ~]$ ls -l myhosts
-rw-r--r-- 2 root root 186 Jul 11 2015 myhosts
```

To view the inode number of a file, use the **-i** option to the **ls** command:

```
[root@OCS ~]$ ls -i myhosts
263402 myhosts
```

Then use the **find** command to search for files with the same inode:

```
[root@OCS ~]$ find / -inum 263402 -ls 2>/dev/null
263402 4 -rw-r--r-- 2 root root 186 Jul 11 2015 /root/myhosts
263402 4 -rw-r--r-- 2 root root 186 Jul 11 2015 /etc/hosts
```

unlink

The **unlink** command does essentially what the **rm** command does: delete a file. There is a subtle, technical difference between how these two commands perform the task, but in almost all cases, the result is the same.

Note that the **unlink** command lacks the options that the **rm** command has.

inodes

A file or directory consists of several components. Many of these components, such as the owner and permissions, are stored in a filesystem element called an inode.

Everything about a file, besides the data in the file and the filename, is stored in the inode. Each file is given an inode number that is unique for the filesystem in which the file resides.

The inode of a file contains the following information:

- Unique inode number
- User owner
- Group owner
- Mode (permissions and file type)
- File size
- Timestamps:
    - Last time file contents was modified
    - Last time inode data was modified
    - Last time file was accessed
- Pointers (references to the data block locations that contain the file data)

You can see this inode information with the **stat** command:

```
[root@OCS ~]$ stat /etc/passwd
  File: '/etc/passwd'
  Size: 2597           Blocks: 8           IO Block: 4096 regular file
Device: fc01h/64513d   Inode: 33857        Links: 1
Access: (0644/-rw-r--r--) Uid: (     0/    root)   Gid:
  (    0/    root)
Access: 2018-10-12 12:54:01.126401594 -0700
Modify: 2018-09-08 12:53:48.371710687 -0700
Change: 2018-09-08 12:53:48.371710687 -0700
  Birth: -
```

Inodes are important in terms of symbolic and hard links. See the "Symbolic (soft)" and "Hard" subsections in this chapter for more details.

find

The **find** command will search the live filesystem for files and directories using different criteria. Here's the format of the command:

```
find [options] starting_point criteria action
```

The *starting_point* is the directory to start the search from. The *criteria* is what to search for, and the *action* is what to do with the results.

The following options are designed to modify how the **find** command behaves:

Option	Description
-maxdepth *n*	Limits how deep into subdirectories the search goes; for example, **find-maxdepth 3** will limit the search to three subdirectories deep.
-mount	Prevents searching directories that serve as mount points. This is useful when you're searching from the / directory.
-regextype *type*	When regular expressions (RE) are used, this option specifies what type of RE will be used; *type* can be emacs (default), posix-awk, posix-basic, posix-egrep, or posix-extended.

Most criteria-based options allow you to specify a numeric value as an argument. This can be preceded by a - or + character to indicate "less than" or "greater than." For example, using +5 would mean "more than five." Here are some important criteria-based options:

Option	Description
-amin *n*	Matches files based on access time; for example, **-amin -3** would match files accessed within the past three minutes.
-group *name*	Matches files that are owned by the *name* group.
-name *pattern*	Matches a file or directory based on the *pattern* provided; the *pattern* can be a regular expression.
-mmin *n*	Matches files based on modification time; for example, **-mmin -3** would match files modified within the past three minutes.
-nogroup	Matches files not owned by a group.
-nouser	Matches files not owned by a user.
-perm *mode*	Matches files that match the permission specified by the *mode* (octal or symbolic); see the examples in the next table.
-size *n*	Matches files based on file size; the value *n* can be preceded by a + (more than) or - (less than) and anteceded by a unit modifier: **c** for bytes, **k** for kilobytes, **M** for megabytes, or **G** for gigabytes.
-type *fstype*	Search for file based on file type (use "d" for directory, "f" for plain file, "l" for symbolic link, and so on).
-user *username*	Matches all files owned by the *username* user (for example, **find /home -user bob**).

Here are some examples using the **-perm** option:

Option	Description
-perm 775	Matches files that exactly match the octal permissions of 775 (rwxrwxr-x)
-perm u=rw	Matches files that exactly match the symbolic permissions of read and write for the owner (rw-------)
-perm -444	Matches files that match the octal permissions of 444 but disregards any other permission values (possible matches: rwxrwxr-x, r--r--r--, rwxr--r--)
-perm ugo=r	Matches files that match the symbolic permissions of read for all three permission sets but disregards any other permission values (possible matches: rwxrwxr-x, r--r--r--, rwxr--r--)
-perm /444	Matches files that match any of the octal permissions of 444 and disregards any other permission values (possible matches: r--------, rw-rw-r--, rwxr--r--)

Once a file is found, an action can be taken on the file. Here are some important action-based options:

Option	Description
-delete	Delete all matched files (for example, **find /tmp -name "*.tmp" -delete**).
-exec *command*	Execute a command on each matched file (see the following example).
-ls	List details about each matched file.
-ok	Execute a command on each matched file, but prompt the user before each match; prompt is a yes/no question to determine if the user wants to execute the command.
-print	Print the filename of each matched file; this is the default action option.

Here's an example of the **-exec** option:

```
[root@OCS ~]# find /etc -name "*.cfg" -exec file {} \;
/etc/grub2.cfg: symbolic link to '../boot/grub2/grub.cfg'
/etc/enscript.cfg: ASCII text
/etc/python/cert-verification.cfg: ASCII text
```

The **\;** is used to build a command line. For example, the command that was executed for the previous **find** example was **file /etc/grub2.cfg; file /etc/enscript.cfg; file /etc/python/cert-verification.cfg**. The \ before the **;** is required to escape the meaning of the **;** character for the BASH shell, so the **;** character is passed to the **find** command as a regular argument.

The {} characters represent where in the command the matching filename is placed. This can be used more than once, as demonstrated in the next example, which makes a copy of each matched file:

```
find /etc -name "*.cfg" -exec cp {} /tmp/{}.bak \;
```

locate

The **locate** command searches for files based on a database that is typically created daily. It does not search the live filesystem, which means it can't be used to find recent files. However, the **locate** command performs its searches quicker than the **find** command because searching a database is faster than searching the live filesystem.

Example:

```
[student@OCS ~]$ locate passwd.1.gz
/usr/share/man/cs/man1/gpasswd.1.gz
/usr/share/man/de/man1/gpasswd.1.gz
/usr/share/man/fr/man1/gpasswd.1.gz
/usr/share/man/hu/man1/gpasswd.1.gz
/usr/share/man/it/man1/gpasswd.1.gz
/usr/share/man/ja/man1/gpasswd.1.gz
/usr/share/man/ja/man1/passwd.1.gz
/usr/share/man/man1/gpasswd.1.gz
/usr/share/man/man1/htpasswd.1.gz
/usr/share/man/man1/kpasswd.1.gz
/usr/share/man/man1/ldappasswd.1.gz
/usr/share/man/man1/lpasswd.1.gz
/usr/share/man/man1/lppasswd.1.gz
/usr/share/man/man1/passwd.1.gz
/usr/share/man/pt_BR/man1/gpasswd.1.gz
/usr/share/man/ru/man1/gpasswd.1.gz
/usr/share/man/zh_CN/man1/gpasswd.1.gz
```

Here are some important options of the **locate** command:

Option	Description
-i	Perform a case-insensitive search.
-r	Use regular expressions rather than globbing when matching filenames.

See the "updatedb" subsection in this chapter for more details regarding the database used by the **locate** command.

grep

See the first "grep" subsection in this chapter.

which

The **whereis** command searches for binary executables. It will report back if the command specified is an alias and will search the locations of the **$PATH** variable. Here are some examples:

```
[student@OCS ~]$ echo $PATH
/usr/local/bin:/bin:/usr/bin:/usr/local/sbin:/usr/sbin:
  /home/student/.local/bin:/home/student/bin
[student@OCS ~]$ which ls
alias ls='ls --color=auto'
        /bin/ls
[student@OCS ~]$ which awk
/bin/awk
[student@OCS ~]$ which rougeone
/usr/bin/which: no rougeone in (/usr/local/bin:/bin:/usr/bin:
/usr/local/sbin:/usr/sbin:/home/student/.local/bin:
  /home/student/bin)
```

Here are some important options of the **which** command:

Option	Description
-a	Display all matches; the **which** command normally exits after the first match is made.
--skip-alias	Do not search for the alias.
-s	Search only for the matching source code files.

whereis

The **whereis** command searches for binary executables, source code, and manual pages. It makes use of standard locations as well as variables such as **$PATH** and **$MANPATH** to determine where to search.

Example:

```
[student@OCS ~]$ whereis ls
ls: /usr/bin/ls /usr/share/man/man1/ls.1.gz
  /usr/share/man/man1p/ ls.1p.gz
```

Here are some important options of the **whereis** command:

Option	Description
-b	Search only for matching executable binary files.
-m	Search only for matching man pages.
-s	Search only for matching source code files.

diff

The **diff** command is used to compare two files.

Syntax:

```
diff [options] file1 file2
```

Here are some important options of the **diff** command:

Option	Description
-q	Show differences in brief.
-y	Display files side-by-side (easier to view the differences).
-i	Case insensitive comparison.
-w	Ignore all whitespace characters.

updatedb

The database used by the **locate** command is created by the **updatedb** command. This command is typically executed automatically by a cron job, on a daily basis, but can also be executed manually by the root user.

When the **updatedb** command is executed, it creates a database of all files on the operating system. The database is created based on rules stored in the **/etc/updatedb.conf** file. A typical file will look like the following:

```
[student@OCS ~]$ more /etc/updatedb.conf
PRUNE_BIND_MOUNTS = "yes"
PRUNEFS = "9p afs anon_inodefs auto autofs bdev binfmt_misc
  cgroup cifs coda configfs cpuset debugfs de
vpts ecryptfs exofs fuse fuse.sshfs fusectl gfs gfs2 hugetlbfs
  inotifyfs iso9660 jffs2 lustre mqueue nc
pfs nfs nfs4 nfsd pipefs proc ramfs rootfs rpc_pipefs securityfs
  selinuxfs sfs sockfs sysfs tmpfs ubifs
 udf usbfs"
PRUNENAMES = ".git .hg .svn"
PRUNEPATHS = "/afs /media /mnt /net /sfs /tmp /udev
  /var/cache/ccache /var/lib/yum/yumdb /var/spool/cups
  /var/spool/squid /var/tmp"
```

Important settings in the **/etc/updatedb.conf** file include the following:

Setting	Description
PRUNEFS	Indicates that files on the specified filesystems will not be included in the database
PRUNENAMES	Indicates that files that match the specified patterns will not be included in the database
PRUNEPATHS	Indicates that files in the specified directories will not be included in the database

Bonus: regex

NOTE: Regular expressions are not officially listed as an exam objective. However, questions related to exam topics (such as the **grep**, **sed** and **find** commands) may include regular expressions. As a result, this is a good topic to review and study for the exam.

The term *regex* stands for regular expression (RE), which is a character or set of characters designed to match other characters. For example, in utilities that support REs, a "." character will match a single character of any type, whereas "[a-z]" would match any single lowercase character.

There are two types of REs: basic and extended. Basic REs are the original, and extended REs are the newer additions. Utilities that use REs normally support basic REs by default and have some switch or feature to enable extended REs. Although documentation may refer to basic REs as obsolete, they are still used by most modern utilities.

Commonly used basic REs are described in the following table:

RE	Description
^	Match the beginning of a line.
$	Match the end of a line.
*	Match the preceding character zero or more times.
.	Match exactly one character.
[ ]	Match exactly one character that is within the [ ] characters; a list of characters ([**abc**]) or a range of characters ([**a-c**]) is permitted.
[^]	Match exactly one character that is *not* within the [ ] characters; a list of characters ([**^abc**]) or a range of characters ([**^a-c**]) is permitted.
\	Escape the special meaning of a regular expression; for example, the pattern \.* would match the value ".*".

Commonly used extended REs are described in the following table:

RE	Description
( )	Group sets of characters together to form an expression; for example, (**abc**).
X|*Y*	Match either *X* or *Y*.
+	Match the preceding character or expression one or more times.
{*X*}	Match the preceding character or expression *X* times.
{*X*,}	Match the preceding character or expression *X* or more times.
{*X*,*Y*}	Match the preceding character or expression *X* to *Y* times.
?	The previous character or expression is optional.

## CHAPTER 10

Given a scenario, manage services

This chapter provides information and commands concerning the following topics:

Systemd management

- Systemctl
- Enabled
- Disabled
- Start
- Stop
- Mask
- Restart
- Status
- Daemon-reload

Systemd-analyze blame

Unit files

- Directory locations
- Environment parameters
- Targets
- Hostnamectl
- Automount

SysVinit

- **chkconfig**
  - on
  - off
  - level
- Runlevels
  - Definitions of 0–6
  - **/etc/init.d**
  - **/etc/rc.d**

- **/etc/rc.local**
- **/etc/inittab**
- Commands (**runlevel**, **telinit**)
- Service
  - Restart
  - Status
  - Stop
  - Start
  - Reload

Systemd Management

Instead of the runlevels that SysVinit uses, Systemd uses "targets." Each target has specific services that start. See Figure 10.1 for an example of a typical Systemd boot sequence.

Figure 10.1   Overview of the Systemd Boot Process

Targets are defined in the **/usr/lib/systemd/system** directory. Consider the following example of a target file:

```
# cat /usr/lib/systemd/system/graphical.target
#   This file is part of systemd.
#
#   systemd is free software; you can redistribute it and/or modify it
#   under the terms of the GNU Lesser General Public License
    as published by
#   the Free Software Foundation; either version 2.1 of the License, or
#   (at your option) any later version.


[Unit]
Description=Graphical Interface
Documentation=man:systemd.special(7)
Requires=multi-user.target
Wants=display-manager.service
Conflicts=rescue.service rescue.target
After=multi-user.target rescue.service rescue.target
   display-manager.service
AllowIsolate=yes
```

The default target is defined by a symbolic link from **/etc/systemd/system/ default.target** to the target in the **/usr/lib/systemd/system** directory.

Example:

```
# ls -l /etc/systemd/system/default.target
lrwxrwxrwx. 1 root root 36 Jun 11 20:47
  /etc/systemd/system/default.target ->
   /lib/systemd/system/graphical.target
```

Use the following command to display the default target:

```
# systemctl get-default
multi-user.target
```

Use the **systemctl list-unit-files --type=target** command to list the available targets. This provides a large amount of output, so the following example uses the **head** command to limit output:

```
# systemctl list-unit-files --type=target | head
UNIT FILE               STATE
basic.target            static
bluetooth.target        static
cryptsetup-pre.target   static
cryptsetup.target       static
ctrl-alt-del.target     disabled
cvs.target              static
default.target          enabled
emergency.target        static
final.target            static
```

Use the following command to set the default target:

```
# systemctl set-default graphical-user.target
rm '/etc/systemd/system/default.target'
ln -s '/usr/lib/systemd/system/graphical-
  user.target' '/etc/systemd/system/default.target'
```

Systemctl

The **systemctl** command is used to administer a Systemd-based distribution. For example, to change to another target, execute the following command:

```
systemctl isolate multi-user.target.
```

Enabled

The **enable** option is used with the **systemctl** command to start a service at boot time.

Syntax:

```
systemctl enable service
```

You can determine if the service is currently enabled or disabled by using the following command:

```
# systemctl is-enabled cups
enabled
```

Disabled

The **disable** option is used with the **systemctl** command to change a service this is currently started at boot time so that it won't start automatically then. Syntax: **systemctl disable** *service*.

You can determine if the service is currently enabled or disabled by using the following command:

```
# systemctl is-enabled cups
cnabled
```

Start

The **start** option is used with the **systemctl** command to start a service that is not currently running.

Syntax:

```
systemctl start service
```

You can determine whether or not the service is currently running by using the following command:

```
# systemctl active cups
enabled
```

Stop

The **stop** option is used with the **systemctl** command to stop a service that is currently running.

Syntax:

```
systemctl stop service
```

You can determine whether or not the service is currently running by using the following command:

```
# systemctl active cups
enabled
```

Mask

To mask a service is to make it completely impossible to start or enable. This is commonly done when there is a conflicting service on the system that, for whatever reason, can't or shouldn't be removed from the system.

The syntax to mask a service is **systemctl mask** *service*.

Restart

The **restart** option is used with the **systemctl** command to restart a service that is not currently running.

Syntax:

```
systemctl restart process_name
```

You can determine whether or not the service is currently running by using the following command:

```
# systemctl active cups
enabled
```

Status

The **status** option is used with the **systemctl** command to display the current status of a service.

Syntax:

```
systemctl status process_name
```

Here is an example of displaying the status of the CUPS service:

```
# sysctl status cups
• cups.service - CUPS Scheduler
   Loaded: loaded (/lib/systemd/system/cups.service; enabled;
 vendor preset: enabled)
   Active: active (running) since Mon 2019-01-07 00:10:18 PST;20h ago
     Docs: man:cupsd(8)
 Main PID: 4195 (cupsd)
    Tasks: 1 (limit: 4780)
   CGroup: /system.slice/cups.service
           └─4195 /usr/sbin/cupsd -l

Jan 07 00:10:18 student-VirtualBox systemd[1]: Started CUPS Scheduler.
```

Daemon-reload

A component of Systemd is created by the **systemd.generator** tool, which is used for creating dependency trees and automatically creating unit files based on different criteria. To have **systemd.generator** "restart," you execute the **systemctl daemon-reload** command. This isn't a common task but one you may need to perform when making manual changes to Systemd. It is more often executed when software installs require the **systemd.generator** tool to be restarted.

Systemd-analyze blame

The **systemd-analyze** command can be used to determine if there are any errors in Systemd configuration as well as to debug Systemd. There are many options, but the Linux+ exam focuses on just one, the **blame** option, shown here:

```
# systemd-analyze blame | head
    1min 3.507s clamd.service
       41.478s fail2ban.service
       12.274s mariadb.service
       10.043s httpd.service
        9.510s network.service
        7.033s csf.service
        6.095s postfix.service
        4.774s webmin.service
        4.124s ossec-hids.service
        2.949s rsyslog.service
```

The output of this command displays all currently running services and how long it took for each service to successfully load. You may be able to troubleshoot a service using this tool because a long load time may indicate a problem. However, a long load time might also be a normal part of the startup of a service, so it is best to have a benchmark to compare against.

Unit Files

A unit file is used to define a service. To display which unit files are defined on the system, use the **list-units** option to the **systemctl** command:

```
# sysctl list-units | head
UNIT FILE                                STATE
proc-sys-fs-binfmt_misc.automount        static
-.mount                                  generated
dev-hugepages.mount                      static
dev-mqueue.mount                         static
proc-sys-fs-binfmt_misc.mount            static
snap-core-5662.mount                     enabled
snap-core-5742.mount                     enabled
snap-core-6130.mount                     enabled
snap-gnome\x2d3\x2d26\x2d1604-64.mount   enabled
snap-gnome\x2d3\x2d26\x2d1604-70.mount   enabled
```

To view the contents of a unit file, use the **cat** option to the **systemctl** command:

```
# systemctl cat cups
# /lib/systemd/system/cups.service
[Unit]
Description=CUPS Scheduler
Documentation=man:cupsd(8)

[Service]
ExecStart=/usr/sbin/cupsd -l
Type=simple
Restart=always

[Install]
Also=cups.socket cups.path
WantedBy=printer.target
```

The first line of the preceding output provides the location of the unit file. The "[Unit]" section describes the service. The "[Service]" section specifies what process should be started as well as some options on how the process should be configured.

The "[Install]" section includes the "WantedBy" setting, which indicates which target "wants" to start this service. It also may contain an "Also" setting that is used to indicate additional services that should be started.

> **NOTE:** The term "service" is used here, but unit files can define many different Systemd components, including mount points, devices, sockets, and more.

You shouldn't worry about how to create your own unit file, but you should be familiar with its function and the settings described in this section of this chapter.

Additional unit file commands:

- **systemctl list-dependencies** *unit*: Lists what other features or services are required by this feature or service
- **systemctl show** *unit*: Lists properties of a unit
- **systemctl edit** *unit*: Used to edit a unit file

Directory Locations

Here are a few locations you should be familiar with for Systemd:

- **/lib/systemd/system**: Standard location for the Systemd files. Most of the Systemd files provided by software packages are stored in this location. On some systems (such as Red Hat–based distributions), the **/usr/lib/systemd/system** directory is used instead of the **/lib/systemd/system** directory.

- **/etc/systemd/system**: Alternative location for the Systemd files. Most of the Systemd files created by administrators are stored in this location.

- **/run/systemd/system**: This location contains "runtime units," which are essentially units created on the fly, typically by programs currently executing on the system.

Environment Parameters

Some units (particularly services) require environment parameters to function correctly. These can be set in one of two ways within the unit file. One method is to point to a file that contains the parameters. This can be done with the EnvironmentFile setting in the unit file, as demonstrated here:

```
# systemctl cat cron
# /lib/systemd/system/cron.service
[Unit]
Description=Regular background program processing daemon
Documentation=man:cron(8)

[Service]
EnvironmentFile=-/etc/default/cron
ExecStart=/usr/sbin/cron -f $EXTRA_OPTS
IgnoreSIGPIPE=false
KillMode=process

[Install]
WantedBy=multi-user.target
```

If the service already has a standard or legacy configuration file, then the EnvironmentFile setting is commonly used. To set the parameters directly in the unit file, use the Environment setting, as demonstrated here:

```
[Service]
Environment="Test=value1"
Environment="Demo=value2"
```

Targets

See the "Systemd Management" section in this chapter.

Hostnamectl

The **hostnamectl** command can be used to view and change host and system information. When used with no arguments, information about the system is displayed:

```
# hostnamectl
    Static hostname: student-VirtualBox
        Icon name: computer-vm
          Chassis: vm
```

```
         Machine ID: 7235c52cf8114b8188c985c05afe75c9
            Boot ID: e6ba643d8da44542a90a26c4466adca7
     Virtualization: oracle
   Operating System: Ubuntu 18.04.1 LTS
             Kernel: Linux 4.15.0-43-generic
       Architecture: x86-64
```

The **set-hostname** option allows you to specify one of two types of hostnames:

- **--static**: Changes are made in the **/etc/hostname** file and are persistent across reboots.

- **--transient**: Changes only apply to currently booted system. No changes are made to the **/etc/hostname** file.

There is also a feature in which you can make a more flexible hostname (one that breaks standard network hostname rules). Use the **--pretty** option for this. With **--pretty** and **--static**, changes are made to the **/etc/machine-info** file.

Automount

Automounting is the process of mounting a resource when a process accesses the mount point. After the process stops using the mount point, the resource is unmounted. Typically automounting is set up for mounting remote network shares or for mounting removable media, such as CD-ROMs and USB disks.

Traditionally, the automount function was handled by the **autofs** daemon. Systemd provides this functionality, and it is slowly replacing the **autofs** daemon. Note that Chapter 4, "Given a scenario, manage storage in a Linux environment," covered details on the mounting process itself. This section will only cover the automount process provided by Systemd.

You create an automount by creating the unit files, like the following:

```
$ cat /etc/systemd/system/mnt-test.automount
[Unit]
Description=Automount Test

[Automount]
Where=/mnt/test

[Install]
WantedBy=multi-user.target

$ cat /etc/systemd/system/mnt-test.mount
[Unit]
Description=Test
```

```
[Mount]
What=nfs.example.com:/export/test
Where=/mnt/test
Type=nfs


[Install]
WantedBy=multi-user.target
```

> **NOTE:**   The automount unit filename must match the mount point name
> (**/mnt/test** = **mnt-test.automount**).

Because you have created new unit files, you need to execute the **systemctl daemon-reload** command. See the "Daemon-reload" section in this chapter to learn more about what this command does.

Here is how to disable the mount unit and enable the automount unit:

```
$ systemctl is-enabled mnt-test.mount
disabled
$ systemctl is-enabled mnt-test.automount
enabled
```

To test, use the **cd** command to switch to the automount mount point.

SysVinit

The init process is started by the kernel. It reads the **/etc/inittab** file to determine which runlevel to boot the system to. This is defined by the "initdefault" line.

All sysinit lines are executed first. Then all lines that have the same value in their second field as the second field of the "initdefault" line are executed. For example, **id:5:initdefault:** means "run all lines that have the value 5 in the second field."

The **/etc/rc.d/rc.sysinit** line boots the system to "single-user" mode. The **/etc/rc.d/rc** script boots the system the rest of the way to the runlevel specified as the argument to the script. This **rc** (run control) script executes all files in the **/etc/rcX.d** directory (X = runlevel). Here's an example: **/etc/rc5.d**.

All files in this directory that begin with *K* are executed with a stop argument, effectively killing or stopping the service associated with the script. For example, **/etc/rc5.d/K73ldap** stops the LDAP services if it is currently running.

All files in this directory that begin with *S* are executed with a start argument, effectively starting the service associated with the script. For example, **/etc/rc5.d/S55sshd** starts the SSH services.

All scripts in the **/etc/rcX.d** directories are actually symbolic links to scripts in the **/etc/init.d** directory. See Figure 10.2 for a visual demonstration of the SysVinit process.

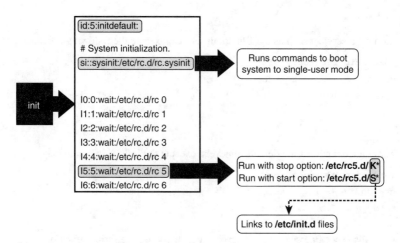

Figure 10.2 Overview of the SysVinit Process

chkconfig

The **chkconfig** command is used to display or modify when services are started or stopped. This section demonstrates the features of this command.

With the **--list** option, the current status of each script is displayed, as shown in the following example:

```
# chkconfig --list | head
NetworkManager 0:off 1:off 2:off 3:off 4:off 5:off 6:off
acpid          0:off 1:off 2:on  3:on  4:on  5:on  6:off
anacron        0:off 1:off 2:on  3:on  4:on  5:on  6:off
atd            0:off 1:off 2:off 3:on  4:on  5:on  6:off
auditd         0:off 1:off 2:on  3:on  4:on  5:on  6:off
autofs         0:off 1:off 2:off 3:on  4:on  5:on  6:off
avahi-daemon   0:off 1:off 2:off 3:on  4:on  5:on  6:off
avahi-dnsconfd 0:off 1:off 2:off 3:off 4:off 5:off 6:off
bluetooth      0:off 1:off 2:on  3:on  4:on  5:on  6:off
capi           0:off 1:off 2:off 3:off 4:off 5:off 6:off
```

on

To turn on a service, such as the Bluetooth service, execute the following command:

```
# chkconfig bluetooth on
# chkconfig --list bluetooth
bluetooth        0:off    1:off    2:on    3:on    4:on    5:on    6:off
```

See the "level" section in this chapter for details as to why this service was turned on for run levels 2, 3, 4, and 5.

off

To turn off a service, such as the Bluetooth service, execute the following command:

```
# chkconfig bluetooth off
# chkconfig --list bluetooth
bluetooth    0:off 1:off 2:off 3:of  4:off 5:off 6:off
```

level

To turn on a default for the default runlevels, execute the following command:

```
# chkconfig bluetooth on
# chkconfig --list bluetooth
bluetooth    0:off 1:off 2:on  3:on  4:o   5:on  6:off
```

You can also specify exactly the runlevel at which you want a script turned on or off:

```
# chkconfig bluetooth --level 2 off
# chkconfig --list bluetooth
bluetooth    0:off 1:off 2:off 3:on  4:on  5:on  6:off
```

Note that default levels are defined in the initialization script itself:

```
# grep chkconfig /etc/rc5.d/S55sshd
# chkconfig: 2345 55 25
```

The 2345 is used to indicate at which runlevels this service should be turned on or started by default.

Runlevels

When SysVinit system is booted, the first process that the kernel starts is called the **init** process. This process is used to start all additional services, depending on the runlevel to which the system is being booted.

Definitions of 0–6

Think of a runlevel as a functional state of the operating system. You can define what services and features are available for each runlevel. You should be aware of three different sets of runlevels: the Linux Standard Base set, the Red Hat set, and the Debian set. The following table outlines these three sets. The standard set is rarely used on Linux distributions anymore, but it gives you a good idea of the original purpose of runlevels. If you are on a Red Hat–based distribution, you should be aware of how the functional state of runlevels differs from Debian-based systems.

Runlevel	Linux Standard Base	Red Hat	Debian
0	Halt the system.	Halt the system.	Halt the system.
1	Single-user mode.	Single-user mode.	Single-user mode.
2	Multiuser mode with no networking and no GUI.	Multiuser mode with no NFS sharing and no GUI.	2–5 are all multi-user mode with GUI.
3	Multiuser mode with no GUI.	Multiuser mode with no GUI.	2–5 are all multi-user mode with GUI.
4	Not defined.	A copy of runlevel 3.	2–5 are all multi-user mode with GUI.
5	Multiuser mode with GUI.	Multiuser mode with GUI.	2–5 are all multi-user mode with GUI.
6	Reboot the system.	Reboot the system.	Reboot the system.

/etc/init.d

See the "SysVinit" subsection in this chapter.

/etc/rc.d

See the "SysVinit" subsection in this chapter.

/etc/rc.local

If you want to issue some commands that will execute during the boot process, you can place them in the **/etc/rc.local** file instead of creating a full init script. Any commands stored in this file will be executed during normal bootup.

/etc/inittab

See the "SysVinit" subsection in this chapter.

Commands: runlevel

To see the current runlevel, execute the **runlevel** command:

```
# runlevel
N 5
```

Commands: telinit

The **telinit** command allows you to change the system to a different runlevel. You can delay a change to the new runlevel by specifying the **-t** option followed by the number of seconds to wait before switching to the new runlevel, like so:

```
# telinit -t 60 3
```

Service

On SysVinit systems, the **service** command can be used to control services on the fly. This section reviews the features of this command.

Restart

The **restart** option to the **service** command will stop and then start a service:

```
# sudo service cups restart
Stopping cups:                                          [   OK   ]
Starting cups:                                          [   OK   ]
```

Status

The **status** option to the **service** command will demonstrate the current status of a service:

```
# sudo service cups status
cups is stopped
```

Stop

The **stop** option to the **service** command will stop a service:

```
# sudo service cups restart
Stopping cups:                                          [   OK   ]
```

Start

The **start** option to the **service** command will start a service:

```
# sudo service cups restart
Starting cups:                                          [   OK   ]
```

Reload

The **restart** option to the **service** command will reload the service's configuration file. This is useful when you have made changes to the configuration file but you don't want to restart the service because it would have adverse actions (such as disconnect existing users from the service):

```
# sudo service cups reload
Reload cups:                                            [   OK   ]
```

NOTE: Not all services support the **reload** option.

## CHAPTER 11

Summarize and explain server roles

This chapter provides information and commands concerning the following topics:

- NTP
- SSH
- Web
- Certificate Authority
- Name server
- DHCP
- File servers
- Authentication server
- Proxy
- Logging
- Containers
- VPN
- Monitoring
- Database
- Print server
- Mail server
- Load balancer
- Clustering

NOTE: For the Linux+ certification exam, it is important to note that for the topics listed under this objective, you are supposed to be able to "**summarize** and **explain** server roles." In other words, you shouldn't be expected to know details regarding setting up, configuring, or administering these servers but rather understand what the functions of the servers are.

In some cases there are other objectives that cover these servers in more detail. Consider this to be a "summary" of services for study purposes.

NTP

NTP (Network Time Protocol) is designed to resolve issues regarding the system time of server and client systems. Having an accurate system time is important for several reasons:

- **Log files**: These files have timestamps embedded within log entries. These timestamps are often critical to determine exactly when an error or security breach occurred. Inaccurate system times will result in inaccurate timestamps, which can lead to issues in determining the cause of problems as well as potential legal issues (log files are sometimes used in legal cases but can be disregarded by the court system if the timestamps are not accurate).

- **Client-server interactions**: Some services require the client and server systems to be in sync regarding system time. If these systems are not in sync, the service may fail completely.

- **Searches for file by timestamp**: Users and administrators will often search for lost or missing files using timestamps. If the system time isn't accurate, the file timestamps won't be accurate, making it difficult to find files.

- **Transaction log timestamps**: Many transaction operations include timestamps. For example, each email that is sent or received has a timestamp of these actions. Another example is banking and credit card transactions. It is critical to ensure these timestamps are as accurate as possible for both security and reliability of the transactions.

The purpose of NTP is to ensure accurate system times. A system is configured as an NTP client, which will set the system time based on data received from one or more NTP servers. Typically three or more NTP servers are used to best ensure the most accurate time.

Organizations may deploy their own NTP servers, but there are also publicly available servers on **pool.ntp.org**. Servers are categorized by how accurate they are. This is done by assigning a "stratum" value to the server. This is a numeric value from 0 to 15, where the lower the value, the more accurate the clock is considered to be.

A clock that advertises itself as a "stratum-0" is one that likely gets its timestamps from an atomic clock and has very little delay in responding to NTP requests. A clock that advertises itself as a "stratum-1" gets its timestamps from "stratum-0" servers.

SSH

SSH (Secure Shell) is a service that allows for secure communication between hosts. The securing features include symmetrical encryption, asymmetrical encryption, and hashing. SSH is used for the following:

- As a secure replacement for telnet and other insecure remote-connection services (such as rlogin). On the client side, the **ssh** command is used for this feature.

- As a secure replacement for file transfer methods such as **ftp** and **rcp**. On the client side, the **sftp** command is used to replace **ftp**, and the **scp** command is used to replace **rcp**.

- As a secure replacement for remote execution methods such as **rsh**. On the client side, the command is used for this feature.

Web

The Web (also called the "World Wide Web") is a component of the Internet that is accessible via web browsers. The term is often used interchangeably with the Internet, but the Internet refers to all the systems connected globally, including servers that provide other features, such as database access and mail services.

Certificate Authority

One of the problems with IT security revolves around the concept of trust. For example, suppose you want to connect to your bank online and you type the bank's URL in a browser. Your browser gets a response from a remote server, but how can you ensure that remote server is actually your bank and not a server that hijacked your connection attempt?

The solution to this is digital certifications. When the browser connects to the server, the server issues a signature that is tied to a digital certificate. A third-party organization called a Certificate Authority (CA) is consulted by the web browser to verify the signature. The trust is built between the client system and the server by using the CA for verification.

Name Server

While users prefer to use hostnames or URL addresses to access other systems, the systems themselves use IP addresses. So when you perform a command like **ping www.google.com**, it needs to be converted into an IP address before the ping request can be sent.

Because there are millions of systems on the Internet, keeping track of all the hostnames and IP addresses can be a daunting task. The Domain Name Service (DNS) protocol provides the solution. DNS uses a series of name servers to perform the hostname-to-IP-address conversion. Name servers are responsible for knowing a subset of hostnames and their corresponding IP addresses, making the task of updating and maintaining these translations easier because the process is distributed over thousands of different systems.

DHCP

Your own system needs networking information that is specific to the network on which you are located. This includes information like the IP address, the gateway IP address, the name server, and the netmask (network mask). These pieces of network information can be assigned manually, which is fine for servers that don't move between networks, but not easy for mobile devices that move from one network to another.

A Dynamic Host Configuration Protocol (DHCP) server provides client systems with this network information automatically. When a client is configured as a DHCP server, it sends a request for DHCP servers to provide this network information. Once this data is received, the client automatically configures itself, allowing the system to communicate on the network.

File Servers

A file server is a system that shares files. Several different file servers are commonly used on Linux systems:

- **FTP server**: While FTP servers provide little security (they don't encrypt network data), they are still widely used in certain situations. For example, you may want to publicly share files on the Internet. An FTP server that uses an anonymous user account (one that doesn't require a password to authenticate) would be a good solution as long as the FTP server has been configured not to permit uploading of files. In terms of accessing an FTP server, an individual user would need to initiate the access via an FTP client program.

- **SFTP server**: SSH (see "SSH" in this chapter) can be used to provide FTP-like access, but in a secured manner. This type of file sharing requires user authentication and secures data transport. In terms of accessing an SFTP server, an individual user would need to initiate the access via an SSH client program.

- **Samba**: Samba is a service that can share both files and printers. It is designed to share files in a manner that allows Microsoft Windows clients the ability to access the shares. It can also be integrated with a Microsoft Server domain. This makes Samba a good solution in an environment that has a mix of operating systems. In terms of accessing an FTP server, an individual user could initiate the access via a Samba client program, but an administrator can also configure access via a mount point (a directory available in the filesystem).

- **NFS**: NFS (Network File System) is primarily designed to share files between Linux or Unix systems (aka, *nix systems). There are some non-*nix client programs available, but these are not commonly used. NFS lacks a lot of the modern security features found in other file servers, but given that it is normally used only on a LAN, these security issues are not as big of a concern. Unlike with FTP or SFTP, users don't initiate access to an NFS server. An administrator would mount an NFS share, making the share available via the filesystem structure on the client system.

Authentication Server

An authentication server is a system that is used to authenticate user accounts on client systems. Several different authentication servers are available on Linux systems:

- **RADIUS**: There are several different options for RADIUS (Remote Authentication Dial-In User Service) servers, including GNU Radius, FreeRADIUS, OpenRADIUS, and BSDRadius. Each has a common collection of features but offers some different features as well. All RADIUS servers are designed to provide centralized AAA (Authentication, Authorization, and Accounting) services. RADIUS servers can be used for a variety of authentication operations, as they are not just limited to Linux.

- **IPA**: Identity, Policy, and Audit (IPA) is a combination of several different technologies that provide the functionality of an authentication server. Several different IPA options are available, but normally the following features are included:

  - **Lightweight Director Access Protocol (LDAP)**: This provides a means to store and retrieve account data.

  - **Kerberos**: A service that provides central authorization of user accounts.

  - **NTP**: See "NTP" in this chapter.

  - **DNS**: See "Name Server" in this chapter.

  - **CA**: See "Certificate Authority" in this chapter.

Proxy

A proxy server acts as a "go between" amid two systems. For example, if you connect to a web server via a web browser, you could use a proxy server to handle the connection to the web server. There are several reasons why a proxy server provides an advantage:

- Proxy servers can monitor network traffic and filter based on the content of the traffic.

- Proxy servers can bypass filters by appearing to be originating from a different system or network.

- Proxy servers can log network traffic and access to remote systems.

- Proxy servers can improve performance by caching static data, either on the client or the server side.

- Proxy servers can provide security features, making the connection more secure.

- Proxy servers can even translate data from one form to another. For example, they could be used to translate data from one language to another.

The most common proxy server on Linux is Squid, but there are also others that perform specific tasks.

Logging

Logging is the process of taking reports from services and storing the data into files or databases for future retrieval. One common logging service is called Syslog (the service itself runs as the **syslogd** process). This service stores its log files in the **/var/log** directory, normally in plain-text files that can be viewed directly. Most modern Linux systems use a newer variation of **syslogd** called **rsyslogd**, a service that is similar to **syslogd** but has more configuration features.

Another logging method often used in conjunction with **rsyslogd** is called **journald**. The **journald** service is a component of **systemd**, a feature that is used to manage processes during the boot procedure. While **journald** also stores log files in the **/var/log** directory, the data is stored in a binary format and displayed via the **journalctl** command.

Containers

You may be familiar with the concept of virtual machines already. Containers share some of the features of virtual machines, but also have some key differences.

A virtual machine (VM) is an operating system (OS) that runs within another OS. The VM is provided virtual components, like CPU and RAM, via an application called a hypervisor. More details on VMs are provided in Chapter 5, "Compare and contrast cloud and virtualization concepts and technologies."

A container is like a lightweight VM. It often acts like a separate system; for example, containers often have their own networking configuration, like IP addresses. However, a container doesn't require all of the components that a VM requires, like a separate virtual CPU, dedicated RAM, or dedicated hard disk space. As a result, your system might be able to support hundreds of containers, whereas it could only support a handful of concurrently running VMs.

One of the most popular container-based software programs is called **docker**. With **docker**, you can create and execute containers on Linux-based systems.

VPN

Virtual Private Network (VPN) is a service that allows for a virtual network over a public network. Thus, data can be shared across public networks in a secure manner. There is a large number of VPN software available for Linux.

Monitoring

Monitoring is a generic term used to describe actively watching activity on your system. A large number of monitoring tools is available for Linux; some of these tools monitor process activity (the **top** command, for example), network activity (**wireshark**, **tcpdump**, and so on), system activity (Nagios, Cacti, and so on) and user activity (**psacct**, **who**, **w**, **lsof**, and so on). Monitoring is a huge topic by itself, but for the exam just be aware of what monitoring is, not the vast number of details and utilities that support it.

Database

A database is a system used to store and return data upon request. This is another of those topics in Linux where a lot of options are available.

In a sense, most of the files stored in the **/etc** directory structure are simple databases (for example, the **/etc/passwd** file). However, most definitions of databases include the need for some database management system to provide controlled access to the data held within the database. You could argue that tools are used to manage the data in the file in **/etc** directly (such as the **useradd** command modifies the **/etc/passwd** file); however, calling these tools "database management systems" is a bit of a stretch.

Most people consider more robust software programs to be database management systems. This includes programs such as Oracle, MySQL, PostgreSQL, Apache Derby, and Firebird.

Print Server

A print server manages print jobs (requests to send data to a printer). The most common print server for Linux is Common Unix Print Service (CUPS). CUPS can be configured to send print jobs to a print queue. When a printer is available, CUPS will send the print job from the queue to the printer.

CUPS also allows for the cancelling of print jobs, print job priority, and the ability to connect to other print servers (like those shared via Samba or from Microsoft Windows print servers).

Mail Server

A mail server is a program responsible for sending, receiving, and storing email messages. Mail servers use system-independent methods, based on Simple Mail Transport Protocol (SMTP), to manage mail messages, which allows one mail server software the ability to interact with another, different mail server.

Sendmail has been a traditionally popular mail server, but most administrators tend to avoid using sendmail because it is difficult (complex) to configure and doesn't have strong security features. However, you should be aware that it is a possible solution and is still in use on many older servers.

Postfix is a more common solution on modern Linux systems. It is considered to be easier to configure and has many features, including good security features.

Load Balancer

A load balancer is a utility that spreads work across multiple servers or systems. Consider a heavily used website like www.google.com. If Google has a single web server, the incoming requests would overwhelm the server very quickly. What happens instead is that each request is farmed out to one of thousands of web servers. Google has never reported how many servers it has, but the estimates are in the millions.

Load balancers are used for many different services, including mail servers, database management servers, and file servers. A group of servers that perform similar functions is called a cluster (see "Clustering" next).

Clustering

The term *clustering* means grouping together a collection of computers to provide a specific service. For example, the collection of web servers that respond to requests to www.google.com is a cluster.

Clusters can be used to provide massive processing power, spread the load between different systems (see "Load Balancer" in this chapter), and provide huge storage space.

## CHAPTER 12

Given a scenario, automate and schedule jobs

This chapter provides information and commands concerning the following topics:

- Manage cron and at jobs
- cron
- **at**
- **crontab**
- **fg**
- **bg**
- **&**
- **kill**
- Ctrl-c
- Ctrl-z
- **nohup**

cron

The cron service allows you to schedule processes to run at specific times. The service makes use of the **crond** daemon, which checks every minute to see what processes should be executed. This section describes how to use this service and how to use the **at** command.

at

The **at** command is used to schedule one or more commands to be executed at one specific time in the future. The syntax for the command is **at** *time*, where *time* indicates when you want to execute a command. For example, the following command will allow you to schedule a command to run at 5 p.m. tomorrow:

```
at 5pm tomorrow
at>
```

When provided the **at>** prompt, enter a command to execute at the specified time. To execute multiple commands, press the Enter key for another **at>** prompt.

When this is complete, hold down the Ctrl key and press the d key. That results in an <EOT> message and creates the at job. Here's an example:

```
[root@OCS ~]$ at 5pm tomorrow
at> /home/bob/rpt.pl
at> echo "report complete" | mail bob
at> <EOT>
job 1 at Thu Feb 23 17:00:00 2017
```

Here are some important options for the **at** command:

Option	Description
-m	Send the user who created the **at** job an email when the job is executed.
-f *filename*	Read commands from *filename*. Useful if running the same **at** jobs on an infrequent basis.
-v	Display the time and date that the **at** job will be executed.

The **atq** command lists the current user's **at** jobs:

```
[root@OCS ~]$ atq
1         Thu Feb 23 17:00:00 2017 a bob
```

The output includes a job number (1 in this example), the date that the command will execute, and the user's name (bob in this example).

The **atq** command has no commonly used options.

To remove an at job before it is executed, run the **atrm** command followed by the job number to remove.

Example:

```
[root@OCS ~]$ atq
1         Thu Feb 23 17:00:00 2017 a bob
[root@OCS ~]$ atrm 1
[root@OCS ~]$ atq
```

The **atrm** command has no commonly used options.

As the administrator, you can use configuration files to determine whether a user can use the command. The **/etc/at.deny** and **/etc/at.allow** files are used to control access to the **at** command.

The format of each of these files is one username per line. Here's an example:

```
[root@OCS ~]$ cat /etc/at.deny
alias
backup
bin
```

```
daemon

ftp

games

gnats

guest

irc

lp

mail

man

nobody

operator

proxy

sync

sys

www-data
```

The following table describes how **the /etc/at.deny** and **/etc/at.allow** files work:

Situation	Description
Only the **/etc/ at.deny** file exists.	All users listed in this file are denied access to the **at** command, whereas all other users can execute the **at** command successfully. Use this file when you want to deny access to a few users but allow access to most users.
Only the **/etc/ at.allow** file exists.	All users listed in this file are allowed access to the **at** command, whereas all other users cannot execute the **at** command successfully. Use this file when you want to allow access to a few users but deny access to most users.
Neither file exists.	On most Linux distributions, this means that only the root user can use the **at** command. However, on some platforms, this results in all users being allowed to use the **at** command.
Both files exist.	Only the **/etc/at.allow** file is consulted, and the **/etc/at.deny** file is completely ignored.

crontab

The **crontab** command allows a user to view or modify her crontab file. The crontab file allows a user to schedule a command to be executed on a regular basis, such as once an hour or twice a month.

Here are some important options for the **crontab** command:

Option	Description
-e	Edit the crontab file.
-l	List the crontab file.
-r	Remove all entries in the crontab file.

Each line of the crontab file is broken into fields, separated by one or more space characters. The following table describes these fields:

Field	Description
First field: Minute	The minute that the command should execute. Values can be 0–59. A single value can be used or a list of values, such as 0,15,30,45. Range values (1–15) can also be used. An * character means "all possible values."
Second field: Hour	The hour that the command should execute. Values can be 0–23. A single value can be used or a list of values, such as 0,6,12,18. Range values (8–16) can also be used. An * character means "all possible values."
Third field: Day of the Month	The day of the month the command should execute. Values can be 1–31. A single value can be used or a list of values, such as 1,15. Range values (1–10) can also be used. An * character means "not specified," unless the fifth field is also an * character, in which case the * character means "all possible values."
Fourth field: Month	The month that the command should execute. Values can be 1–12. A single value can be used or a list of values, such as 6,12. Range values (1–3) can also be used. An * character means "all possible values."
Fifth field: Day of the Week	The day of the week the command should execute. Values can be 0–7 (where 0=Sunday, 1=Monday … 6=Saturday, 7=Sunday). A single value can be used or a list of values, such as 1,3,5. Range values (1–5) can also be used. An * character means "not specified," unless the third field is also an * character, in which case the * character means "all possible values."
Sixth field: Command Name	The name of the command to execute.

For example, the following crontab entry will execute the **/home/bob/rpt.pl** script every weekday (Monday–Friday), every month, starting at 08:00 in the morning and every half hour until 16:30 in the afternoon (4:30 p.m.):

```
0,30 8-16 * 1-12 1-5 /home/bob/rpt.pl
```

As the administrator, you can use configuration files to determine whether a user can use the **crontab** command. The **/etc/cron.deny** and **/etc/cron.allow** files are used to control access to the **crontab** command.

The format of each of these files is one username per line. Here's an example:

```
[root@OCS ~]$ cat /etc/cron.deny
alias
backup
bin
daemon
ftp
```

```
games
gnats
guest
irc
lp
mail
man
nobody
operator
proxy
sync
sys
www-data
```

The following table describes how the **/etc/cron.deny** and **/etc/cron.allow** files work:

Situation	Description
Only the **/etc/ cron.deny** file exists.	All users listed in this file are denied access to the **crontab** command, whereas all other users can execute the **crontab** command successfully. Use this file when you want to deny access to a few users but allow access to most users.
Only the **/etc/ cron.allow** file exists.	All users listed in this file are allowed access to the **crontab** command, whereas all other users cannot execute the **crontab** command successfully. Use this file when you want to allow access to a few users but deny access to most users.
Neither file exists.	On most Linux distributions, this means that only the root user can use the **crontab** command. However, on some platforms, this results in all users being allowed to use the **crontab** command.
Both files exist.	Only the **/etc/cron.allow** file is consulted, and the **/etc /cron.deny** file is completely ignored.

The **/etc/crontab** file acts as the system crontab. The system administrator edits this file to enable the execution of system-critical processes at specific intervals. The following is a sample **/etc/crontab** file:

```
[root@OCS ~]$ cat /etc/crontab
SHELL=/bin/sh
PATH=/usr/local/sbin:/usr/local/bin:/sbin:/bin:/usr/sbin:/usr/bin


#   m   h    dom mon dow user command
17  *          *  *  *      root    cd / && run-parts /etc/cron.hourly
```

Each configuration line describes a process to execute, when to execute it, and what username to execute the process as. Each line is broken into fields, separated by one or more space characters. The following table describes these fields:

Field	Description
First field: Minute	The minute that the command should execute. Values can be 0–59. A single value can be used or a list of values, such as 0,15,30,45. Range values (1–15) can also be used. An * character means "all possible values."
Second field: Hour	The hour that the command should execute. Values can be 0–23. A single value can be used or a list of values, such as 0,6,12,18. Range values (8–16) can also be used. An * character means "all possible values."
Third field: Day of the Month	The day of the month that the command should execute. Values can be 1–31. A single value can be used or a list of values, such as 1,15. Range values (1–10) can also be used. An * character means "not specified," unless the fifth field is also an * character, in which case the * character means "all possible values."
Fourth field: Month	The month that the command should execute. Values can be 1–12. A single value can be used or a list of values, such as 6,12. Range values (1–3) can also be used. An * character means "all possible values."
Fifth field: Day of the Week	The day of the week that the command should execute. Values can be 0–7 (where 0=Sunday, 1=Monday … 6=Saturday, 7=Sunday). A single value can be used or a list of values, such as 1,3,5. Range values (1–5) can also be used. An * character means "not specified," unless the third field is also an * character, in which case the * character means "all possible values."
Sixth field: Username	The name of the user that the command should run as.
Seventh field: Command Name	The name of the command to execute.

fg

A paused process can be restarted in the foreground by using the **fg** command:

```
[student@OCS ~]$ jobs
[1]+  Stopped                 sleep 999
[student@OCS ~]$ fg %1
sleep 999
```

The **fg** command has no commonly used options.

> **NOTE:** You can pause a process that is running in the foreground by holding down the Ctrl key and pressing Z while in that process's window. See the "Ctrl-z" subsection in this chapter for more details.

bg

A paused process can be restarted in the background by using the **bg** command:

```
[student@OCS ~]$ jobs
[1]+ Stopped                        sleep 999
[student@OCS ~]$ bg %1
[1]+ sleep 999 &
[student@OCS ~]$ jobs
[1]+ Running                        sleep 999 &
```

The **bg** command has no commonly used options.

> **NOTE:** You can pause a process that is running in the foreground by holding down the Ctrl key and pressing Z while in that process's window. See the "Ctrl-z" subsection in this chapter for more details.

&

By default, processes started on the command line are run in the foreground. This means that the BASH shell is not accessible until the process that is running in the foreground is terminated.

Running a process in the background allows you to continue to work in the BASH shell and execute additional commands. To execute a process in the background, add an **&** character to the end of the command, like so:

```
[student@OCS ~]$ xeyes &
```

kill

The **kill** command can be used to change the state of a process, including stopping (killing) it.

Syntax:

```
kill PID|jobnumber
```

To stop a process, first determine its process ID or job number and then provide that number as an argument to the **kill** command:

```
[student@OCS ~]$ jobs
 [1]- Running                        sleep 999 &
 [2]+ Running sleep 777 &
 [student@OCS ~]$ kill %2
 [student@OCS ~]$ jobs
 [1]- Running                        sleep 999 &
 [2]+ Terminated                     sleep 777
 [student@OCS ~]$ ps -fe | grep sleep
```

```
student 17846 12540 0 14:30 pts/2          00:00:00 sleep 999
student 17853 12540 0 14:31 pts/2          00:00:00
 grep --color=auto sleep
[student@OCS ~]$ kill 17846
[student@OCS ~]$ ps -fe | grep sleep
student 17856 12540 0 14:31 pts/2          00:00:00
 grep --color=auto sleep
[1]+ Terminated                            sleep 999
```

Here are some important options:

Option	Description
-9	Force kill. Used when the process doesn't exit when a regular **kill** command is executed.
-l	Used to provide a list of other numeric values that can be used to send different kill signals to a process.

Ctrl-c

When a process is running in the foreground, a SIGINT signal can be sent to a process by holding down the Ctrl key and pressing the letter **c**. A SIGINT signal is designed to stop a program prematurely.

Ctrl-z

When a process is running in the foreground, a SIGTSTP signal can be sent to a process by holding down the Ctrl and pressing the letter **z**. A SIGTSTP signal is designed to pause a program. The program can then be restarted by either the **bg** or the **fg** command.

See the "bg" and "fg" subsections in this chapter for more details.

nohup

Each process has a parent process that started it. For example, if you execute a command in a BASH shell, that command's parent process is the BASH shell process.

When a parent process is stopped, a hang-up (HUP) signal is sent to all the child processes. This HUP signal is designed to stop the child processes. By default, a child process will stop when sent an HUP signal.

To avoid this, execute the child process with the **nohup** command:

```
[student@OCS ~]$ nohup some_command
```

This technique is typically used when you remotely log in to a system and want to have some command continue to run even if you are disconnected. When you are disconnected, all of the programs you have running are sent HUP signals. Using the **nohup** command allows this specific process to continue running.

The **nohup** command has no commonly used options.

## CHAPTER 13

Explain the use and operation of Linux devices

This chapter provides information and commands concerning the following topics:

Types of devices

- Bluetooth
- WiFi
- USB
- Monitors
- GPIO
- Network adapters
- PCI
- HBA
- SATA
- SCSI
- Printers
- Video
- Audio

Monitoring and configuration tools

- **lsdev**
- **lsusb**
- **lspci**
- **lsblk**
- **dmesg**
- **lpr**
- **lpq**
- **abrt**
- **CUPS**
- **udevadm** (add, reload-rules, control, trigger)

File locations

- **/proc**
- **/sys**
- **/dev**
- **/dev/mapper**
- **/etc/X11**

Hot pluggable devices

- **/usr/lib/udev/rules.d** (system rules – lowest priority)
- **/run/udev/rules.d** (volatile rules)
- **/etc/udev/rules.d** (local administration – highest priority)
- **/etc/udev/rules.d**

Types of Devices

This section provides a brief description of the systems of devices you should expect to see on Linux systems.

Bluetooth

A Bluetooth device is designed to communicate wirelessly over a very short range. It communicates using a standard that is useful for I/O (input/output) devices like headphones, keyboard and mice.

WiFi

Like Bluetooth, a WiFi device is designed to communicate wirelessly, but this technology has a larger bandwidth and range. You are likely used to WiFi already as the primary means for laptops and tablets to communicate across the network.

USB

The Universal Serial Bus interface provides for wired communication. It has a wide variety of use, from USB-based keyboards and mice to USB external devices.

Monitors

A monitor is used to display the output of a laptop or desktop system. Monitor configuration files are located in the **/etc/X11** directory.

GPIO

General Purpose Input/Output is a programable pin on a chip. Manufacturers provide these pins in order to provide flexibility. A good example is found on a device called the

Raspberry Pi (a device that often uses Linux as a base OS). The Raspberry Pi has a row of GPIO pins, allowing you to connect a variety of programmable devices.

Network Adapters

A network adapter allows for network communication via a wired connection.

PCI

A Peripheral Component Interconnect is a slot on a motherboard. Any device that connects to a PCI slot is referred to as a PCI device. This may include devices like network and audio cards. The **lspci** command displays attached PCI devices (see the "lspci" subsection in this chapter for more details).

HBA

A Host Bus Adapter (HBA) is a card or circuit board that connects to the motherboard, normally through one of the PCI slots.

SATA

Serial AT Attachment (or Serial ATA) is an interface that is often used for mass storage devices. Most modern hard drives and optical drives (CD-ROM, DVD, and so on) are SATA devices. See Chapter 4, "Given a scenario, manage storage in a Linux environment" for more details.

SCSI

Like SATA, SCSI (Small Computer System Interface) is an interface often used for mass storage devices. This interface is rare on laptops and desktop systems, but you may discover it on some high-end servers. See Chapter 4 for more details.

Printers

A printer is a device that allows you to make a physical copy of a digital file or photo. Modern Linux systems use Common Unix Printer Service (CUPS) to manage printers. See the "CUPS" subsection in this chapter for more details.

Video

A video device is also called a graphics card. These devices allow the computer to communicate with the monitor. See Chapter 14, "Compare and contrast Linux graphical user interfaces" and the "/etc/X11" subsection in this chapter for more details.

Audio

An audio device allows the computer to communicate with speakers or headphones. As this is a very well-established means of communication, connecting standard audio devices to Linux rarely requires any configuration. However, very high-end and new audio interface cards may not be supported on Linux.

Monitoring and Configuration Tools

This section focuses on several different utilities designed to display information about hardware devices or configure these devices.

lsdev

The **lsdev** command shows the devices recognized by your system. Here's an example:

```
[root@OCS ~]# lsdev
Device DMA IRQ I/O Ports
-----------------------------------------------
0000:00:1f.0 1000-107f 1180-11bf
acpi 9
cascade 4
e100 2000-203f
eth0 20
eth1 16
[root@OCS ~]# lspci | grep 00:1f.0
00:1f.0 ISA bridge: Intel Corporation 82801BA ISA Bridge(LPC) (rev 12)
```

In the preceding output, you can see that the first device shown occupies two ranges of I/O ports and has a numeric ID, which is a PCI address. The second command in the example searches for that address in the **lspci** command's output, showing that it's a bridge to the legacy ISA bus.

The next device is the advanced configuration and power interface (ACPI), which lets the hardware and software talk together for managing power usage. This communicates to the CPU with interrupt number 9.

Next is a DMA (Direct Memory Access) device called cascade, which is used by the hardware to let two DMA controllers talk to each other. It has DMA channel 4.

The last three entries are for the network peripherals. The first is the network driver, which has some I/O ports reserved. The last two are for the cards; each has an IRQ (Interrupt Request Line).

lsusb

The **lsusb** command displays devices that are attached to the PCI bus.

Syntax:

```
lsusb [options]
```

Here are some key options for the **lsusb** command:

- **-D** displays a specific USB device (specified as an argument) rather than probing the **/dev/bus/usb** directory and displaying all USB devices.
- **-t** displays USB devices in a tree-like format.
- **-v** shows "verbose" messages.

Example:

```
[root@OCS Desktop]# lsusb
Bus 001 Device 002: ID 1221:3234 Unknown manufacturer Disk(Thumb drive)
Bus 001 Device 001: ID 1d6b:0002 Linux Foundation 2.0 root hub
Bus 002 Device 001: ID 1d6b:0001 Linux Foundation 1.1 root hub
```

lspci

The **lspci** command displays devices attached to the PCI bus.

Syntax:

```
lspci [options]
```

Here are some key options for the **lspci** command:

- **-b** is "bus centric," meaning it displays IRQ (Interrupt Request Line) numbers.
- **-n** displays device numbers rather than names; names typically are stored in **/usr/share/hwdata/pci.ids** or **/usr/share/hwdata/pci.ids.gz**.
- **-nn** displays both device numbers and names.
- **-v** shows "verbose" messages.
- **-vv** shows even more "verbose" messages.
- **-vvv** shows the most "verbose" messages.

Example:

```
[root@OCS ~]# lspci
00:00.0 Host bridge: Intel Corporation 440FX - 82441FX
   PMC [Natoma] (rev 02)
00:01.0 ISA bridge: Intel Corporation 82371SB PIIX3 ISA
   [Natoma/ Triton II]
00:01.1 IDE interface: Intel Corporation 82371AB/EB/MB PIIX4
   IDE (rev 01)
00:02.0 VGA compatible controller: InnoTek Systemberatung
   GmbH VirtualBox Graphics Adapter
00:03.0 Ethernet controller: Intel Corporation 82540EM
   Gigabit Ethernet Controller (rev 02)
00:04.0 System peripheral: InnoTek Systemberatung GmbH
   VirtualBox Guest Service
00:05.0 Multimedia audio controller: Intel Corporation
   82801AA AC'97 Audio Controller (rev 01)
00:06.0 USB controller: Apple Inc. KeyLargo/Intrepid USB
00:07.0 Bridge: Intel Corporation 82371AB/EB/MB PIIX4 ACPI (rev 08)
00:0b.0 USB controller: Intel Corporation 82801FB/FBM/FR
   /FW/FRW (ICH6 Family) USB2 EHCI Controller
```

```
00:0d.0 SATA controller: Intel Corporation 82801HM/HEM
    (ICH8M/ICH8M-E) SATA Controller [AHCI mode] (rev 02)
```

lsblk

The **lsblk** command displays the block devices attached to the system. For example, the following command was executed on a virtual machine and displays a single virtual hard disk (vda) and two partitions (vda1 and vda2):

```
[root@OCS ~]# lsblk
NAME     MAJ:MIN RM  SIZE RO TYPE MOUNTPOINT
vda       252:0    0  254G  0 disk
├─vda1 252:1    0  250G  0 part /
└─vda2 252:2    0    4G  0 part [SWAP]
```

Important options for the **lsblk** command include the following:

Option	Description
-a	List all devices, including empty devices.
-l	Display output in list format, rather than a tree format.
-p	Display full device name paths (for example, "/dev/vda" rather than just "vda").

dmesg

The **dmesg** command displays the in-memory copy of the kernel ring buffer.

Example:

```
[root@OCS log]# dmesg | head
Initializing cgroup subsys cpuset
Initializing cgroup subsys cpu
Linux version 2.6.32-573.7.1.el6.x86_64
    (mockbuild@c6b8.bsys.dev.centos.org)  (gcc version 4.4.7 20120313
    (Red Hat 4.4.7-16) (GCC) ) #1 SMP Tue Sep 2222:00:00 UTC 2015
Command line: ro root=/dev/mapper/VolGroup-lv_root
    rd_NO_LUKS LANG=en_US.UTF-8 rd_NO_MD
    rd_LVM_LV=VolGroup/lv_swap SYSFONT=latarcyrheb-sun16
    crashkernel=auto rd_LVM_LV=VolGroup/ lv_root
    KEYBOARDTYPE=pc KEYTABLE=us rd_NO_DM rhgb quiet
KERNEL supported cpus:
      Intel GenuineIntel
      AMD AuthenticAMD
      Centaur CentaurHauls
BIOS-provided physical RAM map:
    BIOS-e820: 0000000000000000 - 000000000009fc00 (usable)
```

lpr

See the "CUPS" subsection in this chapter.

lpq

See the "CUPS" subsection in this chapter.

abrt

See the "CUPS" subsection in this chapter.

CUPS

The Common Unix Printing System (CUPS) can be configured via command-line tools, a web-based interface, or (depending on your distribution) a GUI-based tool. Because of the nature of the Linux+ multiple-choice exam, the questions focus on the command-line tools.

To create a printer, use the **lpadmin** command, as shown here:

```
lpadmin -p printer_name -E -v device_name
```

Here are some important options for the **lpadmin** command:

Option	Description
-p	Used to specify the name of the printer.
-E	Enables the printer and sets the print queue to accept mode.
-v	Used to specify the device name (called the **device-uri**); use the following device name for a remote printer: **socket://***IP_address*.
-d	Sets the system default printer.
-x	Deletes the printer.

Some CUPS configuration can be performed by executing the **cupsctl** command. By default, it displays the current settings:

```
[root@OCS ~]# cupsctl
_debug_logging=1
_remote_admin=0
_remote_any=0
_share_printers=0
_user_cancel_any=0
BrowseLocalProtocols=dnssd
DefaultAuthType=Basic
JobPrivateAccess=default
JobPrivateValues=default
MaxLogSize=0
SubscriptionPrivateAccess=default
```

```
SubscriptionPrivateValues=default
WebInterface=Yes
```

The following table describes the important settings that can be made with the **cupsctl** command and associated files:

File	Description
_debug_logging	Enable (**--debug-logging**) or disable (**--no-debug-logging**) debugging mode for more or fewer log messages.
_remote_admin	Allow (**--remote-admin**) or disallow (**--no-remote-admin**) remote access to the administration features of CUPS.
_remote_any	Allow (**--remote-any**) or disallow (**--no-remote-any**) remote access to the CUPS service from the Internet (remote systems).
_share_printers	Automatically share printers (**--share-printers**) or don't share printers (**--no-share-printers**).
_user_cancel_any	Allow (**--user-cancel-any**) or disallow (**--no-user-cancel-any**) users to cancel any print job (disallowing still permits a user to cancel her own print job).

The **/etc/cups** directory is the location of the CUPS configuration files. The following table describes these files:

File	Description
classes.conf	Defines printer classes (collections of printers)
cupsd.conf	The primary configuration file for the CUPS service
printers.conf	The configuration file that defines the printers configured on the system

A printer that is ready to print is considered to be accepting print requests and is enabled. You can block print requests from being sent to the print queue by executing the following command:

```
cupsreject printer
```

When a printer is rejecting, the print jobs in the queue are still sent to the printer, but no new print jobs will be sent to the print queue. When you're using the **cupsreject** command, use the **-r** option to provide a reason for rejecting jobs:

```
cupsreject -r "printer down for repairs" printer
```

To allow print jobs to be sent to the printer, use the following command:

```
cupsaccept printer
```

In some cases, you may want to stop print jobs from going from the print queue to the printer. This may be for a quick repair, such as a paper jam. To stop print jobs from being sent to the printer, use the following command:

cupsdisable *printer*

Users can still print to the print queue as long as the printer is in accept mode. To allow print jobs to go from the queue to the printer, use the following command:

cupsenable *printer*

The following demonstrates the difference between accept/reject versus enable/disable:

```
print request -> [accept|reject] -> print queue -> [enable|disable] ->
printer
```

Although the CUPS commands can handle all the printing tasks for modern Linux distributions, older printer commands are still available:

- **lpr:** A command-line tool to send print jobs to the printer. Syntax: **lpr -P** *printer_name file_to_print*.

- **lpq:** A command-line tool that displays the status of a printer. Use the **-a** option to display the status of all printers.

- **lprm:** A command-line tool that removes print jobs from the print queue. Older versions of printer interfaces may have used a command called **abrt**.

udevadm

If you change a **udev** rule (see the "/etc/udev/rules.d" subsection in this chapter for adding udev rules), then execute the following command to load the new rule into the kernel's memory:

```
# udevadm control --reload
```

You can verify the rule after a device has been created by using the following command:

```
# udevadm trigger
```

add

See the "/etc/udev/rules.d" subsection in this chapter for adding **udev** rules and the "udevadm" subsection in this chapter for loading new rules.

reload-rules

See the "udevadm" subsection in this chapter for information on reloading new rules for **udev**.

control

See the "udevadm" subsection in this chapter.

trigger

See the "udevadm" subsection in this chapter.

File Locations

Several locations in the filesystem contain useful information about devices. This section explores some of the key locations and the data they contain.

/proc

The **/proc** filesystem provides information regarding processes, kernel features, and system hardware. The **/proc** filesystem is memory based, not stored on the hard drive.

Here are the key files and directories in **/proc**:

File/Directory	Description
/proc/cmdline	The kernel parameters used to boot the system.
/proc/cpuinfo	Information about the CPUs.
/proc/devices	A list of each character and block device file the kernel has recognized.
/proc/mdstat	Information about RAID devices.
/proc/meminfo	Information about system memory.
/proc/modules	A list of all kernel modules currently loaded into memory.
/proc/partitions	The kernel's partition table. Note that this may be different from what is in the hard disk's partition table.
/proc/swaps	A list of all swap space recognized by the kernel.
/proc/vmstat	Virtual memory information.
/proc/sys	A directory that contains tunable kernel parameters.

/sys

The **/sys** filesystem is designed to provide important information regarding devices and buses that the kernel is aware of. The **/sys** filesystem is memory based, not stored on the hard drive.

Here are the key files and directories in **/sys**:

File/Directory	Description
/sys/block	Describes block devices, such as hard drives, CD-ROMs, DVDs, and RAID and LVM devices. Examples: sda (first SATA or USB drive), dm-0 (first LVM device), and sr0 (first CD-ROM or DVD).
/sys/bus	Describes devices that are attached to the system bus.
/sys/bus/cpu	Describes the CPUs that are attached to the system. Look under **/sys/bus/cpu/devices** to see details about each CPU.
/sys/bus/cpu /devices	Describes the USB devices that are attached to the system.

/dev

The **/dev** filesystem contains device files. Device files are used to access physical devices (such as hard drives, keyboards, and CPUs) and virtual devices (such as LVM devices, pseudo-terminals, and software RAID devices). The **/dev** filesystem is memory based, not stored on the hard drive.

Here are the key files in **/dev**:

File	Description
/dev/sd*	Devices that begin with "sd" in the **/dev** directory are either SATA, SCSI, or USB devices. The device name **/dev/sda** refers to the first device, **/dev/sdb** refers to the second device, and so on. If a device has partitions, they are numbered starting with the value of 1.
/dev/sda1	Example: The first partition of the first SATA, SCSI, or USB device.
/dev/hd*	Devices that begin with "hd" in the **/dev** directory are IDE-based devices. The device name **/dev/hda** refers to the first device, **/dev/hdb** refers to the second device, and so on. If a device has partitions, they are numbered starting with the value of 1.
/dev/hda1	Example: The first partition of the first IDE-based device.
/dev/cdrom	Symbolic link that points to the first CD-ROM on the system.
/dev/dm*	Devices that begin with "dm" in the **/dev** directory are either software RAID or LVM devices. The device name **/dev/dm-0** refers to the first device, **/dev/dm-1** refers to the second device, and so on.
/dev/tty*	Devices that begin with "tty" in the **/dev** directory are terminal devices. The device name **/dev/tty0** refers to the first device, **/dev/tty1** refers to the second device, and so on.

/dev/mapper

Regular partitions are automatically assigned device names that are predictable. The first disk on the system is assigned to **/dev/sda** (unless it is an older IDE device, in which case it is assigned the device file **/dev/hda**). The second disk on the system is assigned to **/dev/sdb**.

Other device types, such as Logical Volume Manager (LVM), don't have predictable, automatically assigned device names. Instead, they use a feature called the device mapper.

See the "/dev/mapper" subsection in Chapter 4 for more details.

/etc/X11

The **/etc/X11/xorg.conf** file is the primary configuration file for the X server. The file is broken into different configuration sections, including the following:

Section	Description
Files	Used to specify pathnames to files needed by the server; for example, the **FontPath** entry is used to indicate the location for fonts.
ServerFlags	Provides global X server options.
Module	Loads X server modules; for example, to load the DRI module, include **Load "dri"** in the **Module** section.
Extensions	Enables X11 protocol extensions.
InputDevice	Used to define input devices such as a mouse and keyboard.
Device	Used to define output devices such as video cards.
Monitor	Defines the monitor or monitors connected to the system.
Screen	Matches the device (video card) to the corresponding attached monitor.

Here's a sample **/etc/X11/xorg.conf** file:

```
Section "Module"
     Load          "dbe"
     Load          "ddc"
EndSection
Section "Extensions"
    Option "Composite" "Enable"
EndSection
Section "Files"
    FontPath      "/usr/X11/lib/X11/fonts/75dpi/:unscaled"
    FontPath      "/usr/X11/lib/X11/fonts/100dpi/:unscaled"
    FontPath      "/usr/X11/lib/X11/fonts/misc/"
EndSection
Section "InputDevice"
    Identifier    "Keyboard1"
    Driver        "kbd"
EndSection
Section "InputDevice"
    Identifier "Mouse1"
    Driver "mouse"
    Option "Protocol"    "Microsoft"
    Option "Device"      "/dev/input/mice"
EndSection
Section "Monitor"
    Identifier "Monitor1"
EndSection
```

```
Section "Device"
    Identifier "Card1"
    Driver "fbdev"
    Option "fbdev" "/dev/fb0"
EndSection
Section "Screen"
    Identifier "Screen1"
    Device "Card1"
    Monitor "Monitor1"
    DefaultDepth 24
    Subsection "Display"
      Modes "1024x768" "800x600" "640x480"
    EndSubsection
  EndSection
Section "ServerLayout"
    Identifier "Simple Layout"
    Screen "Screen1"
    InputDevice "Mouse1" "CorePointer"
    InputDevice "Keyboard1" "CoreKeyboard"
EndSection
```

> **NOTE:**   Although **xorg.conf** is typically located in the **/etc/X11** directory, its location may vary across operating system distributions. (See manual page "man xorg.conf" for details and further possible locations.)

Hot Pluggable Devices

udev is the Linux kernel's device manager. It manages the device files under **/dev** using information about the device from **sysfs**. Every accessible device on the system will have a corresponding device file under **/dev**. If a device is plugged in to the computer while it is running, **udev** can configure it and make it available to the system. Devices that support being plugged in at runtime are also called *hot plug* devices, as opposed to *cold plug* devices, which require the computer to be rebooted for them to be used.

/usr/lib/udev/rules.d (System Rules – Lowest Priority)

These are rules for the **udev** device manager that should not be modified because they are created by developers. The rules in the **/etc/udev/rules.d** have a higher priority and can be used to overwrite rules in the **/usr/lib/udev/rules.d** directory. See the "/etc/udev/rules.d" section in this chapter for more details regarding **udev** rules.

/run/udev/rules.d (Volatile Rules)

These are rules for the **udev** device manager that are created and destroyed dynamically by applications and daemons. See the "/etc/udev/rules.d" section in this chapter for more details regarding udev rules.

/etc/udev/rules.d (Local Administration – Highest Priority)

See the "/etc/udev/rules.d" section in this chapter for details.

/etc/udev/rules.d

The udev device manager is managed by configuration files in the **/etc/udev/rules.d** directory. Each file in this directory can include entries that modify the behavior of a device file, such as the ownership or permissions placed on the device file. A typical system may have some files in the **/etc/udev/ruled.d** directory by default, depending on how the installation was performed.

If you want to create custom rules, they should be placed in the **/etc/udev/rules.d/10-local.rules** file. There are many possible rules; the following is provided as a simple example:

```
KERNEL=="hdb", GROUP="users"
```

The previous rule means "if the **/dev/hdb** device is created (likely a secondary drive, like a USB drive), then give group ownership to the 'users' group."

Also see the "udevadm" subsection in this chapter for more details.

## CHAPTER 14

Compare and Contrast Linux Graphical User Interfaces

This chapter provides information and commands concerning the following topics:

Servers

- Wayland
- X11

GUI

- Gnome
- Unity
- Cinnamon
- MATE
- KDE

Remote desktop

- VNC
- XRDP
- NX
- Spice

Console redirection

- SSH port forwarding (local, remote, X11 forwarding, VNC)

Accessibility

It is important to realize that the objective related to the following topic is to "compare and contrast Linux graphical user interfaces." This means you are not expected to configure, administer, or know specifics of using graphical user interfaces or related concepts, but rather be able to answer questions regarding what these components consist of.

Servers

Graphical user interfaces (GUIs) provide the means for users to interact with the operating system using methods beyond just the keyboard. GUIs take advantages of hardware, such as a computer mouse or a touch screen, to allow users to more easily provide input to programs. Additionally, GUIs provide a more flexible visual display than the terminal displays of previous generations of operating systems.

In Linux, a GUI server is the software that provides the interface between the hardware and the desktop. This section describes two common Linux GUI servers: Wayland and X11.

Wayland

The goal of Wayland is to provide a more simple structure than X11 (see the "X11" section in this chapter next for more details). Newer features in the kernel are able to provide many of the capabilities that X11 has traditionally provided. As a result, the implementation of X11 tends to be "bloated" when compared to the lightweight Wayland.

Some distributions, such as Ubuntu, have already adopted Wayland. It is likely that more will follow in order to streamline the Linux Windows platform.

X11

The X11 software (also called the X Window System or just X) is a legacy system created in 1984 by MIT (Massachusetts Institute of Technology). The program now includes an open source version that is maintained by the X.Org Foundation.

The X11 software includes drivers to interact with hardware components used with GUI-based systems, such as the monitor and mouse. X11 also provides basic GUI operations, such as the ability to draw, resize, and move GUI-based applications on the screen.

It is important to note that X11 does not provide an actual desktop. This software is provided by different projects. See the "GUI" section next.

GUI

KDE (now called KDE Plasma) was the first Linux desktop environment, and GNOME was primarily invented because its author wasn't happy with the licensing of the libraries used for the KDE desktop.

It doesn't really matter which one you use, but many people feel that KDE is more aesthetically pleasing, whereas GNOME does things from an architecturally correct perspective. Both get the job done.

A desktop environment can be defined by the following common criteria (to name a few):

- File manager
- Control panel/center
- Window manager
- Common look and feel
- Integrated office suite
- Media players

Three other popular desktops—Unity, Cinnamon, and MATE—are listed on the exam objectives. Keep in mind that you do not need to know details about these desktops, but rather be able to compare and contrast them. The following table provides a brief comparison of each of these desktops.

Desktop	Features	Example distros
KDE Plasma	Highly customizable. Includes many tools, tabbed browsing file manager, desktop widgets, and live windows previews.	OpenSUSE and Kubuntu
GNOME	Only includes FOSS (free and open source) software. More simple and easy to use, and follows HIG (Human Interface Guidelines). Support for Wayland has been included.	Fedora and Debian
Cinnamon	Newer desktop designed initially for Linux Mint to enhance/replace GNOME. Contains GNOME components and is known for a good user experience, with focus on graphics, effects, and animations.	Linux Mint
MATE	Newer desktop, originally an extension to GNOME. More lightweight than other desktops, normally uses less system resources, and is good for hardware with limited resources.	Manjaro Linux and Linux Mint MATE
Unity	Uses existing desktop applications, with focus on the interface (not apps). Originally designed for Ubuntu, but development is now handled by other organizations.	Previous versions of Ubuntu

Gnome

See the "GUI" section in this chapter.

Unity

See the "GUI" section in this chapter.

Cinnamon

See the "GUI" section in this chapter.

MATE

See the "GUI" section in this chapter.

KDE

See the "GUI" section in this chapter.

Remote Desktop

The idea of a remote desktop is to be able to have a desktop that is running on one system displayed on another system. The following table provides a brief comparison of different remote desktop applications available in Linux.

Application	Description
VNC	This protocol is very popular, not only in Linux, but also on Microsoft Windows (although connections between different platforms are problematic). On one system a VNC server is started, which can then be connected to from one or more VNC client utilities. VNC, which stands for Virtual Network Computing, is an established protocol, with origins in the early 2000s.
XRDP	This desktop protocol is based on the FreeRDP and rdesktop projects. One notable advantage is that you can use an XRDP client utility on Microsoft Windows to connect to a Linux desktop running the XRDP server software.
NX	NX, or NoMachine, is a cross-platform (Linux, Windows, and Mac) remote desktop software suite known for its flexibility and features. It not only can be used on native installations, but also on virtualized installations.
Spice	Originally a closed source product, Spice (Simple Protocol for Independent Computing Environments) was acquired by Red Hat and released as an open source product in 2009. Although it is Linux specific (Linux and Android), there is some support for Microsoft Windows. It also includes some support for virtualized environments.

VNC

See the "Remote Desktop" section in this chapter.

XRDP

See the "Remote Desktop" section in this chapter.

NX

See the "Remote Desktop" section in this chapter.

Spice

See the "Remote Desktop" section in this chapter.

Console Redirection

Console redirection is a term on the Linux+ exam objectives that is referring to the process of SSH port forwarding. This section covers the topic of port forwarding.

SSH Port Forwarding

The term *SSH port forwarding* is often called *SSH tunneling*. This technique provides the means to create a secure connection between two systems using software provided by Secure Shell (SSH). This subsection explores several commonly used SSH port-forwarding techniques.

Local

When the SSH forwarding process originates from the client machine, this is referred to as *local port forwarding*. In this scenario, an outgoing port on the local system is configured to connect via SSH to a specific port on a remote system. This is typically configured on the local system with a command like the following:

```
ssh -L 9000:onecoursesource.com:80 localhost
```

Now any connections from the SSH client are forwarded *via the SSH server* to the destination server.

Remote

While the command to create a remote SSH tunnel looks very much like the command to establish a local SSH tunnel, the results are a bit different:

```
sh -R 9001:localhost:9001 name@remote
```

Now any connections from the SSH client are forwarded *via the SSH client* to the destination server.

> **NOTE:** This feature normally requires a change to the **/etc/ssh/sshd_config** file as the "GatewayPorts" value must be set to "yes".

X11 Forwarding

When you connect to a remote server via SSH, you can execute commands and see the output of the commands within your local terminal. However, if you attempt to execute any program that results in GUI output, the X server on your local system will refuse to display the output.

An X11 forward tunnel will give all the SSH client programs the ability to receive data from the GUI-based program to display on the local X server. This just requires including the **-X** option when connection is via the **ssh** command.

VNC

VNC, or Virtual Network Computing, allows for an entire remote desktop to be displayed on your local X server. There are many VNC software solutions available, including the following:

- TigerVNC
- TightVNC
- RealVNC
- NoMachine

VNC software (also called a VNC server) must be installed on the client system. Not all Linux desktops come with this software installed by default.

Accessibility

Many features are available on desktops that allow users to have a richer experience. These features cater to many individuals who would benefit from such *accessibility options*. The following list describe the most common of these features/utilities:

- **Sticky Keys**: A feature that allows the user to perform keyboard combinations, such as **Ctrl-c**, without having to hold down the modifier button while pressing the combination.

- **Repeat Keys**: A feature that continuously inserts a key value when a user holds down a key on the keyboard.

- **Slow Keys**: A feature for people who have "heavy hands" when typing on a keyboard. Often they find that extra (unwanted) characters appear when they move their hands from one key to another and accidently press another key. With Slow Keys, a key press only results in a displayed character if the key is held down for a short period of time.

- **Bounce Keys**: If a user has "shaky hands" and accidentally types keys repeatedly, Bounce Keys prevents this from happening. However, this makes it more difficult to type words like "difficult," which has repeating f's.

- **Toggle Keys**: This feature is used to provide a sound when modifier keys, such as the Shift key, are pressed. This makes it easier for users to know whether they have pressed a modifier key.

- **Mouse Keys**: When the Mouse Keys feature is enabled, the user can move the mouse cursor by using keys on the keyboard.

- **Screen Reader**: A screen reader verbalizes the text shown on the screen. Several screen readers are available, including Orca, Emacspeak, eSpeak, and festival.

- **Braille Display**: A Braille display is a "monitor" that provides Braille output.

- **Screen Magnifier**: A screen magnifier allows the user to better see the screen by magnifying a portion of it. An example of a screen magnifier is KMagnifier, a program available on KDE desktops.

- **Onscreen Keyboard**: An onscreen keyboard allows the user to "type" using a mouse with a virtual keyboard or using a touch-enabled screen. An example of an onscreen keyboard is Gnome's GOK.

## CHAPTER 15

Given a scenario, apply or acquire the appropriate user and/or group permissions and ownership

This chapter provides information and commands concerning the following topics:

File and directory permissions

- Read, write, execute
- User, group, other
- SUID
- Octal notation
- umask
- Sticky bit
- GUID
- Inheritance
- Utilities (chmod, chown, chgrp, getfacl, setfacl, ls, ulimit, chage)

Context-based permissions

- SELinux configurations (disabled, permissive, enforcing)
- SELinux policy (targeted)
- SELinux tools (setenforce, getenforce, sestatus, setsebool, getsebool, chcon, restorecon, ls -Z, ps -Z)
- AppArmor (aa-disable, aa-complain, aa-unconfined, /etc/apparmor.d/, /etc/apparmor.d/tunables)

Privilege escalation

- su
- sudo
- wheel
- visudo
- sudoedit

User types

- Root
- Standard
- Service

File and Directory Permissions

The user who owns a file or directory has the ability to allow or deny access to the file or directory using permissions. Additionally, the root user has the ability to change the permissions of any file or directory on the system. This section focuses on these permissions and how to apply them.

Read, Write, Execute

Every file and directory has standard permissions (also called "read, write, and execute" permissions) that either allow or disallow a user access. Using these standard permissions is something that every Linux user should understand how to do, as this is the primary way a user will protect his files from other users.

To view the permissions of a file or directory, use the **ls -l** command:

```
[student@OCS ~]$ ls -l /etc/chrony.keys
-rw-r-----. 1 root chrony 62 May  9  2018 /etc/chrony.keys
```

The first ten characters of the output denote the file type (recall that a hyphen [–] as the character in the first position denotes a plain file, whereas a **d** denotes a directory) and the permissions for the file. Permissions are broken into three sets: the user owner of the file (root in the previous example), the group owner (chrony), and all other users (referred to as "others").

Each set has three possible permissions: read (symbolized by **r**), write (**w**), and execute (**x**). If the permission is set, the character that symbolizes the permission is displayed. Otherwise, a hyphen (–) character is displayed to indicate that permission is not set. Thus, **r-x** means "read and execute are set, but write is not set."

What read, write, and execute permissions really mean depends on whether the object is a file or directory. For files, these permissions mean the following:

- **Read**: Can view or copy file contents.
- **Write**: Can modify file contents.
- **Execute**: Can run the file like a program. After you create a program, you must make it executable before you can run it.

For directories, they mean the following:

- **Read**: Can list files in the directory.
- **Write**: Can add and delete files in the directory (requires execute permission).
- **Execute**: Can "**cd**" into the directory or use it in a pathname.

User, Group, Other

See the "Read, Write, Execute" subsection in this chapter.

SUID

The following table describes the special permission sets of **suid**, **sgid**, and the sticky bit:

	suid	sgid	Sticky Bit
Description	When set on executable files, **suid** allows a program to access files using the permissions of the user owner of the executable file.	When set on executable files, **sgid** allows a program to access files using the permissions of the group owner of the executable file. When it's set on directories, all new files in the directory inherit the group ownership of the directory.	When the sticky bit is set on directories, files in the directory can only be removed by the user owner of the file, the owner of the directory, or the root user.
Set	**chmod u+s** *file* or **chmod 4**xxx *file* (*xxx* refers to regular read, write, and execute permissions.)	**chmod g+s** *file* or **chmod 2**xxx *file* (*xxx* refers to regular read, write, and execute permissions.)	**chmod o+t** *file* or **chmod 1**xxx *file* (*xxx* refers to regular read, write, and execute permissions). Note: Sticky bit permissions are almost always set to the octal value of 1777.
Remove	**chmod u-s** *file* or **chmod 0**xxx *file*	**chmod g-s** *file* or **chmod 0**xxx *file*	**chmod o-t** *file* or **chmod 0**xxx *file*

See the "chmod" subsection in this chapter for details about the **chmod** command.

Octal Notation

See the "chmod" subsection in this chapter for details about octal notation.

umask

The **umask** command sets default permissions for files and directories. These default permissions are applied only when the file or directory is initially created.

The **umask** command accepts one argument: the mask value. The mask value is an octal value that is applied against the maximum possible permissions for new files or new directories, as shown in the following table:

Type	Maximum Possible Permission for New Item
File	**rw-rw-rw-**
Directory	**rwxrwxrwx**

Figure 15.1 describes how a umask value of **027** would apply to new files versus how it would apply to new directories.

Description	File			Directories		
Maximum	rw-	rw-	rw-	rwx	rwx	rwx
Umask Applied	---	-M-	MM-	---	-M-	MM-
Result	rw-	r--	---	rwx	r-x	--x

Figure 15-1   How umask Is Applied

> **NOTE:**   Each shell has its own umask value. If you change the umask in one shell, it will not affect the umask value in any other shell. To make a persistent change to your umask across logins, add the **umask** command to the **~/.bash_profile** file.

Sticky Bit

See the "SUID" subsection in this chapter for details about the sticky bit.

GUID

See the "SUID" subsection in this chapter for details about GUID.

Inheritance

Unlike in some operating systems, basic and advanced Linux permissions don't utilize inheritance. The idea of inheritance is when a new file or directory inherits the permissions from the directory that the item is created in.

There is a way to have permissions inherit from the parent directory: by using ACLs (access control lists). See the "setfacl" subsection for details.

Utilities

Several utilities or commands allow you to manage permissions. The utilities that are testable for the Linux+ exam are covered in this section.

chmod

The **chmod** command is used to change permissions on files. It can be used in two ways: symbolic method and octal method. With the octal method, the permissions are assigned numeric values:

- Read = 4
- Write = 2
- Execute = 1

With these numeric values, one number can be used to describe an entire permission set:

- 7 = **rwx**
- 6 = **rw-**
- 5 = **r-x**
- 4 = **r--**
- 3 = **-wx**
- 2 = **-w-**
- 1 = **--x**
- 0 = **---**

So, to change the permissions of a file to **rwxr-xr--**, you would execute the following command:

```
chmod 754 filename
```

The following table demonstrates some examples using the octal method:

Example	Description
chmod 755 file	Sets the permissions of **rwxr-xr-x**.
chmod 511 file	Sets the permissions of **r-x--x--x**.
chmod 600 file	Sets the permissions of **rw-------**.

With octal permissions, you should always provide three numbers, which will change all the permissions. But, what if you only want to change a single permission of the set? For that, use the symbolic method by passing three values to the **chmod** command, as shown in the following table:

Who	What	Permission
u = user owner	+	**r**
g = group owner	-	**w**
o = other	=	**x**
a = all sets		

The following demonstrates adding execute permission to all three sets (user owner, group owner, and others) using the symbolic method:

```
[student@OCS ~]$ ls -l display.sh
-rw-rw-r--. 1 student student 291 Apr 30 20:09 display.sh
[student@OCS ~]$ chmod a+x display.sh
[student@OCS ~]$ ls -l display.sh
-rwxrwxr-x. 1 student student 291 Apr 30 20:09 display.sh
```

Here are some important options for the **chmod** command:

Option	Description
-R	Recursively apply changes to an entire directory structure.
-v	Verbose. Produce output demonstrating the changes that are made.

chown

The **chown** command is used to change the user owner or group owner of a file or directory. The following table demonstrates different ways to use this command:

Example	Description
chown tim abc.txt	Changes the user owner of the **abc.txt** file to tim user.
chown tim:staff abc.txt	Changes the user owner of the **abc.txt** file to tim user and the group owner to the staff group.
chown :staff abc.txt	Changes the group owner of the **abc.txt** file to the staff group.

NOTE: Only the root user can change the user owner of a file. To change the group owner of a file, the user who executes the command must own the file and be a member of the group that the ownership is being changed to.

Here are some important options for the **chown** command:

Option	Description
-R	Recursively apply changes to an entire directory structure.
--reference=_file_	Change the user and group owner to the ownership of _file_.
-v	Verbose. Produce output demonstrating the changes that are made.

chgrp

The **chgrp** command is designed to change the group ownership of a file. The syntax of this command is **chgrp** [_options_] _group_name file_. In the following example, the group ownership of the **abc.txt** file is changed to the staff group:

```
[student@OCS ~]$ chgrp staff abc.txt
```

NOTE: To change the group owner of a file, the user who executes the command must own the file and be a member of the group that the ownership is being changed to.

Here are some important options for the **chgrp** command:

Option	Description
-R	Recursively apply changes to an entire directory structure.
--reference=*file*	Change the user and group owner to the ownership of *file*.
-v	Verbose. Produce output demonstrating the changes that are made.

getfacl

See the "setfacl" subsection next.

setfacl

ACLs (access control lists) allow the owner of a file to give permissions for specific users and groups. The **setfacl** command is used to create an ACL on a file or directory:

```
sarah@OCS:~$ setfacl -m user:dane:r-- sales_report
```

The **-m** option is used to make a new ACL for the file. The format of the argument to the **-m** option is *what*:*who*:*permission*. The value for *what* can be one of the following:

- **user** or **u** when applying an ACL for a specific user.
- **group** or **g** when applying an ACL for a specific group.
- **others** or **o** when applying an ACL for "others."
- **mask** or **m** when setting the mask for the ACL. (The mask will be explained later in this section.)

The value for *who* will be the user or group to which the permission will be applied. The permission can be provided as either a symbolic value (**r--**) or an octal value (**4**).

Once an ACL has been applied on a file or directory, a plus sign (**+**) character will appear after the permissions when the **ls -l** command is executed, as shown here:

```
sarah@OCS:~$ ls -l sales_report
-rw-rw-r--+ 1 sarah sales 98970 Dec 27 16:45 sales_report
```

To view the ACL, use the **getfacl** command:

```
sarah@OCS:~$ getfacl sales_report
# file: sales_report
# owner: sarah
# group: sarah
user::rw-
user:william:r--
group::rw-
mask::rw-
other::r--
```

The following example demonstrates setting an ACL for a group:

```
sarah@OCS:~$ setfacl -m g:games:6 sales_report
sarah@OCS:~$ getfacl sales_report
# file: sales_report
# owner: sarah
# group: sarah
user::rw-
user:william:r--
group::rw-
group:games:rw-
mask::rw-
other::r--
```

For regular permissions, the **umask** value is used to determine the default permissions applied for new files and directories. For ACLs, you can define a default ACL set for all new files and directories that are created within a shell by using the **-m** option with the **setfacl** command. In this case, the following syntax is used for the argument: **default:*what:who:permission***.

The following example will create a default ACL for the **reports** directory:

```
sarah@OCS:~$ mkdir reports
sarah@OCS:~$ setfacl -m default:g:games:r-x reports
sarah@OCS:~$ setfacl -m default:u:bin:rwx reports
sarah@OCS:~$ getfacl reports
# file: reports
# owner: sarah
# group: sarah
user::rwx
group::rwx
other::r-x
default:user::rwx
default:user:bin:rwx
default:group::rwx
default:group:games:r-x
default:mask::rwx
default:other::r-x
```

The following example demonstrates how new files and directories will inherit the ACLs that were created in the commands executed in the previous example:

```
sarah@OCS:~$ mkdir reports/test
sarah@OCS:~$ getfacl reports/test
# file: reports/test
# owner: sarah
# group: sarah
```

```
user::rwx
user:bin:rwx
group::rwx
group:games:r-x
mask::rwx
other::r-x
default:user::rwx
default:user:bin:rwx
default:group::rwx
default:group:games:r-x
default:mask::rwx
default:other::r-x
sarah@OCS:~$ touch reports/sample1
sarah@OCS:~$ getfacl reports/sample1
# file: reports/sample1
# owner: sarah
# group: sarah
user::rw-
user:bin:rwx                        #effective:rw-
group::rwx                          #effective:rw-
group:games:r-x                     #effective:r--
mask::rw-
other::r--
```

Here are some important options for the **setfacl** command:

Option	Description
-b	Remove all ACLs.
-d	Set a default ACL on a directory; this will be inherited by any new file or directory created with this directory.
-R	Apply recursively.

ls

See the "Read, Write, Execute" subsection in this chapter to see how the **ls** command is important for displaying permissions.

ulimit

The **ulimit** command lists or sets a user's account limits:

```
[root@OCS ~]# ulimit -a
core file size              (blocks, -c)   0
data seg size               (kbytes,  -d)   unlimited
scheduling priority         (-e)    0
file size                   (blocks, -f)   unlimited
```

```
pending signals                (-i)     15439
max locked memory              (kbytes, -l)    64
max memory size                (kbytes, -m)       unlimited
open files                     (-n)        1024
pipe size                      (512 bytes, -p)    8
POSIX message queues           (bytes, -q)    819200
real-time priority             (-r)    0
stack size                     (kbytes, -s)    8192
cpu time                       (seconds, -t)   unlimited
max user processes             (-u)   4096
virtual memory                 (kbytes, -v)   unlimited
file locks                     (-x)   unlimited
```

These limits are normally configured by the system administrator using a PAM (Pluggable Authentication Modules) configuration file:

```
[root@OCS ~]# tail -n 12 /etc/security/limits.conf
#<domain>         <type>          <item>            <value>
#

#*                soft            core              0
#*                hard            rss               10000
#@student         hard            nproc             20
#@faculty         soft            nproc             20
#@faculty         hard            nproc             50
#ftp              hard            nproc             0
# End of file
```

For example, you may want to limit how many concurrent logins an account can have:

```
student              -            maxlogins         4
```

Users rarely use the **ulimit** command to limit their own account, so the options for this command are not as important as understanding what the output displays. Additionally, some of the limits are very rarely used. The commonly used limits are described in the following table:

Limit	Description
fsize	Maximum file size allowed in memory
cpu	Maximum CPU time allowed
nproc	Maximum number of concurrently running processes
maxlogins	Maximum number of concurrent logins

chage

See the "chage" section in Chapter 8, "Given a scenario, manage users and groups."

Context-Based Permissions

Files and directories may be compromised by users who either do not understand permissions or accidently provide more access than intended. This is a reflection of an old system administration saying, "If we didn't have users, nothing would break and the system would be more secure." Of course, the response to this saying is, "Without users, we wouldn't have a job!" Users' mistakes often do provide unintended access to the data that is stored in files.

Note that traditional Linux permissions make use of Discretionary Access Control (DAC), while context-based permissions utilize Mandatory Access Control (MAC). However, when a context-based solution is enabled, DAC still applies (both MAC and DAC are enforced).

Context-based permissions can be configured to accommodate for this flaw by providing an additional level of security when processes (programs) are used to access files. This section covers two commonly used context-based methods: SELinux and AppArmor.

SELinux Configurations

An SELinux security policy can be applied that will require processes to be a part of an SELinux security context (think "security group") in order to be able to access files and directories. Regular permissions will still be used to further define access, but for accessing the file/directory, this SELinux policy would be applied first.

A bigger concern, and one that most SELinux policies are designed to address, is how daemon (or system) processes present a security risk. Consider a situation where you have many active processes that provide a variety of services. For example, one of these processes may be a web server, as shown in the following example:

```
root@OCS:~# ps -fe | grep httpd
root      1109     1  0  2018  ?         00:51:56 /usr/sbin/httpd
apache    1412  1109  0  Dec24 ?         00:00:09 /usr/sbin/httpd
apache    4085  1109  0  05:40 ?         00:00:12 /usr/sbin/httpd
apache    8868  1109  0  08:41 ?         00:00:06 /usr/sbin/httpd
apache    9263  1109  0  08:57 ?         00:00:04 /usr/sbin/httpd
apache   12388  1109  0  Dec26 ?         00:00:47 /usr/sbin/httpd
apache   18707  1109  0  14:41 ?         00:00:00 /usr/sbin/httpd
apache   18708  1109  0  14:41 ?         00:00:00 /usr/sbin/httpd
apache   19769  1109  0  Dec27 ?         00:00:15 /usr/sbin/httpd
apache   29802  1109  0  01:43 ?         00:00:17 /usr/sbin/httpd
apache   29811  1109  0  01:43 ?         00:00:11 /usr/sbin/httpd
apache   29898  1109  0  01:44 ?         00:00:10 /usr/sbin/httpd
```

Note that in the preceding output, each line describes one Apache Web Server process (**/usr/sbin/httpd**) that is running on the system. The first part of the line is the user who initiated the process. The process that runs as root is only used to spawn additional **/usr/sbin/httpd** processes. The others, however, respond to incoming web page requests from client utilities (web browsers).

Imagine for a moment that a security flaw is discovered in the software for the Apache Web Server that allows a client utility to gain control of one of the **/usr/sbin/httpd** processes and issue custom commands or operations to that process. One of those operations could be to view the content of the **/etc/passwd** file, which would be successful because of the permissions placed on this file:

```
root@OCS:~# ls -l /etc/passwd
-rw-r--r-- 1 root root 2690 Dec 11  2018 /etc/passwd
```

As you can see from the output of the preceding command, all users have the ability to view the contents of the **/etc/passwd** file. Ask yourself this: Do you want some random person (usually called a hacker) to have the ability to view the contents of the file that stores user account data?

With an SELinux policy, the **/usr/sbin/httpd** processes can be "locked down" so each can only access a certain set of files. This is what most administrators use SELinux for: to secure processes that may be compromised by hackers making use of known (or, perhaps, unknown) exploits.

This subsection covers the essentials of managing an SELinux security policy.

disabled

When in disabled mode, SELinux is not functional at all. No checks are performed when users attempt to access files or directories. See the "setenforce" and "getenforce" subsections in this chapter for more details on viewing and changing the SELinux mode.

permissive

When in permissive mode, SELinux performs checks but will never block access to a file or directory. This mode is designed for troubleshooting problems as log messages are created when in this mode. See the "setenforce" and "getenforce" subsections in this chapter for more details on viewing and changing the SELinux mode.

enforcing

When in enforcing mode, SELinux performs checks and will block access to files or directories if necessary. See the "setenforce" and "getenforce" subsections in this chapter for more details on viewing and changing the SELinux mode.

SELinux Policy

An SELinux policy is a collection of rules that determine what restrictions are imposed by the policy. The policy itself is often very complex, and details are beyond the scope of the Linux+ exam. It is, however, important to know that the policy sets the restrictions based on rules.

You should also know that one of the most commonly used policies is the "targeted" policy. This policy normally exists by default on systems that have SELinux installed, and it is typically the default policy that is enabled when SELinux is first enabled.

A targeted policy contains rules designed to protect the system from services, rather than regular users. Each service is assigned one or more security contexts, Boolean values, and additional rules that limit the service's ability to access files and directories.

targeted

See the "SELinux Policy" subsection in this chapter.

SELinux Tools

A large number of tools are used to manage SELinux. This subsection covers the tools you should know for the Linux+ exam.

setenforce

You can disable the security policy (useful when testing a new policy or troubleshooting SELinux problems) with the **setenforce** command:

```
root@OCS:~# setenforce 0
root@OCS:~# getenforce
Permissive
```

While in "Permissive" mode, SELinux will not block any access to files and directories, but warnings will be issued and viewable in the system log files.

getenforce

Use the **getenforce** command to determine the current SELinux mode:

```
root@OCS:~# getenforce
Enforcing
```

The result "Enforcing" means SELinux is installed and the security policy is currently active. See the "disabled," "permissive," and "enforcing" subsections in this chapter for more details regarding SELinux modes.

sestatus

The **sestatus** command provides overall status information about SELinux:

```
root@OCS:~# sestatus
SELinux status:                 enabled
SELinuxfs mount:                /sys/fs/selinux
SELinux root directory:         /etc/selinux
Loaded policy name:             targeted
Current mode:                   enforcing
Mode from config file:          enforcing
Policy MLS status:              enabled
Policy deny_unknown status:     allowed
Max kernel policy version:      28
```

setsebool

To set an SELinux Boolean, use the **setsebool** command:

```
root@OCS:~# getsebool -a | grep abrt_anon_write
abrt_anon_write --> off
root@OCS:~# setsebool abrt_anon_write 1
root@OCS:~# getsebool -a | grep abrt_anon_write
abrt_anon_write --> on
```

See the "getsebool" subsection next for information about Boolean values.

getsebool

Part of an SELinux security policy includes Booleans. A Boolean is a setting that can be assigned either a true or a false value. This value can affect the behavior of the SELinux policy.

```
root@OCS:~# getsebool -a | head
abrt_anon_write --> off
abrt_handle_event --> off
abrt_upload_watch_anon_write --> on
antivirus_can_scan_system --> off
antivirus_use_jit --> off
auditadm_exec_content --> on
authlogin_nsswitch_use_ldap --> off
authlogin_radius --> off
authlogin_yubikey --> off
awstats_purge_apache_log_files --> off
```

In order to determine what a Boolean is used for, use the **semanage** command:

```
root@OCS:~# semanage boolean -l | head
```

SELinux boolean	State	Default	Description
privoxy_connect_any 　Allow privoxy to connect any	(on	, on)	
smartmon_3ware 　to 3ware	(off	, off)	Allow smartmon
mpd_enable_homedirs 　enable homedirs	(off	, off)	Allow mpd to
xdm_sysadm_login 　sysadm login	(off	, off)	Allow xdm to
xen_use_nfs	(off	, off)	Allow xen to use nfs
mozilla_read_content 　to read content	(off	, off)	Allow mozilla
ssh_chroot_rw_homedirs 　chroot rw homedirs	(off	, off)	Allow ssh to
mount_anyfile	(on	, on)	Allow mount to anyfile

See the "setsebool" subsection in this chapter for information on how to set a Boolean value.

chcon

Use the **chcon** command to change the context of a file or directory:

```
root@OCS:~# chcon -t user_home_t /var/www/html/index.html
```

See the "ls -Z" subsection in this chapter for more details regarding security contexts.

restorecon

There are SELinux rules that define the default security contexts for a majority of the system files. The **restorecon** command is used to reset the default security context on a file or directory.

Example:

```
root@OCS:~# restorecon /var/www/html/index.html
```

A commonly used option to the **restorecon** command is the **-R** option, which performs the changes recursively on a directory structure.

See the "ls -Z" subsection in this chapter for more details regarding security contexts.

ls -Z

Each process runs with a security context. To see this, use the **-Z** option to the **ps** command (the **head** command is used here simply to limit the output of the command):

```
root@OCS:~# ps -fe | grep httpd | head -2
system_u:system_r:httpd_t:s0 root    1109    1   0   2018 ?
  00:51:56 /usr/sbin/httpd
system_u:system_r:httpd_t:s0 apache 1412 1109   0 Dec24 ?
  00:00:09 /usr/sbin/httpd
```

The security context (**system_u:system_r:httpd_t:s0**) is complicated, but for understanding the basics of SELinux, the important part is **httpd_t**, which is like a security group or domain. As part of this security domain, the **/usr/sbin/httpd** process can only access files that are allowed by the security policy for **httpd_t**. This policy is typically written by someone who is an SELinux expert, and that expert should have proven experience regarding which processes should be able to access specific files and directories on the system.

Files and directories also have an SELinux security context that is defined by the policy. To see a security context for a specific file, use the -Z option to the **ls** command (note that the SELinux context contains so much data that the filename cannot fit on the same line):

```
root@OCS:~# ls -Z /var/www/html/index.html
unconfined_u:object_r:httpd_sys_content_t:s0/var/www/html/index.html
```

ps -Z

See the "ls -Z" subsection in this chapter.

AppArmor

AppArmor is a MAC system that plays a similar role to SELinux in that it provides a context-based permission model. This subsection describes the key components of AppArmor that are exam testable.

aa-disable

An AppArmor profile is a rule set that describes how AppArmor should restrict a process. A profile can be disabled for a specific profile by using the **aa-disable** command. Here's an example:

```
root@OCS:~# ln -s /etc/apparmor.d/usr.sbin.mysqld
  /etc/apparmor.d/disable
root@OCS:~#  apparmor_parser -R /etc/apparmor.d/usr.sbin.mysqld
```

> **NOTE:** To view the status of a profile, use the **aa-status** command. To enable a profile again, use the following commands:

```
root@OCS:~# rm /etc/apparmor.d/disable/usr.sbin.mysqld
root@OCS:~#  apparmor_parser -r
  /etc/apparmor.d/usr.sbin.mysqld
```

aa-complain

If you need to troubleshoot an AppArmor profile, it is best to put it into complain mode. In this mode, there are no restrictions enforced, but any problems will be reported.

Use the **aa-complain** command to put a profile into complain mode:

```
root@OCS:~#  aa-complain /usr/sbin/mysqld
Setting /usr/sbin/mysqld to complain mode.
```

To put the profile back into the "enforcing" mode, use the following command:

```
root@OCS:~#  sudo aa-enforce /usr/sbin/mysqld
Setting /usr/sbin/mysqld to enforce mode
```

aa-unconfined

Use the **aa-unconfined** command to list processes that are not restricted by the AppArmor profiles.

/etc/apparmor.d/

The **/etc/apparmor.d** directory is the location of the definitions of the AppArmor profiles. Note that knowing how to create or read these files is beyond the scope of the Linux+ exam, but it is important to know the location of these profiles in order to determine which profiles are available and to use the AppArmor commands, such as the **aa-disable** command.

/etc/apparmor.d/tunables

The **/etc/apparmor.d/tunables** directory is the location of files that can be used to fine-tune the behavior of AppArmor. Note that knowing how to create or read these files is beyond the scope of the Linux+ exam.

Privilege Escalation

The concept behind privilege escalation is that a user may need to be able to execute commands using an account that has more privileges than the user's account normally has. For example, a regular user may need to execute a command that requires root user access. There are several techniques that can provide privilege access; this subsection covers the techniques that are exam testable.

su

The **su** command allows a user to shift user accounts:

```
[student@OCS ~]# id
uid=1000(student) gid=1000(student) groups=1000(student)
context=unconfined_u:unconfined_r:unconfined_t:s0-s0:c0.c1023
[student@localhost ~]# su root
Password:
[root@OCS ~]# id
uid=0(root) gid=0(root) groups=0(root)
context=unconfined_u:unconfined_r:unconfined_t:s0-s0:c0.c1023
```

One option is permitted when executing the **su** command: the - option. When you execute the **su** command with the - option, a new login shell will be provided. When you're not using the - character, a non-login shell will be provided.

sudo

When properly configured by the administrator, users can use the **sudo** command to run commands as other users (typically as the root user). To execute a command as root, enter the following:

```
sudo command
```

You will be prompted for your own password and, if the settings in the **/etc/sudoers** file are correct, the command will execute correctly. If the settings are not correct, an error message will appear.

The following table describes common options for the **sudo** command:

Option	Description
-b	Run the command in the background.
-e	Run like the **sudoedit** command. See the "sudoedit" subsection in this chapter.
-l	List which commands are allowed for this user.
-u *user*	Run the command as *user* rather than as the root user.

Also see the "visudo" section in this chapter for details regarding the **/etc/sudoers** file.

wheel

A common method for providing non-root users with root access is to use the wheel group. If enabled in the **/etc/sudoers** file (normally this line is "commented out"), anyone in the wheel group will have the ability to run any command as the root user via the **sudo** command:

```
%wheel    ALL=(ALL)    ALL
```

visudo

The **/etc/sudoers** file is used to determine which users can use the **sudo** command to execute commands as other users (typically as the root user). To edit this file, you must be logged in as the root user and should use the **visudo** command rather than edit the file directly.

The following table describes important definitions for the **/etc/sudoers** file:

Option	Description
User_Alias	A name that represents a group of users (for example, **User_Alias ADMINS = julia, sarah**)
Cmnd_Alias	A name that represents a group of commands (for example, **Cmnd_Alias SOFTWARE = /bin/rpm, /usr/bin/yum**).

The format of an entry for the **/etc/sudoers** file uses the following syntax:

```
user              machine=commands
```

To allow the student user the ability to execute the **/usr/bin/yum** command as the root user, add an entry like the following to the **/etc/sudoers** file:

```
student       ALL=/usr/bin/yum
```

To allow all members of ADMINS the ability to execute all of the **SOFTWARE** command as the root user, add an entry like the following to the **/etc/sudoers** file:

```
ADMINS       ALL=SOFTWARE
```

sudoedit

If you want to edit a file using sudo access, consider using the **sudoedit** or **sudo -e** command. Using this feature requires having the ability to edit a file using a command designed to edit files (such as **nano**, **vi**, or **vim**).

Example:

```
sudoedit file1
```

Note that the editor that will be chosen depends on variables. The following variables are consulted:

- SUDO_EDITOR
- VISUAL
- EDITOR

If none of these variables is set, then the vi editor is typically the default.

User Types

This section breaks down the different user types you are likely to encounter on Linux-based systems.

Root

The root account is the system administrator account. It is important to note that what makes the root account special is the UID of 0. Any user with a UID of 0 is a full system administrator. As a security note, when you're performing audits, look for any user with a UID of 0, as this is a common hacking technique.

Standard

Any account with a UID of 1000 or higher is considered a standard or regular user account. People are normally assigned standard user accounts so they can log in to the system and perform tasks.

Service

A typical Linux system will have many service user accounts. These service user accounts typically have UID values under 1000, making it easy for an administrator to recognize these as special accounts.

Some of these service accounts are often referred to as "daemon accounts" because they are used by daemon-based software. *Daemons* are programs that run in the background, performing specific system tasks.

Other service accounts may exist to provide features for the operating system. For example, the "nobody" account is used to apply permissions for files that are shared via NFS (Network File System).

Additionally, if you add new software to the system, more users might be added because software vendors make use of both user and group accounts to provide controlled access to files that are part of the software.

## CHAPTER 16

Given a scenario, configure and implement appropriate access and authentication methods

This chapter provides information and commands concerning the following topics:

PAM

- Password policies
- LDAP integration
- User lockouts
- Required, allowed, or sufficient
- **/etc/pam.d/**
- pam_tally2
- faillock

SSH

- **~/.ssh/**
- **known_hosts**
- **authorized_keys**
- config
- **id_rsa**
- **id_rsa.pub**
- User-specific access
- TCP Wrappers
- **/etc/ssh/ (ssh_config, sshd_config)**
- **ssh-copy-id**
- **ssh-keygen**
- **ssh-add**

TTYs

- **/etc/securetty**
- **/dev/tty#**

PTYs

PKI

- Self-signed
- Private keys
- Public keys
- Hashing
- Digital signatures
- Message digest

VPN as a client

- SSL/TLS
- Transport mode
- Tunnel mode
- IPSec
- DTLS

PAM

PAM (Pluggable Authentication Modules) is already used by almost all the Linux utilities that attempt to authenticate users. This is important because you don't need to make adjustments to the utilities to change how users are authenticated, but rather the PAM configuration files.

To understand how beneficial PAM is, you should realize some of the things you can have PAM do. While we won't cover all these in detail, here are some examples of what you can do with PAM:

- PAM can be used to enforce more robust password requirements.
- You can limit what days and times users can log in to the system with PAM.
- PAM can limit where users log in from.
- PAM can set or unset environment variables. Because you can have different PAM rules for different utilities, this means you would have one set of environment variables for local login, one set for SSH logins, and one for FTP logins.
- User accounts can have restrictions placed on them with PAM. For example, the number of processes a user can execute could be limited.
- You can limit where the root user can log in from. This can make your system more secure by only allowing the root user to log in locally or use the **su** command to gain access to the root account.

Keep in mind that these are just a few of the things you can do with PAM. Dozens of different PAM modules provide many different authentication features.

NOTE: PAM can be a complicated system. Remember that the goal of the contents of this book is to provide a summary, not a complete description, of each topic.

Password Policies

The pam_unix module provides a lot of features that modify how passwords are set. For example, consider the following commands:

```
[root@OCS ~]# grep ^password /etc/pam.d/passwd
password      include        system-auth
[root@OCS ~]# grep ^password /etc/pam.d/system-auth
password      requisite      pam_cracklib.so try_first_pass retry=3
password      sufficient     pam_unix.so md5 shadow nullok
  try_first_pass use_authtok
password      required       pam_deny.so
```

The shadow option to the pam_unix module makes it so passwords are stored using the shadow system. Passwords are stored in the **/etc/shadow** file, not the **/etc/passwd** file.

You can make some changes to this module to make your system more secure. For example, if you modify the pam_unix line in the **/etc/pam.d/system-auth** file to match the following, the system does not allow users to reuse the same passwords:

```
password      sufficient     pam_unix.so md5 shadow nullok
  try_first_pass use_authtok remember=5
```

Now the last five passwords for each user are remembered, and the user cannot use one of these five passwords when changing to a new password. This prevents users from using the same passwords over and over.

The following table describes some additional important pam_unix options:

Option	Description
md5	Encrypt the password using the MD5 encryption algorithm.
sha256	Encrypt the password using the SHA256 encryption algorithm.
nullok	Allow the root user to provide users with null (empty) passwords.
remember=x	Remember old user passwords and don't allow users to use these passwords when changing passwords.

LDAP Integration

Note that Lightweight Directory Access Protocol (LDAP) client configuration includes more than just adding the PAM component. However, the exam objective is to know how to enable LDAP integration for PAM, so that is what is covered in this subsection.

LDAP can also be implemented at different levels. For example, you can have LDAP create home directories for users when a user logs in (or you could use an entirely different technique by using the automount utility to mount network drives). At the very minimum, the following bold lines should be added to the **/etc/pam.d/system-auth** file:

```
auth        sufficient pam_ldap.so
auth            required         pam_env.so
auth            sufficient       pam_unix.so try_first_pass nullok
auth            required         pam_deny.so


account     sufficient pam_ldap.so
account         required         pam_unix.so


password    sufficient pam_ldap.so
password        requisite        pam_pwquality.so try_first_pass local_use
rs_only retry=3 authtok_type=
password        sufficient       pam_unix.so try_first_pass use_authtok nu
llok sha512 shadow
password        required         pam_deny.so


session         optional         pam_keyinit.so revoke
session         required         pam_limits.so
-session        optional         pam_systemd.so
session     optional   pam_ldap.so
session         [success=1 default=ignore] pam_succeed_if.so service in
 crond quiet use_uid
session         required         pam_unix.so
```

The following list describes additional configurations that could be enabled when LDAP is enabled in PAM:

- **"auth   sufficient   pam_ldap.so" in the /etc/pam.d/su and /etc/pam.d/su-l files**: Enables LDAP for the **su** command

- **"password   sufficient   pam_ldap.so" in the /etc/pam.d/passwd file**: Allows users to change their LDAP passwords

- **"session   required   pam_mkhomedir.so skel=/etc/skel umask=0022" in the /etc/pam.d/system-login file**: Creates a home directory, with files from the skeleton directory, for the user at login

- **"auth   sufficient   pam_ldap.so" in the /etc/pam.d/sudo file**: Allows LDAP users to use the **sudo** command (provided other configuration settings have been made for sudo access for the user)

User Lockouts

See the "faillock" and "pam_tally2" subsections in this chapter.

Required, Allowed, or Sufficient

To understand what the contents of a PAM configuration file mean, you first have to understand the first column of data. There are four possible types in the first column: auth, account, session, and password. How they are used is visually described in Figure 16.1.

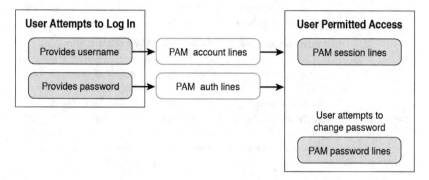

Figure 16.1   PAM Types

The first value of each line in a PAM configuration file, the type, is basically when to use the module. The last value of each line is the PAM module to run (or another configuration file to consult). The middle value is called the control value. When the PAM module returns successful or unsuccessful, how this return value is used depends on the control value.

The following table describes the different traditional control values. When you're reading the descriptions in this table, it is important to note that when a set of rules is parsed, the end result must be successful for the action to take place. For example, consider the following rules:

```
account    required    pam_nologin.so
account    include     system-auth
```

For the user account to be validated, the end result of the chain of rules must be successful. This chain of rules is also referred to as the rule stack.

Value	Description
required	**Returns successful**: If the current PAM module returns successful, the next rule is checked in the list. If this is the final rule, the stack returns with a value of successful (except when a previous requisite rule is unsuccessful).
	Returns unsuccessful: If the current PAM module returns unsuccessful, no additional modules are executed. The stack returns with a value of unsuccessful. In other words, the modules run with the required value must return success for the stack to return success.

Value	Description
requisite	In some ways this value is like required. The difference is highlighted in italics.
	Returns successful: If the current PAM module returns successful, the next rule is checked in the list. If this is the final rule, the stack returns with a value of successful.
	Returns unsuccessful: If the current PAM module returns unsuccessful, *additional modules are executed; however, regardless of what happens with these other modules, the stack returns with a value of unsuccessful.* This is useful sometimes because the additional modules may provide more information in the log files.
optional	**Returns successful**: If the current PAM module returns successful, the next rule is checked in the list. If this is the final rule, the stack returns with a value of successful (except when a previous requisite rule is unsuccessful).
	Returns unsuccessful: If the current PAM module returns unsuccessful, the next rule is checked in the list. If this is the final rule, the stack returns with a value of successful (except when a previous requisite rule is unsuccessful).
	In other words, the return value of the module has no impact on the success or failure of the stack. Exception: If this is the only rule in the stack, optional acts like required.
sufficient	**Returns successful**: If the current PAM module returns successful, then no additional rules are checked. The stack immediately returns with a value of successful (except when a previous requisite rule is unsuccessful).
	Returns unsuccessful: If the current PAM module returns unsuccessful, the next rule is checked in the list. If this is the final rule, the stack returns with a value of successful (except when a previous requisite rule is unsuccessful).
	In other words, if the return value of the module is successful, no other modules are checked and the stack is automatically successful. A return of unsuccessful has no impact on the overall return value of the stack.
include	This value tells PAM to use all the rules from the file specified. Only the rules for the current type (auth, account, and so on) are used.

For those of you who like more visual examples, look at the flow chart diagram in Figure 16.2. Note that this figure makes use of the following information:

```
[root@OCS ~]# grep ^account /etc/pam.d/sshd
account      required       pam_nologin.so
account      include        system-auth
[root@OCS ~]# grep ^account /etc/pam.d/system-auth
account      required       pam_unix.so
account      sufficient     pam_succeed_if.so uid < 500 quiet
account      required       pam_permit.so
```

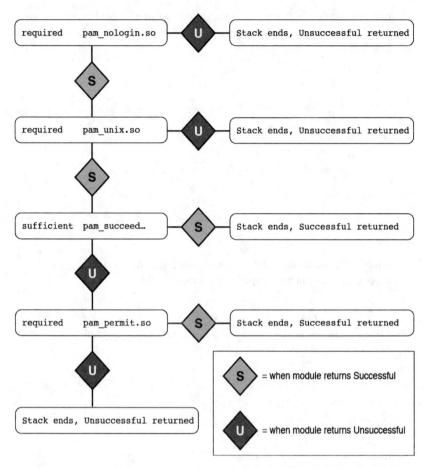

Figure 16.2 PAM Control Values Example

/etc/pam.d/

If you view the contents of the **/etc/pam.d** directory, it looks something like the
following output:

```
[root@OCS ~]# ls /etc/pam.d
atd                 other            runuser-l        su-l
chfn                passwd           screen           system-auth
chsh                password-auth    smartcard-auth   systemd-user
config-util         polkit-1         smtp             usermin
crond               postgresql       smtp.postfix     vlock
cups                postlogin        smtp.sendmail    vsftpd
cvs                 ppp              sshd             webmin
dovecot             proftpd          su               xserver
fingerprint-auth    remote           sudo
login               runuser          sudo-i
```

Each file is designed to configure a command or utility that uses PAM to authenticate user accounts. For example, the following file is used to configure how the Secure Shell server uses PAM:

```
[root@OCS ~]# more /etc/pam.d/sshd
#%PAM-1.0
auth          include       system-auth
account       required      pam_nologin.so
account       include       system-auth
password      include       system-auth
session       optional      pam_keyinit.so force revoke
session       include       system-auth
session       required      pam_loginuid.so
```

pam_tally2

You can lock out a user as the result of unsuccessful login attempts by using the following bolded setting in the **/etc/pam.d/password-auth** file:

```
auth          required       pam_env.so
auth          required       pam_tally2.so file=
  /var/log/tallylog deny=3 even_deny_root unlock_time=1200
auth          sufficient     pam_unix.so try_first_pass nullok
auth          required       pam_deny.so
account       required       pam_unix.so
account       required       pam_tally2.so
```

Here are the key value of these lines:

- **file**: The name of the file to store the failed login attempts
- **deny**: When to lock out the user (after this number of unsuccessful attempts)
- **even_deny_root**: Makes this apply to the root account as well as regular users
- **unlock_time**: The time, in seconds, in which to keep the account locked

faillock

You can lock out a user as the result of unsuccessful login attempts by using the following bolded settings in the **/etc/pam.d/system-auth** file:

```
auth          required       pam_env.so
auth       required       pam_faillock.so preauth
  silent audit deny=4 unlock_time=1200
auth          sufficient     pam_unix.so try_first_pass nullok
auth       [default=die]   pam_faillock.so authfail
  audit deny=4 unlock_time=1200
auth          required       pam_deny.so
```

Here are the key values of these lines:

- **deny**: When to lock out the user (after this number of unsuccessful attempts)
- **unlock_time**: The time, in seconds, in which to keep the account locked

SSH

The **ssh** command is a utility that allows you to connect to a Secure Shell (SSH) server. The syntax of the command is as follows:

```
ssh user@hostname
```

Replace *user* with the username you want to use to log in as and replace *hostname* with a system hostname or IP address.

The first time you use the **ssh** command to connect to a system, it will issue the following prompt:

```
[root@OCS ~]# ssh bob@server1
The authenticity of host 'server1' can't be established.
ECDSA key fingerprint is
   8a:d9:88:b0:e8:05:d6:2b:85:df:53:10:54:66:5f:0f.
Are you sure you want to continue connecting (yes/no)?
```

This is to ensure you are logging in to the correct system. Typically users answer "yes" to this prompt, assuming they are logging in to the correct machine, but this information can also be verified independently by contacting the system administrator of the remote system.

After the user answers "yes" to this prompt, the SSH server fingerprint is stored in the **known_hosts** file in the ~/**.ssh** directory.

The following table describes common options for the **ssh** command:

Option	Description
-F *configfile*	Specify the configuration file to use for the ssh client utility. The default configuration file is **/etc/ssh/ssh_config**. See the "ssh_config" section in this chapter for details regarding this file.
-4	Only use IPv4 addresses.
-6	Only use IPv6 addresses.
-E *logfile*	Place errors in the specified log file rather than displaying them to standard output.

~/.ssh/

SSH data for individual users is stored in each user's home directory under the **.ssh** subdirectory. This directory is used by SSH to store important data, and users can modify configurations in this directory. This subsection focuses on the files that may be stored in the ~/**.ssh** directory.

known_hosts

After a connection is established with an SSH server, the SSH client stores the server's unique "fingerprint" key in the user's **.ssh/known_hosts** file:

```
[root@OCS ~]# cat .ssh/known_hosts
|1|trm4BuvRfOHzJ6wusHssj6HcJKg=|EruYJY709DXorogeN5Hdcf6jTCo=
  ecdsa-sha2-nistp256AAAAE2VjZHNhLXNoYTItbmlzdHAyNTYAAAAIbmlzd
  HAyNTYAAABBBG3/rARemyZrhIuirJtfpfPjUVnph9S1w2NPfEWec/f59V7nA
  ztn5rbcGynNYOdnozdGNNizYAiZ2VEhJ3Y3JcE=
```

Typically the contents of this file should be left undisturbed; however, if the SSH server is reinstalled, then it would have a new "fingerprint" key. This would require all users to remove the entry for the SSH server in the **.ssh/known_hosts** file.

authorized_keys

When a user wants to use password-based SSH authentication, the first step is to create authentication keys by using the **ssh-keygen** command. See the "ssh-keygen" section for details regarding this process.

After the authentication key files have been created, the public key (the contents of either the **~/.ssh/id_dsa.pub** or **~/.ssh/id_rsa.pub** file) needs to be copied to the system that the user is attempting to log in to. This requires placing the public key into the **~/.ssh/authorized_keys** file on the SSH server. This can be accomplished by manually copying over the content of the public key file from the client system and pasting it into the **~/.ssh/authorized_keys** file on the SSH server. Alternatively, you can use the **ssh-copy-id** command: **ssh-copy-id** *user@server*.

config

Users can customize how commands like **ssh**, **scp**, and **sftp** work by creating the **~/.ssh/config** file. The format and settings in this file are the same as those found in the **/etc/sshd/ssh.conf** file. See the "ssh_conf" subsection in this chapter for more details.

id_rsa

The content of the **~/.ssh/id_rsa** and **id_rsa.pub** files is used for password authentication in conjunction with the **ssh-agent** and **ssh-add** utilities. See the "ssh-add" subsection in this chapter for details regarding these utilities.

id_rsa.pub

The content of the **~/.ssh/id_rsa** and **id_rsa.pub** files is used for password authentication in conjunction with the **ssh-agent** and **ssh-add** utilities. See the "ssh-add" subsection in this chapter for details regarding these utilities.

User-Specific Access

This subsection refers to a feature called passwordless login. If a user routinely logs in to a specific SSH server, that user may want to set up passwordless logins. To do this, you would follow these steps:

Step 1. On the SSH client machine, execute the **ssh-keygen** command, as shown the "ssh-keygen" subsection in this chapter. When prompted for a passphrase, press the Enter key to leave this blank (or, you could use the **-N** option with the **ssh-keygen** command, which results in no passphrase prompt).

Step 2. There is now a public key in the **~/.ssh/id_rsa.pub** file. This needs to be copied to the remote server, into the **~/.ssh/authorized_keys** file of your account on the remote machine (you may need to create this directory and set the permissions to **770**). This can be done with the following command:

```
[student@OCS ~]$ cat .ssh/id_rsa.pub |
ssh 192.168.1.22 'cat >> .ssh/authorized_keys'
student@192.168.1.22's password:
```

Step 3. Set the permissions of the **authorized_keys** file to **640**:

```
[student@OCS ~]$ ssh 192.168.1.22 'chmod 640
/home/student/.ssh/authorized_keys'
student@192.168.1.22's password:
```

On some distributions, you can use the **ssh-copy-id** command to complete both Step 2 and Step 3 (see the "ssh-copy-id" subsection in this chapter for more details). However, you should also know how to use the manual method described in these steps.

You now should be able to log in to the SSH server without a password:

```
[student@OCS ~]$ ssh 192.168.1.22 date
Mon Jan 11 16:59:32 PST 2019
```

Some security experts point out that having no passphrase for your key poses a security risk. However, if you do have a passphrase, each time you try to connect to the SSH server from the client, instead of being asked for your password, you are asked for the passphrase (and having to type a password/passphrase is what you were trying to avoid in the first place):

```
[student@OCS ~]$ ssh 192.168.1.22 date
Enter passphrase for key '/home/student/.ssh/id_rsa':
Mon Jan 11 17:17:00 PST 2019
```

A method that you can use to have a passphrase for the RSA key and avoid having to type it for each connection is to use a utility called **ssh-agent**. The following steps demonstrate how this works:

Step 1. Start a new BASH shell with the **ssh-agent** utility:

```
ssh-agent /bin/bash
```

Step 2.   Execute the following command:

```
ssh - add ~/.ssh/id_rsa
```

From this point on, when you use the **ssh-agent** shell to remotely connect to the SSH server, the connection takes place without the passphrase.

TCP Wrappers

One of the techniques to filter access to services on a host is a library called TCP Wrappers. This library uses simple configuration files (the **/etc/hosts.allow** and **/etc/hosts.deny** files) to either allow or deny access from specific hosts or networks.

Only services that use the TCP Wrappers library will be affected by the **/etc/hosts.allow** and **/etc/hosts.deny** files. You can determine if a program uses this library by using the **ldd** command:

```
[root@OCS ~]# which sshd
/usr/sbin/sshd
[root@OCS ~]# ldd /usr/sbin/sshd | grep libwrap
   libwrap.so.0 => /lib64/libwrap.so.0 (0x00002b003df03000)
```

TCP Wrappers uses the following steps to determine whether access should be allowed or denied:

1. If a match is made in the **/etc/hosts.allow** file, then access is granted. If not, then the next step is consulted.

2. If a match is made in the **/etc/hosts.deny** file, then access is denied. If not, then the next step is consulted.

3. If no matches are made in either file, then access is granted.

The format of the **/etc/hosts.allow** and **/etc/hosts.deny** files is as follows:

```
service:        hosts|network
```

The following explicitly allows access to the SSHD server for the 192.168.1.1 hosts and the 192.168.99.0/24 network:

```
[root@OCS ~]# cat /etc/hosts.allow
sshd:    192.168.1.1
sshd:    192.168.99.0/24cat
```

The following table describes how the service can be specified:

Item	Description
service	Matches a single service.
service,service	Matches any of the services listed. (Note that there's no space between services.)
ALL	Matches all services.

The following table describes how the host or network can be specified:

Item	Description
IP	An IP address.
Hostname	A hostname that can be resolved.
@group	A NIS group.
Network	Any of these formats are permitted: 192.168.1, 192.168.99.0/24, 192.168.99.0/255.255.255.0, or .example.com.

/etc/ssh/

The **/etc/ssh** directory contains files that can be used to administer both the SSH server and SSH client utilities. This subsection covers the essentials of these files.

ssh_conf

The **/etc/ssh/ssh.conf** file is used to modify the behavior of the SSH client utilities, such as ssh, scp, and sftp. This file affects all users, but users can override these settings by creating their own configuration file in their home directory (the **~/.ssh/config** file).

A few components of the **ssh_config** file are different from the **sshd_config** file (consider reviewing the "sshd_config" subsection in this chapter before continuing). To begin with, there is the systemwide **/etc/ssh/ssh_config** file, which applies to all users. Additionally, each user can create a file in their home directory (**~/.ssh/config**) that can be used to override the settings in the **/etc/ssh/ssh_config** file.

In addition to the files, command-line options can override the values specified in the configuration files. Here is the order in which all this information is parsed:

1. Command-line options
2. The user's **~/.ssh/config** file
3. The **/etc/ssh/ssh_config** file

The first parameter found is the one used. For example, if **ConnectTimeout** is set in the user's **~/.ssh/config** file and a different value is set in the **/etc/ssh/ssh_config** file, the user's configuration file is used to set this value.

Another important difference between the **ssh_config** file and the **sshd_config** file is that most of the settings in the **ssh_config** file are subsettings of the **Host** setting. The **Host** setting allows you to specify different rules for different SSH servers you are connecting to. For example, the following would apply the **ConnectTimeout** value of **0** when connecting to server1.localhost.com and a value of **600** when connecting to test.example.com:

```
Host server1.localhost.com
ConnectTimeout 0
Host test.example.com
ConnectTimeout 600
```

Many of the settings in the **ssh_config** file are related to settings in the SSH server configuration file, such as the following **/etc/ssh/sshd_config** file setting:

```
X11Forwarding yes
```

On the client side, this feature is typically enabled by using the **-X** or **-Y** option when executing the **ssh**-based commands. However, if you want this feature to be the default, the following settings could be used in either the **/etc/ssh/ssd_config** or the **~/.ssh/config** file:

```
ForwardX11 and ForwardX11Trusted
```

sshd_conf

The **sshd_conf** file is used to configure the SSH server. Important settings in this file include the following:

- **Protocol**: Set to either "1", "2", or "1,2", this setting defines the protocol type for the SSH server. Protocol 1 is no longer supported, so this value normally should be set to "2".

- **ListenAddress**: Specifies the IP address assigned to the network cards that SSH should accept connections on. Example: **ListenAddress 192.168.1.100:192.168.1.101**.

- **Port**: The port on which the SSH server will listen for inbound connections. Example: **Port 2096**.

- **LogLevel**: The logs you want the SSH server to record. The following values are permitted:
  - **QUIET**
  - **FATAL**
  - **ERROR**
  - **INFO**
  - **VERBOSE**
  - **DEBUG**
  - **DEBUG1** (same as **DEBUG**)
  - **DEBUG2**
  - **DEBUG3**

- **PermitRootLogin**: When this is set to "no", the root user cannot log in directly via SSH.

- **AllowUsers** or **DenyUsers:** Defines what users can log in via SSH (**AllowUsers**) or which users cannot login via SSH (**DenyUsers**). Example: **AllowUsers bob sue ted**.

- **PasswordAuthentication**: When set to "yes" (the default), this setting allows users to log in by providing their username and password. If it's set to "no", users can log in using an authentication key only.

- **PubkeyAuthentication**: When this is set to "yes", a user can store a public key on the server. The public key is generated by the **ssh-keygen** command on the user's client system. See the "ssh-keygen" section in this chapter for more details.

- **Banner**: Specifies a file of which the contents are displayed prior to the user authentication process.

- **PrintMotd**: If this is set to yes (the default), the contents of the **/etc/motd** file are displayed when a user logs in to the system via SSH. See the "MOTD" section in Chapter 17, "Summarize security best practices in a Linux environment," for more details about the **/etc/motd** file.

- **X11Forwarding**: If set to yes (the default is no), this provides an easy way to allow graphical programs to be executed on the SSH server and displayed on the SSH client. This requires the SSH client command (the **ssh** command) be executed with the **-X** or **-Y** option. See the "SSH Port Forwarding" subsection in Chapter 14, "Compare and contrast Linux graphical user interfaces," for more information.

- **MaxAuthTries**: Set to a numeric value that indicates how many attempts a user has to enter the correct password. The default is 6.

- **PermitEmptyPasswords**: If this is set to no (the default), users cannot log in via SSH if the password field for the user account is empty.

ssh-copy-id

The **ssh-copy-id** command is used to copy the login keys that are created by the **ssh-keygen** command to a remote system (also see the "ssh-keygen" subsection in this chapter). The format for this command is as follows:

```
ssh-copy-id user@hostname
```

ssh-keygen

The **ssh-keygen** command can be used to generate authentication keys. A common use for this command is to create the authentication files used for passwordless authentication:

```
[julia@OCS ~]$ ssh-keygen
Generating public/private rsa key pair.
Enter file in which to save the key (/home/julia/.ssh/id_rsa):
Enter passphrase (empty for no passphrase):
Enter same passphrase again:
Your identification has been saved in /home/julia/.ssh/id_rsa.
Your public key has been saved in /home/julia/.ssh/id_rsa.pub.
The key fingerprint is:
6d:40:24:e2:3e:62:7f:a4:f0:5d:d5:05:1b:06:fd:d7 bo@ubuntu
The key's randomart image is:
+--[ RSA 2048]----      +
|        . ..o .o+.. |
|   . . o   o.+      |
|   .         . . o. .|
```

```
|    .    +      . E|
|  + o  .  S o        . |
|  . = = . .          |
|    + o              |
|      .              |
|                     |
+-----------------    +
```

The result of this command is two new files: **~/.ssh/id_rsa** and **~/.ssh.id_rsa.pub**. The content of these files is used for password authentication in conjunction with the **~/.ssh/ authorized_keys** file.

RSA is an encryption algorithm. Another popular encryption algorithm is DSA. To use DSA instead of RSA, use the **-t DSA** option to the **ssh-keygen** command. The result of using this option is two new files: **~/.ssh/id_dsa** and **~/.ssh.id_dsa.pub**.

> **NOTE:** If a passphrase is requested during the execution of the **ssh-keygen** command, this passphrase would need to be entered in place of a password whenever an SSH connection is established. Repeatedly entering this passphrase can be avoided by using the **ssh-agent** and **ssh-add** utilities. See the "ssh-add" sections in this chapter for details regarding these utilities.

ssh-add

The **ssh-agent** utility is used to avoid needing to enter a passphrase whenever password-less SSH authentication is used. See the "ssh-keygen" section in this chapter for details regarding setting up passwordless SSH authentication.

One way to use this feature is to execute the following command: **ssh-agent bash**. A shell is started in which the SSH agent will cache added RSA and DSA encryption keys. These keys can be added to the SSH agent cache with the **ssh-add** command.

After the **ssh-agent** utility has been started, the **ssh-add** command can be used to add RSA and DSA encryption keys to the SSH agent's cache.

To use the **ssh-add** utility, execute the command with no arguments:

```
[julia@OCS ~]$ ssh-add
Identity added: /home/julia/.ssh/id_rsa (/home/julia/.ssh/id_rsa)
```

After the keys have been added, they are automatically used in future SSH connections.

TTYs

A "TTY" is a device file that is associated with a terminal display. A terminal display is traditionally a command-line login screen, but modern Linux systems with graphics cards can also display a GUI or Windows-based output to a TTY file.

See the "/dev/tty#" subsection in this chapter for further information.

/etc/securetty

The **/etc/securetty** file lists all the device files in which the root user can log in to the system. For example, if you remove all the **/etc/tty#** device filenames from this file, then the root user wouldn't be able to log in when the user is sitting in front of the system.

By default, this file will contain all the possible device files a user could log in from. On systems where security is paramount, this file is normally heavily altered to prevent the root user from logging in directly. This provides better security because in order to gain root access, someone would have to know the password of both a regular user and the root user (regular user password to log in and root password to use the **su** command to switch to the root account).

/dev/tty#

The TTY device files are all named **/dev/tty#**, where # is actually a number:

```
[julia@OCS ~]$ ls /dev/tty*
/dev/tty      /dev/tty20   /dev/tty33   /dev/tty46   /dev/tty59
/dev/tty0     /dev/tty21   /dev/tty34   /dev/tty47   /dev/tty6
/dev/tty1     /dev/tty22   /dev/tty35   /dev/tty48   /dev/tty60
/dev/tty10    /dev/tty23   /dev/tty36   /dev/tty49   /dev/tty61
/dev/tty11    /dev/tty24   /dev/tty37   /dev/tty5    /dev/tty62
/dev/tty12    /dev/tty25   /dev/tty38   /dev/tty50   /dev/tty63
/dev/tty13    /dev/tty26   /dev/tty39   /dev/tty51   /dev/tty7
/dev/tty14    /dev/tty27   /dev/tty4    /dev/tty52   /dev/tty8
/dev/tty15    /dev/tty28   /dev/tty40   /dev/tty53   /dev/tty9
/dev/tty16    /dev/tty29   /dev/tty41   /dev/tty54   /dev/ttyS0
/dev/tty17    /dev/tty3    /dev/tty42   /dev/tty55   /dev/ttyS1
/dev/tty18    /dev/tty30   /dev/tty43   /dev/tty56   /dev/ttyS2
/dev/tty19    /dev/tty31   /dev/tty44   /dev/tty57   /dev/ttyS3
/dev/tty2     /dev/tty32   /dev/tty45   /dev/tty58
```

While there are many TTY files, typically only seven are in use on standard Linux distributions. One of these is reserved for GUI-based logins, and the other six provide a command-line login. Normally either **/dev/tty1** or **/dev/tty7** provides the GUI-based login, but this varies from one distribution to another. You can switch between these TTY interfaces by holding down the Ctrl and Alt keys and pressing a function key. For example, Ctrl-Alt-F1 will switch to the **/dev/tty1** device interface.

Note that **/dev/ttyS#** devices are for physical serial port access.

It is important to know about these device files because of a security feature that can limit where the root user can log in to the system. See the "/etc/securetty" subsection for more details about this feature.

PTYs

The term "PTY" refers to pseudo-terminals. These are the terminals that are provided to a shell when a user logs in remotely (such as an SSH connection) or when a user opens a new terminal window in a GUI-based environment. PTY device files are normally created as needed, and they appear in the **/dev/pts** directory. Each PTY device file is given a number for a name; for example, **/dev/pts/0** would be the first PTY device file.

It is important to know about these device files because of a security feature that can limit where the root user can log in to the system. See the "/etc/securetty" subsection for more details about this feature.

PKI

Public Key Infrastructure (PKI) is used when a user attempts to connect to a server, such as a web server, to ensure that the server is really where the user intended to go rather than a rogue server. Often this structure will also provide the means to encrypt data between the server and the user.

The technique used by TLS (see the "SSL/TLS" subsection in this chapter) is called asymmetric cryptography (it is also referred to as PKC, or public key cryptography). With asymmetric cryptography, two keys are used: a *public key* and a *private key*. These keys are used to encrypt and decrypt data.

The public key is used to encrypt the data sent to the Apache Web Server. This key is provided to all systems upon request. For example, when a web browser first connects to an Apache Web Server that is using TLS, the web browser asks for the public key of the server. This public key is freely given to the web browser.

Any additional data sent from the web browser to the server, such as account names and passwords, is encrypted using this public key. This data can only be decrypted by the server using the private key (this is a process called *hashing*). This is where the term *asymmetric cryptography* comes into play. With symmetric cryptography, the same key is used to encrypt and decrypt data. Two separate keys are needed when asymmetric cryptography is used: one to encrypt data and the other to decrypt. This means that only the web server can decrypt the data sent by the web browser.

You might be wondering how the web browser really know that it reached the correct web server and not some "rogue" web server. When the web server sends its public key, it includes a *digital signature* (also called a *message digest*). This digital signature can be sent to a CA (Certificate Authority) server, a trusted third-party system used to verify the digital signature. In some cases the server itself provides the signature in a process called a *self-signed* certificate.

From the user's perspective, all this takes place behind the scenes and is completely transparent—at least until something goes wrong and warning messages are displayed by the web browser. Because digital certificates typically have an expiration date, the most common problem is when the CA does not have an updated digital certificate or when the user changes the date on the computer.

See Figure 16.3 for a visual example of this process.

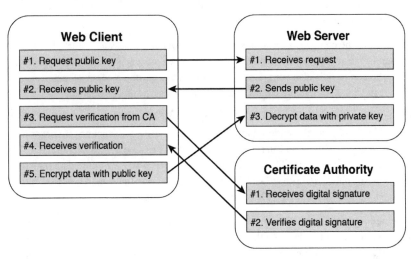

Figure 16.3   SSL Process

Self-Signed

See the "PKI" section in this chapter.

Private Keys

See the "PKI" section in this chapter.

Public Keys

See the "PKI" section in this chapter.

Hashing

See the "PKI" section in this chapter.

Digital Signatures

See the "PKI" section in this chapter.

Message Digest

See the "PKI" section in this chapter.

VPN as a Client

Consider an organization that is geographically located in a single building in San Diego, California. This organization provides its employees access to sensitive data from a locally administered database. By keeping all of the data transfer of this sensitive data within the company's physical network (on the local area network, or LAN), the company enjoys a higher level of security than if the data were transmitted over the Internet (a wide area network, or WAN).

However, as the company grows, this method of providing access to the data becomes a hindrance. Employees who need to travel to meet clients cannot access this important data. The company is also considering expanding by acquiring a company based in New York City, but there are concerns as to how the data would be shared.

You are the system administrator for the company, and it is your responsibility to develop a viable (and secure) solution. Fortunately for you, there is virtual private network (VPN). With this VPN, you can securely transfer data between a VPN server and a VPN client. This feature is much like how Secure Shell (SSH) provides secure data transfer; it makes use of public and private keys to encrypt and decrypt the data. All of the routers between the VPN server and VPN client only see encrypted data.

There are many different VPN software solutions available, so for the Linux+ exam the important thing is to understand the concepts. If you want to get some hands-on practice, OpenVPN is a good choice, but realize that any exam question should be focused on the technology, not any specific software solution.

This section covers the different concepts you should know when working with a VPN.

SSL/TLS

Transport Layer Security (TLS) is a cryptographic protocol that is used by VPNs to provide secure transport of data. Secure Sockets Layer (SSL) is the predecessor to TLS and is considered deprecated.

TLS isn't just used for VPNs; it is also commonly used in web server communications, email transport, and Voice over IP (VoIP).

Transport Mode

For a VPN, transport mode is when only the data is encrypted. In transport mode, IP information in the packet is not encrypted. This is a common method used when a site-to-site VPN is configured. Site-to-site VPNs are common in large organizations in which network traffic must transverse the Internet to get from one network to another. The use of a site-to-site VPN makes the data transfer more secure.

Tunnel Mode

For a VPN, tunnel mode is when both the data and the metadata (IP data in the packet) are encrypted. This is a common method used when a client-to-site VPN is configured.

IPSec

Internet Protocol Security (IPSec) is used in VPNs for authentication and to encrypt network packets. IPSec differs from TLS (see the "SSL/TLS" subsection in this chapter) in several ways, but the primary difference is where in the OSI model the security enhancements take place. TLS performs its operations above Layer 3, whereas IPSec performs its operations at Layer 3. This is an important different because some networking appliances have Layer 3 functionality but don't work above Layer 3, making it difficult to implement VPN on these devices.

DTLS

Datagram Transport Layer Security (DTLS) utilizes datagram-based security features to provide a secure VPN transport. A datagram is used on packet-switched networks as the basic unit of transfer and uses a connectionless communication method. DTLS is based on TLS (see the "SSL/TLS" subsection in this chapter).

## CHAPTER 17

Summarize security best practices in a Linux environment

This chapter provides information and commands concerning the following topics:

Boot security

- Boot loader password
- UEFI/BIOS password

Additional authentication methods

- Multifactor authentication (tokens, hardware, software, OTP, biometrics)
- RADIUS
- TACACS+
- LDAP
- Kerberos (kinit, klist)

Importance of disabling root login via SSH

Password less login (Enforce use of PKI)

Chroot jail services

No shared IDs

Importance of denying hosts

Separation of OS data from application data (disk partition to maximize system availability)

Change default ports

Importance of disabling or uninstalling unused and unsecure services

- FTP
- Telnet
- Finger
- Sendmail
- Postfix

Importance of enabling SSL/TLS

Importance of enabling auditd

CVE monitoring

Discouraging use of USB devices

Disk encryption (LUKS)

Restrict cron access

Disable Ctrl-Alt-Del

Add banner

MOTD

> **NOTE:**   For the Linux+ certification exam, it is important to note that for the topics listed under this objective, you are supposed to be able to "**summarize security best practices in a Linux environment.**" In other words, you shouldn't be expected to know details regarding setting up, configuring, or administering security best practices, but rather understand what the function of security best practices is.

Boot Security

An often-overlooked security weakness is the boot process. If someone has physical access to the system, this person could compromise the operating system during the boot process. This section describes methods that can be used to address the vulnerabilities of the boot process.

Boot Loader Password

The boot loader allows an individual to perform custom operations during the boot process. This can include booting to alternate kernels or booting to a runlevel where the root user is automatically logged in.

As a result, it is a security best practice to enable a password on the boot loader. See Chapter 1, "Explain Linux boot process concepts," for additional details on how to configure this feature.

UEFI/BIOS Password

The x86 platform includes a tool that initiates the boot process. This is often referred to as the BIOS, or on newer systems the UEFI. Regardless of the specific tool, every UEFI/BIOS provides an individual with the ability to perform custom booting operations.

For example, an individual could use UEFI/BIOS to boot from a removable media device, such as a CD-ROM or USB drive. This could enable the person to mount the Linux filesystems on the hard drive and access data that would normally not be accessible. In other words, this technique could be used to hack into a system that is physically accessible.

To prevent this, it is a security best practice to place a password on the UEFI/BIOS. The exact technique for this operation varies as hardware vendors provide a variety of different UEFI/BIOS interfaces.

Additional Authentication Methods

The standard authentication method is to use local user accounts and passwords. This method lacks some of the security features that more complex methods provide. This section explores alternative authentication methods that should be considered when developing a security best practice policy.

Multifactor Authentication

With multifactor authentication, the user is requested to provide multiple bits of evidence that prove the user's identity. One common multifactor authentication method is called two-factor authentication, or 2FA. For this method, the user is required to provide two forms of identity, which could include the following:

- Something the user knows
- Something the user has
- Something the user "is"

This subsection covers different techniques used with multifactor authentication.

Tokens

A token is a unique value (typically either a number or alphanumeric value) that is generated by either a hardware device or a software program. Tokens are typically automatically generated on an ongoing basis and normally are only valid for short periods of time, such as 30 seconds.

Hardware

A hardware token is one that is generated by a hardware device. Typically this is a very small device, such as a key fob. The hardware device may have additional authentication methods, such as a fingerprint scanner, but this tends to be somewhat rare.

Software

A software token is one that is generated by a program. A common example is an app on a mobile device.

OTP

OTP stands for one-time password. This is an authentication technique that is often incorporated in two-factor authentication. It is also a technique that can be used in the event that a user has lost or forgotten a password.

Biometrics

Biometrics takes advantage of the "something that the person is" component of multifactor authentication. A user's fingerprint, iris scan, or other biological data could be used to verify a user's identity.

RADIUS

Remote Authentication Dial-In Service (RADIUS) is a protocol that allows a client system to make use of a server to authenticate users. This service provides AAA (Authentication, Authorization, and Accounting) management in a centralized location.

RADIUS is often compared to TACACS+, but knowing the differences between these protocols is beyond the scope of the Linux+ exam. Most importantly, realize that RADIUS can provide very powerful functions within a security policy because it offers centralized AAA management. Also, you should realize that RADIUS is more vendor agnostic than TACACS+.

TACACS+

Terminal Access Controller Access-Control System Plus (TACACS+) is a protocol that allows client systems to make use of a server to authenticate users. This service provides AAA (Authentication, Authorization, and Accounting) management in a centralized location.

TACACS+ is often compared to RADIUS, but knowing the differences between these protocols is beyond the scope of the Linux+ exam. Most importantly, realize that TACACS+ can provide very powerful functions within a security policy because it offers centralized AAA management. Also, you should realize that TACACS+ was developed by Cisco and is not as vendor agnostic as RADIUS.

LDAP

Lightweight Directory Access Protocol (LDAP) is a protocol that provides directory services information. This means the protocol can be used to provide user account information, but it does not provide the full AAA functionality that RADIUS or TACACS+ does. LDAP is also often used to store other information not directly related to user accounts, such as hostnames.

LDAP can be used to authenticate users, but when considering a security policy, you should realize that RADIUS and TACACS+ provide a more robust solution. For example, LDAP does not provide the "Accounting" that AAA protocols like RADIUS and TACACS+ do.

Kerberos

The Kerberos protocol is used to authenticate users by utilizing a ticket-based system. When a client system initially gains the credentials from the user to authenticate the user, this information is sent to a Kerberos Authentication Server for verification.

The Authentication Server then passes information to a Key Distribution Center, which issues a Ticket-Granting Ticket, or TGT. The TGT is encrypted using the Ticketing-Granting Service, and the secret key for the encrypting in passed back to the client system.

This secret key will now be used for further authentication requests (for example, if the user attempts to log in to another system that is within the Kerberos realm).

kinit

The **kinit** utility is used by Kerberos to obtain an individual ticket. This ticket is then cached on the local system for future authentication attempts.

klist

The **klist** utility is used to display a list of cached Kerberos tickets.

Importance of Disabling Root Login via SSH

By default, SSH servers will allow the root user to log in directly. For servers that are directly accessible to the Internet, this poses a security risk as hackers can attempt to log in to the root account directly. By disabling direct root login, a hacker would first need to compromise a non-root account and then compromise the root account via a different method (such as the **su** or **sudo** command).

Disabling direct root login via SSH is accomplished by modifying the following setting in the **/etc/ssh/sshd_config** file:

```
PermitRootLogin no
```

Passwordless Login

A passwordless login is when a system allows a user to log in without the need for a password. This is normally associated with SSH and considered both a convenient feature and a security feature.

The concept behind this feature is to utilize SSH keys to verify the identity of the user. The following steps are performed:

Step 1. Execute the **ssh-keygen** command on the client system to create a public-private key pair.

Step 2. Copy the public SSH key to the remote system in the **.ssh** directory for the user on the remote system. Most systems provide an **ssh-copy-id** to perform this task, but it can also be performed by manually copying the pubic key.

Step 3. Log in to the remote system to verify access is provided without the need for a password. The combination of the private key on the local system and the corresponding public key on the remote system is used to verify the identity of the user.

Enforce Use of PKI

Public Key Infrastructure (PKI) can be applied to SSH; this utilizes public SSH keys for user account authentication (see the "Password less Login" section in this chapter for more details on SSH keys). On systems with security policies that encourage the use of SSH keys for authentication, it is best to enforce the use of PKI to ensure all users make use of this method.

This can be accomplished by making the following changes to the **/etc/ssh/sshd_config** file:

```
PasswordAuthentication no
RSAAuthentication yes
PubkeyAuthentication yes
```

Chroot Jail Services

A chroot jail service is a service that only has access to a small portion of the filesystem. Instead of being able to access the complete filesystem, the service will only be able to access a subdirectory, which typically holds its configuration data.

The primary security advantage of a chroot jail service is that the service won't be able to see or modify critical system data. For example, if a service can only see the content in the **/var/chroot** directory, then files like the **/etc/passwd** and **/etc/shadow** files are not available to the service. This is especially important on Internet-facing servers, which are prone to hacker attacks.

Some services, such as BIND, have built-in chroot jail configurations. Others may require the administrator to manually create the jail with commands like the **chroot** command.

No Shared IDs

Consider the following output:

```
[root@OCS ~]# grep "x:1099:" /etc/passwd
ted:x:1099:1099:Ted Jones:/home/ted:/bin/bash
bob:x:1099:1099:Bob Smith:/home/bob:/bin/bash
```

Because both users share the same user ID (UID), there is no way to account for their actions. The identity of a user is tied to the account UID, not to the account name. Any audit policies will associate actions with the UID, making it impossible in this situation to determine which person performed specific events when the users have the same UID associated with their accounts. This breaks best security measures.

Importance of Denying Hosts

There are several different methods to deny access to a system, service, or network, including the following:

- Firewalls
- TCP Wrappers

- PAM (Pluggable Authentication Modules)
- Individual service configuration

The importance of denying hosts in a security policy stems from the fact that there are systems known to be used as launching points for hacker attacks. These hosts should always be denied access to your systems. Note: Several sites provide lists of compromised systems (search for "blacklist sites"). One example is https://mxtoolbox.com.

Separation of OS Data from Application Data

Suppose a new application that you are testing goes "out of control" and compromises the filesystem it is stored on. This could be anything from filling up the filesystem with huge log files to performing unsafe filesystem operations.

A compromised filesystem could render the entire operating system (OS) unusable. As a result, it is best to separate OS data from application data. The primary means of accomplishing this is by using separate partitions (see the "Disk Partition to Maximize System Availability" in this chapter next for more details).

Disk Partition to Maximize System Availability

You have some new software that your IT department is testing on a nonproduction system and you want to avoid it causing any harm to the files that are required for the OS. The best course of action is to create a separate partition (or logical volume) and install the new software in that location.

Even on production systems, you should keep the application installation location separate from the OS data. This means you should create the following partitions or volumes at a minimum:

- **/usr**: Most software is installed here.
- **/opt**: Some software is installed here (typically third-party software).
- **/var**: For separation of log files and other spooling data.
- **/boot**: To keep the boot files separate from everything else.
- **/home**: To keep any user-generated or installed software separate from the OS data.
- **/**: The location of the rest of the system data (mostly OS data).

Change Default Ports

Services listen to network ports for inbound connections. The **/etc/services** file lists the standard port numbers by service type. For example:

```
[root@OCS ~]# egrep "22/tcp| 22/udp" /etc/services
ssh    22/tcp      # The Secure Shell (SSH) Protocol
ssh    22/udp      # The Secure Shell (SSH) Protocol
```

The ports used by standard services, such as the SSH server shown in the previous example, are called "well-known ports." The disadvantage of using these well-known ports is that hackers will attempt to brute-force attack services on these ports. As a result, one way of providing a higher level of security is by using a different port than the standard. For example, the SSH server can be configured to listen to a different port than port 22.

The disadvantage of this security technique is that hackers can still determine the correct port by performing port-scanning attacks. So, while this technique may be successful in stopping a novice or automated attack, it isn't foolproof.

Importance of Disabling or Uninstalling Unused and Unsecure Services

Some services should either never be used or used sparingly. This next section focuses on unsecure services and the limited use in which they should be used.

FTP

File Transport Protocol (FTP) is a commonly used protocol designed to transfer files between systems. Because data is sent between the FTP client and server unencrypted, the protocol is not secure. This data includes any user account information, meaning anyone who can "snoop" the network can see a user's name and password.

FTP servers do provide an important and useful function: anonymous FTP service. An anonymous FTP server doesn't require any user authentication and should only allow for the downloading of content (no upload permitted). This allows someone to create a repository that holds content that is designed for anyone to download (like the ISO files for a Linux distribution).

Telnet

The telnet protocol permits remote login, but unlike ssh, it provides no encryption. While the **telnet** command may be used to test connections to remote ports, a telnet server should not be used on modern systems where security is important.

Finger

The term finger is related to the Name/Finger protocol, which is designed to provide information about computers and users. The **finger** command has long been used as a way to provide a report on a user. However, because this information is sent via the network unencrypted, this command and protocol should never be used on modern systems where security is important.

Sendmail

See the "Postfix" subsection next.

Postfix

Both sendmail and postfix are email servers. Often there is no need for email services on the local system, or at least no email should be needed externally. A real email server should be configured to send and receive messages to and from remote email servers.

Desktop systems and most non-email servers should not be configured to handle external email. This may require some configuration changes to these services.

In reality, you really should consider disabling or limiting all services, unless there is a need for them to have remote access. For example, on most Linux distributions the CUPS print server is installed and configured to start by default. If the system in question has no need for printing, consider disabling and perhaps removing the software for CUPS.

Importance of Enabling SSL/TLS

Secure Sockets Layer (SSL) and Transport Layer Security (TLS) are the technologies behind Hypertext Transfer Protocol Secure (HTTPS). HTTPS allows web clients and servers to connect in a secure manner. On a web server where sensitive data is accessed, such as a bank account site or online shopping site, enabling these technologies is critical. Information-only websites where a user may log in to the site should also have these technologies enabled to secure user account data. These technologies ensure that the web client is accessing the correct web server, not some rogue web server masquerading as the real website.

Importance of Enabling auditd

The **auditd** daemon is used to log user account activity. It allows an administrator to determine if a user has performed any unauthorized activity.

CVE Monitoring

Common Vulnerabilities and Exposures (CVE) is a system that provides information about publicly known vulnerabilities. Once a vulnerability has been discovered in a software program or operating system, a CVE report is created. For security purposes, administrators should monitor relevant reports and implement fixes to vulnerabilities as quickly as possible. Failure to do so can result in a compromised system.

Discouraging Use of USB Devices

USB devices are commonly used to store and transport data on desktop systems. However, on servers they can pose a security risk because a hacker may be able to inject data into or steal data directly from the server. As a result, it is common practice to disable USB devices, typically by using settings in the BIOS.

Even on desktop systems, the use of USB devices poses risks. If a desktop system has access to sensitive information, the USB device may be used to steal the data.

Additionally, users may bring in viruses or worm software unintentionally on USB devices. In some organizations, USB devices are not just discouraged, but prohibited.

Disk Encryption

Disk encryption is a technology that makes it nearly impossible to access the data on a hard disk unless it is unencrypted. This protects the data on a hard disk in the event that the system is stolen, so it is commonly used on laptop devices.

When the system boots, the filesystem on the disk is unencrypted. This means that the disk is not encrypted when a user is currently logged in; instead, it is only encrypted when the system is not up and running.

See the "LUKS" subsection next for more details.

LUKS

Linux Unified Key Setup (LUKS) is a disk encryption method commonly used on Linux systems. Current versions of LUKS make use of a kernel module (dm-crypt) to perform the encryption and decryption operations.

Restrict cron Access

Regular users will sometimes use cron to perform system operations and execute code during off hours. This is designed to take advantage of times when there is limited activity on the system.

Sometimes users will abuse this service, executing code that they are not supposed to on critical systems. As an administrator, you can restrict cron access by adding usernames to the **/etc/cron.deny** file.

Disable Ctrl-Alt-Del

There are a variety of methods designed to disable someone from performing a Ctrl-Alt-Del (depending on your specific Linux distribution). The purpose of disabling Ctrl-Alt-Del is, however, similar on all Linux distributions: You want to prevent users from rebooting the system by using the "three finger salute."

On x86 systems, holding down the Ctrl and Alt keys while pressing the Del key will result in rebooting the system. This may not be a bad thing on desktop systems, but on servers, this can certainly cause problems.

If you have servers that are physically accessible (any server that has a keyboard, really), then research how to disable Ctrl-Alt-Del and enable this change as part of your regular security policy.

Add Banner

Many services that provide remote access (such as FTP, SSH or web servers) have the concept of a banner. A banner is a message this is displayed typically prior to the user attempting to log in to the system. Normally this is used to provide the user with a warning about accessing the system, such as the fact that only authorized users should attempt to access the system. In some cases, these banner messages are required by law.

Each service has a specific manner to set up the banner. You will need to consult the documentation to determine exactly how to perform this action.

MOTD

After a user logs in to the system, the contents of the **/etc/motd** file are displayed. The purpose of the "Message Of The Day" (MOTD) file is for the administrator to provide the user with useful information regarding the system just logged in to.

## CHAPTER 18

Given a scenario, implement logging services

This chapter provides information and commands concerning the following topics:

Key file locations

- /var/log/secure
- /var/log/messages
- /var/log/[application]
- /var/log/kern.log

Log management

- Third-party agents
- **logrotate**
- **/etc/rsyslog.conf**
- **journald, journalctl**
- **lastb**

Key File Locations

The **/var/log** directory is the standard location for log files to be placed. Some of these log files are created by the logging daemons, while others are created by individual applications. This section covers some of the key log files.

/var/log/secure

The **/var/log/secure** file contains log entries related to authentication and authorization operations. This can include entries of when users log in, attempts to gain escalated privileges, and other security-related tasks.

The following example demonstrates a successful login via SSH:

```
[root@OCS ~]# tail -n 2 /var/log/secure
Oct 13 16:34:55 OCS sshd[7547]: Accepted password
  for sarah from 72.220.222.74 port 63970 ssh2
Oct 13 16:34:55 OCS sshd[7547]: pam_unix(sshd:session):
  session opened for user sarah by (uid=0)
```

Note that **/var/log/secure** entries are generated by a logging daemon. See the "Third-Party Agents" subsection in this chapter for details about these daemons.

/var/log/messages

The **/var/log/secure** file contains a large variety of log entries. You can expect to see messages from numerous services and daemons, including crond, the kernel, and mail servers.

The following example demonstrates the crond daemon being restarted:

```
[root@OCS ~]# tail -n 2 /var/log/messages
Oct 13 16:46:13 mail systemd: Stopping Command Scheduler...
Oct 13 16:46:13 mail systemd: Starting Command Scheduler...
```

Note that **/var/log/messages** entries are generated by a logging daemon. See the "Third-Party Agents" subsection in this chapter for details about these daemons.

/var/log/[application]

Most modern applications or servers create log files without the assistance of a logging service. For instance, consider the following command output:

```
[root@OCS ~]# ls /var/log
audit              journal            ppp
boot.log           lfd.log            proftpd
btmp               mail               README
clamav             maillog            sa-update.log
cron               mailman            secure
cups               mariadb            tallylog
drupal.log         messages           wtmp
gateone            mysqld-queries.log xferlog
grubby             ntpstats           yum.log
httpd
```

Of the log files displayed in the previous output, only a handful are managed by a logging daemon (see the "Third-Party Agents" subsection in this chapter to learn which files are managed by logging daemons). Most of them are managed by individual applications. For example:

- The **yum** utility writes messages to the **/var/log/yum.log** file.
- The MariaDB database program stores log files in the **/var/log/mariadb** directory.
- The CUPS print server stores log files in the **/var/log/cups** directory.

Whether application log files exist depends on what software you install and enable on your system.

/var/log/kern.log

The **/var/log/kern.log** file contains messages from the kernel. For example, the following demonstrates some of the kernel messages generated during the boot process:

```
[root@OCS ~]# ls /var/kern.log
Jun 22 04:03:53 mail kernel: [    0.000000] Initializing
   cgroup subsys cpuset
Jun 22 04:03:53 mail kernel: [    0.000000] Initializing
   cgroup subsys cpu
Jun 22 04:03:53 mail kernel: [    0.000000] Initializing
   cgroup subsys cpuacct
Jun 22 04:03:53 mail kernel: [    0.000000] Linux
   version 3.19.8-100.fc20.x86_64 (mockbuild@bkernel01.phx2
   .fedoraproject.org) gcc version 4.8.3 20140911 (Red Hat 4.8.3-7)
   (GCC) ) #1 SMP Tue May 12 17:08:50 UTC 2015
Jun 22 04:03:53 mail kernel: [    0.000000] Command line:
   root=LABEL=root ro quiet biosdevname=0 LANG=en_US.utf8
```

Note that **/var/log/kern.log** entries are generated by a logging daemon (although some Linux distributions don't create this file, leaving kernel messages to be stored in the **/var/log/messages** file instead). See the "Third-Party Agents" subsection in this chapter for details about these daemons.

Log Management

Not only do you need to know where to file log files, as an administrator you also need to know how to manage the log files. This includes configuring what logs are generated as well as how often to back up and discard older log entries. This section focuses on these important tasks.

Third-Party Agents

The syslog service has existed since 1980. Although it was advanced at the time it was created, its limitations have grown over time as more complex logging techniques became required.

In the mid-2000s, the rsyslog service was created, also as an extension of the traditional syslog service. The rsyslog service includes the ability to extend the capabilities by including modules.

The configuration of these services (the format of the **syslog.conf** file) is consistent, with the exception of slightly different naming conventions (**rsyslog.conf**, for example) and additional features available in the log files.

The **syslogd** or **rsyslogd** daemon is responsible for logging of application and system events. It determines which events to log and where to place log entries by configuration settings that are located in the **/etc/syslog.conf** file.

Here are some important options to the **syslogd** and **rsyslogd** command:

Option	Description
-d	Enable debugging mode.
-f	Specify the configuration file (**/etc/syslog.conf** is the default).
-m *x*	Create a timestamp in the log files every *x* minutes. Set this to 0 to omit timestamps.
-r	Enable the **syslogd** daemon to accept logs from remote systems.
-s	Enable verbose mode.
-x	Disable DNS lookups for IP addresses.

logrotate

The **logrotate** command is a utility designed to ensure the partition that holds the log files has enough room to handle them. Log file size increases over time. The **logrotate** command rotates log files over time to limit the filesystem space that the logs use.

This command is configured by the **/etc/logrotate.conf** file and files in the **/etc/logrotate.d** directory. Typically, the **logrotate** command is configured to run automatically as a cron job:

```
[root@OCS ~]# cat /etc/cron.daily/logrotate
#!/bin/sh

/usr/sbin/logrotate /etc/logrotate.conf
EXITVALUE=$?
if [ $EXITVALUE != 0 ]; then
     /usr/bin/logger -t logrotate "ALERT exited
  abnormally with [$EXITVALUE]"
fi
exit 0
```

The **/etc/logrotate.conf** file is the primary configuration file for the **logrotate** command. Here's an example of a typical **/etc/logrotate.conf** file:

```
[root@OCS ~]# cat /etc/logrotate.conf
# see "man logrotate" for details
# rotate log files weekly
weekly

# keep 4 weeks' worth of backlogs
rotate 4

# create new (empty) log files after rotating old ones
create

# uncomment this if you want your log files compressed
```

```
#compress

# RPM packages drop log rotation information into this directory
include /etc/logrotate.d

# no packages own wtmp -- we'll rotate them here
/var/log/wtmp {
    monthly
    minsize 1M
    create 0664 root utmp
    rotate 1
}
```

The top part of this file is used to enable global settings that apply to all files rotated by the **logrotate** utility. These global settings can be overridden for individual files by a section defined like the following:

```
/var/log/wtmp {
    monthly
    minsize 1M
    create 0664 root utmp
    rotate 1
}
```

These sections are also found in files located in the **/etc/logrotate.d** directory. See more on that later in this subsection.

The following table details some important settings in the **/etc/logrotate.conf** file:

Settings	Description
daily|weekly|monthly	How often to rotate files.
rotate *x*	Keep *x* number of old (backup) files.
create	Create a new log file when backing up the old log file.
compress	Compress the backup log file, using gzip by default; the **compress** command can be changed by the **compresscmd** setting.
compresscmd	Specify the compression utility to use when compressing backup log files.
datetext	Backup log files are normally named by the convention **logfile.***x*, where *x* represents a number (0, 1, 2, and so on); using **datetext** will change the extension to a date value (YYYYMMDD).
mail *address*	Mail backup log file to *address*.
minsize *x*	Only rotate log file if its size is at least the value specified by *x*.

Settings	Description
nocompress	Do not compress the backup copy of the log file.
olddir *dir*	Place backup log files in the *dir* directory.

Files in the **/etc/logrotate.d** directory are used to override the default settings in the **/etc/logrotate.conf** file for the **logrotate** utility. The settings for these files are the same as the settings for the **/etc/logrotate.conf** file.

/etc/rsyslog.conf

The **/etc/rsyslog.conf** file is one of the configuration files for the **syslogd** daemon. The following demonstrates a typical **rsyslog.conf** file with the comments and blank lines removed (also note that more advanced features called modules were also removed from the following output):

```
[root@OCS ~]# grep -v "^$" /etc/rsyslog.conf | grep -v "^#"
*.info;mail.none;authpriv.none;cron.none   /var/log/messages
authpriv.*                                 /var/log/secure
mail.*                                     -/var/log/maillog
cron.*                                     /var/log/cron
*.emerg                                    *
uucp,news.crit                             /var/log/spooler
local7.*                                   /var/log/boot.log
```

Every line represents one logging rule that is broken into two primary parts: the selector (for example, **uucp,news.crit**) and action (**/var/log/spooler**). The selector is also broken into two parts: the facility (**uucp,news**) and priority (**crit**).

The following list shows the available facilities:

- auth (or security)
- authpriv
- cron
- daemon
- kern
- lpr
- mail
- mark
- news
- syslog
- user

- uucp
- local0 through local7

The following list shows the available priority levels:

- debug
- info
- notice
- warning (or warn)
- err (or error)
- crit
- alert
- emerg (or panic)

The following list shows the available actions:

- Regular file (using "-" before the filename omits syncing with every log entry, thus reducing hard drive writes)
- Named pipes
- Console or terminal devices
- Remote hosts
- User(s), which writes to the specified user's terminal windows (use * for all users)

journald

The **journald** service (also sometimes called **systemd-journald**) stores log entries in a special file format in order to optimize the log file entries. This section introduces the **journalctl** command, which is used to display **journald** log entries.

journalctl

On modern Linux systems, the logging process is handled by the **systemd-journald** service. To query systemd log entries, use the **journalctl** command:

```
[root@OCS ~]# journalctl | head
-- Logs begin at Tue 2017-01-24 13:43:18 PST, end
   at Sat 2017-03-04 16:00:32 PST. --
Jan 24 13:43:18 localhost.localdomain
   systemd-journal[88]: Runtime journal is using 8.0M
   (max allowed 194.4M, trying to leave 291.7M free
   of 1.8G available → current limit 194.4M).
Jan 24 13:43:18 localhost.localdomain
   systemd-journal[88]: Runtime journal is using 8.0M
   (max allowed 194.4M, trying to leave 291.7M free of 1.8G
   available → current limit 194.4M).
```

```
Jan 24 13:43:18 localhost.localdomain kernel:
  Initializing cgroup subsys cpuset
Jan 24 13:43:18 localhost.localdomain kernel:
  Initializing cgroup subsys cpu
Jan 24 13:43:18 localhost.localdomain kernel:
  Initializing cgroup subsys cpuacct
Jan 24 13:43:18 localhost.localdomain kernel:
  Linux version 3.10.0-327.18.2.el7.x86_64
  (builder@kbuilder.dev.centos.org) (gcc version
  4.8.3 20140911 (Red Hat 4.8.3-9) (GCC) ) #1 SMP
  Thu May 12 11:03:55 UTC 2016
Jan 24 13:43:18 localhost.localdomain kernel: Command
  line: BOOT_IMAGE=/vmlinuz-3.10.0-327.18.2.
  el7.x86_64 root=/dev/mapper/centos-root ro
  rd.lvm.lv=centos/root rd.lvm.lv=centos/swap
  crashkernel=auto rhgb quiet LANG=en_US.UTF-8
Jan 24 13:43:18 localhost.localdomain kernel:
  e820: BIOS-provided physical RAM map:
Jan 24 13:43:18 localhost.localdomain kernel:
  BIOS-e820: [mem 0x0000000000000000-0x000000000009fbff] usable
```

Here are some important options for the **journalctl** command:

Option	Description
--all or **-a**	Show all fields in full format.
-r	Reverse the log order so newest entries are displayed first.
-k	Show only kernel messages.
--priority=*value*	Only show messages that match the priority *value* (**emerg, alert, crit, err, warning, notice, info,** or **debug**).

The **/etc/systemd/journald.conf** file is used to configure the **systemd-journald** service. Typically, this file contains all commented-out values by default. Here are some important settings for the **/etc/systemd/journald.conf** file:

Setting	Description
Storage=*value*	Indicates where to store the journal date; *value* can be **volatile, persistent, auto,** or **none.**
compress=[1|0]	If set to **1** (true), this option indicates compression of journal entries before writing to the file.

The **/var/log/journal** directory is where the **systemd-journald** service stores journal entries if the **Storage=persistent** setting is placed in the **/etc/systemd/journald.conf** file.

lastb

The **lastb** command displays failed login attempts.

Example:

```
[root@OCS ~]# lastb -n 8
zabbix ssh:notty 203.153.32.67  Mon Oct 1 05:03 - 05:03 (00:00)
zabbix ssh:notty 203.153.32.67  Mon Oct 1 05:03 - 05:03 (00:00)
steven ssh:notty 211.73.25.162  Mon Oct 1 04:45 - 04:45 (00:00)
steven ssh:notty 211.73.25.162  Mon Oct 1 04:45 - 04:45 (00:00)
admin  ssh:notty 41.41.98.82    Mon Oct 1 03:42 - 03:42 (00:00)
admin  ssh:notty 41.41.98.82    Mon Oct 1 03:42 - 03:42 (00:00)
admin  ssh:notty 143.255.154.98 Mon Oct 1 03:42 - 03:42 (00:00)
admin  ssh:notty 143.255.154.98 Mon Oct 1 03:42 - 03:42 (00:00)

btmp begins Mon Oct  1 03:42:01 2018
```

Here are some important options for the **lastb** command:

Option	Description
-a	Display the hostname or IP address in the last column of the display.
-d	Display the hostname as the result of a DNS lookup (may take a long time to query all entries).
-F	Display full date timestamps.
-n x	Display the last x entries (replace x with a number).

## CHAPTER 19

Given a scenario, implement and configure Linux firewalls

This chapter provides information and commands concerning the following topics:

Access control lists

- Source
- Destination
- Ports
- Protocol
- Logging
- Stateful vs. stateless
- Accept
- Reject
- Drop
- Log

Technologies

- firewalld (zones, run time)
- iptables (persistency, chains)
- ufw (**/etc/default/ufw, /etc/ufw/**)
- Netfilter

IP forwarding

- **/proc/sys/net/ipv4/ip_forward**
- **/proc/sys/net/ipv6/conf/all/forwarding**

Dynamic rule sets

- DenyHost
- Fail2ban
- IPset

Common application

- Firewall configurations (**/etc/services**, privileged ports)

Access Control Lists

A *firewall* (aka, access control list) is a network appliance (either hardware or software based) that is designed to either allow or block network traffic. Firewalls can be implemented on a variety of devices, including routers, network servers, and users' systems. This section explores the basic concepts of firewalls. Note that specific examples are provided in the "iptables" subsection in this chapter.

Source

The term *source* refers to where a network packet originated from. Firewall rules can be created to filter network traffic from the source by using the source's IP address, port, or MAC address.

Destination

The term *destination* refers to where a network packet is being sent to. Firewall rules can be created to filter network traffic for the destination by using either the destination's IP address, port, or MAC address.

Ports

A port is a unique number used to address a service on a system. Network packets contain a source port and a destination port. Firewall rules can be created to filter network traffic by using the source or destination port number.

Also see the "Privileged Ports" subsection in this chapter.

Protocol

It is common to filter packets by the protocol. This could either be a protocol like ICMP, TCP, or UDP, or be a protocol associated with a specific port (like telnet, which uses port 22).

Logging

Firewall rules are normally used to allow or block a network packet; however, there are also rules that are designed to log information regarding a network packet. This is useful when you want to see information about a packet that you will block with a later rule.

Stateful vs. Stateless

A stateful rule is one that applies to any previously established connection. Consider when you have a firewall like the following:

- Allow most outbound connections, including to websites, SSH access, FTP sites, and so on.
- Block most inbound connections, so outside users can't connect to services you may have running.

The problem with this scenario is that when you connect to a remote system, both outbound and inbound rules will apply. The outbound rules apply when you establish a connection, and the inbound rules apply when the remote server responds. If you have a rule that blocks most inbound connections, you may never receive the response from that website you are trying to visit.

You can overcome this by creating "stateful rules." Stateful rules essentially mean "if a network packet is responding to a request that the local machine initiated, let it through the firewall."

A stateless rule is one that applies regardless of any previously established connection.

Accept

Once a network packet matches the criteria of a firewall rule, a target is used to determine what action to take. There are four standard targets for iptables: Accept, Reject, Drop, and Log.

The Accept target tells iptables to allow the packet to advance to the next filtering point.

Reject

The Reject target tells iptables to return the packet to the source with an error message. The message is not advanced to the next filtering point.

Also see the "Accept" subsection in this chapter.

Drop

The Drop target tells iptables to discard the packet. No response is sent to the source, and the message is not advanced to the next filtering point.

Also see the "Accept" subsection in this chapter.

Log

The Log target tells iptables to create a log entry that contains detailed information about the packet. With this target, the packet is neither explicitly allowed nor blocked, but further rules in the rule set (the chain) may determine this result.

Also see the "Accept" subsection in this chapter.

Technologies

A large number of firewall technologies can be implemented on Linux systems. This section focuses on the technologies you will find on the exam.

firewalld

On Red Hat–based distributions, it is common to use a utility called firewalld to configure iptables rules. Rules are configured into categories called "zones," and the rules are managed by the **firewall-cmd** command.

Zones

For example, you can execute the command **firewall-cmd --get-zones** to display all available zones:

```
root@OCS:~# firewall-cmd --get-zones
block dmz drop external home internal public trusted work
```

You can set different rules on each zone and assign the zone rule set to different interfaces. For example, your **eth0** interface may connect to your internal network, so you may apply the "trusted" or "internal" zone, which should have less-restrictive rules. Conversely, your **eth1** interface may connect to the Internet, which means the "dmz" or "external" zone may be a better solution.

Run Time

Rules created on the command line using the **firewall-cmd** command affect the active firewall on the system. This is referred to as the "run time" firewall. If the system is rebooted or the firewall service is restarted, these rules would be lost.

To make "run time" rules persist after a system or firewall reset, use the following command:

```
root@OCS:~# firewall-cmd --runtime-to-permanent
```

iptables

Rule sets (called *chains*) are applied at different places (called *filter points*), allowing for more flexibility in this ACL software. Figure 19.1 demonstrates these filter points.

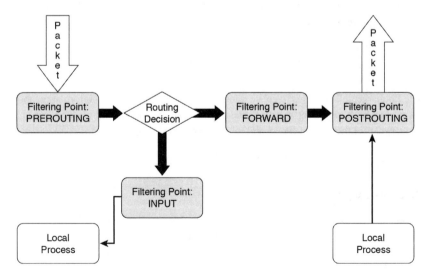

Figure 19.1   Packet Filtering—Outbound Packets

Types of rules, referred to as a *table*, can be placed on a filtering point. A filtering point can have one or more sets of rules because iptables performs multiple functions: either filter (block or allow) the data, perform a NAT operation on the packet, or mangle the packet. The combination of the filtering point plus the table (filter, nat, or mangle) form a single set of rules called a *chain*.

Consider a chain to be a set of *rules* that determines what actions to take on a specific packet. For example, a rule on the "filter INPUT" chain could block an incoming packet based on the source IP address. Another rule could be used to allow packets destined for a specific network port.

The order of the rules is also important. Once a matching rule is found, an action (called a *target*) takes place, and additional rules are ignored (with one exception, as noted next).

See the "Accept," "Drop," "Reject," and "Log" subsections in this chapter for more details about the targets.

The following table describes several common iptables rules:

Rule	Description
iptables -t filter -L INPUT	Display all the rules for the INPUT-filter chain.
iptables -D INPUT 1	Delete rule 1 from the INPUT-filter chain.
iptables -F INPUT	Flush all the rules of the INPUT-filter chain.
iptables -A INPUT -s 192.168.10.100 -j DROP	Append a rule at the end of the INPUT-filter chain that drops any packet from the 192.168.10.100 system.
iptables -A INPUT -s 192.168.20.0/24 -j DROP	Append a rule at the end of the INPUT-filter chain that drops any packet from the 192.168.10.0/24 network.
iptables -I INPUT 2 -s 192.168.20.125 -j ACCEPT	Insert this rule as rule 2 and move all remaining rules down by one.
iptables -A INPUT -p icmp -j DROP	Create a rule that drops packets that match the ICMP protocol.
iptables -A INPUT -m tcp -p tcp --dport 23 -j DROP	Create a rule that drops packages that are destined for port 23.
iptables -A INPUT -p icmp -s 192.168.125.125 -j DROP	Create a rule that must match all criteria (ICMP protocol and source IP address of 192.168.125.125).
iptables -A INPUT -i eth0 -s 192.168.100.0/24 -j DROP	Create a rule that filters based on network interface.
iptables -L INPUT -v	Display detailed information about the rules.
iptables -P INPUT DROP	Set the default chain policy. If no rules match, this default target will be used.

Persistency

All changes that are made by the **iptables** command only affect the currently running firewall. If the system was rebooted, all changes made using the **iptables** command would be lost, and the rules would revert back to the default.

You can save the rules into a file by using the **iptables-save** command. Normally the output of this command is sent to the screen, but you can redirect the output to a file:

```
root@OCS:~# iptables-save > /etc/iptables.rules
```

Chains

See the "iptables" subsection in this chapter.

ufw

On Debian-based distributions, you will likely have the ability to use **ufw** (uncomplicated firewall). Similar to **firewalld**, the goal of this utility is to act as a front-end interface to create iptables rules.

For example, the following would create a rule to allow for both inbound and outbound SSH connections:

```
root@OCS:~# ufw allow ssh
```

The ufw firewall rules are stored here:

- **/etc/default/ufw**
- **/etc/ufw**

Note that the **/etc/default/ufw** rules should not be modified manually. The rules in **/etc/ufw** are designed for system administrators to modify and override the default rules from the **/etc/default/ufw** directory.

Netfilter

The component of the kernel that performs NAT and IP forwarding is called Netfilter. There are a few different forms of NAT:

- **DNAT**: Destination NAT; used when you want to place servers behind a firewall and still provide access from an external network. DNAT rules are placed on the PREROUTING filtering point. Further discussion of this topic is beyond the scope of this book.

- **SNAT**: Source NAT; used when you have an internal network with *statically assigned* private IP addresses. Using SNAT, you can funnel access to the Internet via a single machine that has a live IP address (an address that is routable on the Internet). This system is configured with SNAT, which is used to map an internal address with external communication. SNAT rules are placed on the POSTROUTING filtering point. Further discussion of this topic is beyond the scope of this book.

- **MASQUERADE**: Used when you have an internal network with *dynamically assigned* private IP addresses (for example, using DHCP). Using MASQUERADE, you can funnel access to the Internet via a single machine that has a live IP address (an address that is routable on the Internet). This system is configured with MASQUERADE, which is used to map an internal address with external communication. MASQUERADE rules are placed on the POSTROUTING filtering point.

Because most internal networks use DHCP to assign IP addresses, MASQUERADE is more common than SNAT. It is also easier to configure because SNAT requires you to create rules for each internal system. With MASQUERADE, a single command handles all the internal systems:

```
root@OCS:~# iptables -t nat -A POSTROUTING -j MASQUERADE
```

Note that NAT by itself isn't enough. You also have to implement the IP forwarding feature in the kernel. See the "IP Forwarding" section next.

IP Forwarding

IP forwarding is a kernel feature that allows network packets to be passed from one network to another. This feature is commonly used to create a router on a server.

This is a simple matter, as you just need to set the value of the following files to "1":

- **/proc/sys/net/ipv4/ip_forward**: This enables IP forwarding for IPV4 network packets.

- **/proc/sys/net/ipv6/conf/all/forwarding**: This enables IP forwarding for IPV6 network packets.

Dynamic Rule Sets

Not all rules are created by hand. Several utilities will dynamically create firewall rules. The goal of these utilities is to recognize when a system is under attack and create rules to block the hacking attempt.

DenyHost

The **DenyHost** utility is similar to **fail2ban,** but it is designed especially to protect SSH servers, and it doesn't create **iptables** rules, but rather TCP Wrapper rules. If it appears that a remote system is attempting a brute-force attack (using a dictionary of possible passwords as a means of guessing a user's password), then **DenyHost** will create a rule in the **/etc/hosts.deny** file to block the remote system.

Fail2ban

The **fail2ban** daemon will scan specific log files, searching for IP addresses of systems that attempt to breach the system by repeated connection attempts.

The primary configuration file is the **/etc/fail2ban/jails.conf** file. However, if you look at this file, you will likely see the following message:

```
# HOW TO ACTIVATE JAILS:
#
# YOU SHOULD NOT MODIFY THIS FILE.
#
# It will probably be overwritten or improved in a
  distribution update.
#
# Provide customizations in a jail.local file or
  a jail.d/customisation.local.
# For example, to change the default bantime for all jails
  and to enable the
# ssh-iptables jail, the following (uncommented) would appear
  in the .local file.
# See man 5 jail.conf for details.
```

The problem that you run into in modifying this file directly is that updates to the fail2ban software package could result in overriding this file. As the warning in this file recommends, you can create **.local** files with customizations.

The file is called **jails.conf** because remote hosts are placed in a "jail" due to suspicious activity. As with a real jail, the intent is to let the host out of jail after a specific period of time.

The following table describes some key settings in this file:

Setting	Description
bantime	How long in seconds a host is banned.
maxretry	The number of failures in connecting within the "findtime" before a host is banned.
findtime	The period of time, in seconds, that the "maxretry" entry uses. For example, if the settings bantime = 600 findtime = 600 maxretry = 5 are applied, then five failures within 600 seconds would result in a ban for 600 seconds.
enabled	If **enabled** is set to "true", then the jail is enabled. This is a very important setting because the default value for this setting in the **jail.conf** file is "false". Only specific sections should be enabled (the ones you want to use).
ignoreip	Allows you to create "white lists" of IP address to never ban.

IPset

The IPset utility is designed to create "sets" of IP addresses and then use this set to apply rules to a collection of systems. For example, the following command will create a set:

```
root@OCS:~#ipset create test hash:net
```

The next set of rules will add IP addresses to the "test" set:

```
root@OCS:~#ipset add test 192.168.100.0/24
root@OCS:~#ipset add test 192.168.110.0/24
root@OCS:~#ipset add test 192.168.120.0/24
```

And the next command will apply a rule to this set:

```
root@OCS:~#iptables -I INPUT -m set --match-set test src -j LOG
```

Common Application

See the "iptables" subsection in this chapter—specifically the table that shows common examples of **iptables** rules.

Firewall Configurations

See the "iptables" subsection in this chapter—specifically the table that shows common examples of **iptables** rules.

/etc/services

The **/etc/services** file is the traditional location where services are mapped to ports. It is considered traditional in the sense that, historically, services would look to this file to determine which port they should use. However, most modern services have a setting in their configuration file that is used to determine the specific port they will use.

The **/etc/services** file is still useful to administrators in that it contains ports that have been assigned to services by the Internet Assigned Numbers Authority (IANA).

Each line in this file describes one service-to-port mapping. Here's the format of the line:

```
service_name port/protocol [alias]
```

For example:

```
[root@OCS ~]# grep smtp /etc/services
smtp            25/tcp              mail
smtp            25/udp              mail
urd             465/tcp             smtps # URL Rendesvous
   Directory for SSM / SMTP over SSL (TLS)
rsmtp           2390/tcp            # RSMTP
rsmtp           2390/udp            # RSMTP
```

Privileged Ports

Network ports 1–1023 are considered privileged ports. This is because they have been reserved for commonly used protocols.

## CHAPTER 20

Given a scenario, backup, restore, and compress files

This chapter provides information and commands concerning the following topics:

Archive and restore utilities

- **tar**
- **cpio**
- **dd**

Compression

- **gzip**
- **xz**
- **bzip2**
- **zip**

Backup types

- Incremental
- Full
- Snapshot clones
- Differential
- Image

Off-site/off-system storage

- SFTP
- SCP
- **rsync**

Integrity checks

- MD5
- SHA

Archive and Restore Utilities

When disaster strikes, such as a hard disk failure or a natural disaster, data may become corrupted. Using archive and restore utilities helps limit the risks involved with data loss and makes it easier to transfer information from one system to another. This section focuses on these utilities.

tar

The purpose of the **tar** command is to merge multiple files into a single file. To create a tar file named **sample.tar**, execute the following:

```
tar -cf sample.tar files_to_merge
```

To list the contents of a **.tar** file:

```
tar -tf sample.tar
```

To extract the contents of a **.tar** file:

```
tar -xf sample.tar
```

The following table details some important options:

Option	Description
-c	Create a **.tar** file.
-t	List the contents of a **.tar** file.
-x	Extract the contents of a **.tar** file.
-f	Specify the name of the **.tar** file.
-v	Be verbose (provide more details as to what the command is doing).
-A	Append new files to an existing **.tar** file.
-d	Compare the difference between a **.tar** file and the files in a directory.
-u	Update; only append newer files into an existing **.tar** file.
-j	Compress/uncompress the **.tar** file using the **bzip2** utility.
-J	Compress/uncompress the **.tar** file using the **xz** utility.
-z	Compress/uncompress the **.tar** file using the **gzip** utility.

cpio

The purpose of the **cpio** command is to create archives. You can create an archive of files by sending the filenames into the command as STDIN, as in the following example:

```
[student@OCS ~]$ find /etc -name "*.conf" | cpio -ov > conf.cpio
```

The following table details some important options:

Option	Description
-d	Used with the **-i** option to extract the directory structure as well as the files in the **cpio** file.
-i	Extract data from a **cpio** file; the file should be provided via STDIN (for example, **cpio -i < conf.cpio**).
-o	Create an archive (output file).
-t	List the table of contents of a **cpio** file.
-v	Verbose mode.

dd

The **dd** command can perform multiple operations related to backing up data and creating files. One common use is to make a backup of an entire drive; for example, the following backs up the entire **/dev/sdb** device to the **/dev/sdc** device:

```
[student@OCS ~]$ dd if=/dev/sdb of=/dev/sdc bs=4096
```

Another use of the **dd** command is to create a large file that can be used as a swap file:

```
[student@OCS ~]$ dd if=/dev/zero of=/var/swapfile bs=1M count=50
```

The following table details some important options:

Option	Description
if=	Specify the input file.
of=	Specify the output file.
bs=	Specify the block size.
count=	Indicate the number of blocks to create/transfer.

Compression

Archive files, log files, and mail spools can become very large over time. Use the compression tools covered in this section to reduce the size of these files.

gzip

Use the **gzip** command to compress files:

```
[student@OCS ~]$ ls -lh juju
-rwxr-xr-x 1 vagrant vagrant 109M Jan 10 09:20 juju
[student@OCS ~]$ gzip juju
[student@OCS ~]$ ls -lh juju.gz
-rwxr-xr-x 1 vagrant vagrant 17M Jan 10 09:20 juju.gz
```

Note that the **gzip** command replaces the original file with the compressed file.

The following table details some important options:

Option	Description
-c	Write output to STDOUT and do not replace the original file. Use redirection to place output data into a new file (for example, **gzip -c juju > juju.gz**).
-d	Decompress the file (you can also use the **gunzip** command).
-r	Recursive: Used when a directory argument is given to compress all files in the directory (and its subdirectories).
-v	Verbose: Display percentage of compression.

The **gzip**, **xz**, and **bzip2** commands are very similar. The biggest difference is the technique used to compress files. The **gzip** command uses the Lempel-Ziv coding method, whereas the **bzip2** command uses the Burrows-Wheeler block-sorting text-compression algorithm and Huffman coding. The **xz** command uses the LZMA and LZMA2 compression methods.

Use the **gzip** command to decompress gzipped files:

```
[student@OCS ~]$ ls -lh juju.gz
-rwxr-xr-x 1 vagrant vagrant 17M Jan 10 09:20 juju.gz
[student@OCS ~]$ gunzip juju
[student@OCS ~]$ ls -lh juju
-rwxr-xr-x 1 vagrant vagrant 109M Jan 10 09:20 juju
```

XZ

Use the **xz** command to compress files:

```
[student@OCS ~]$ ls -lh juju
-rwxr-xr-x 1 vagrant vagrant 109M Jan 10 09:20 juju
[student@OCS ~]$ xz juju
[student@OCS ~]$ ls -lh juju.xz
-rwxr-xr-x 1 vagrant vagrant 11M Jan 10 09:20 juju.xz
```

The following table details some important options:

Option	Description
-c	Write output to STDOUT and do not replace the original file. Use redirection to place output data into a new file (for example, **xz -c juju > juju.xz**).
-d	Decompress the file (you can also use the **unxz** command).
-l	List information about an existing compressed file (for example, **xz [nd]l juju.xz**).
-v	Verbose: Display percentage of compression.

The **gzip, xz**, and **bzip2** commands are very similar. The biggest difference is the technique used to compress files. The **gzip** command uses the Lempel-Ziv coding method, whereas the **bzip2** command uses the Burrows-Wheeler block-sorting text-compression algorithm and Huffman coding. The **xz** command uses the LZMA and LZMA2 compression methods.

bzip2

Use the **bzip2** command to compress files:

```
[student@OCS ~]$ ls -lh juju
-rwxr-xr-x 1 vagrant vagrant 109M Jan 10 09:20 juju
[student@OCS ~]$ bzip2 juju
[student@OCS ~]$ ls -lh juju.bz2
-rwxr-xr-x 1 vagrant vagrant 14M Jan 10 09:20 juju.bz2
```

Note that the **bzip2** command replaces the original file with the compressed file.

The following table details some important options:

Option	Description
-c	Write output to STDOUT and do not replace the original file. Use redirection to place output data into a new file (for example, **bzip2 -c juju > juju.bz**).
-d	Decompress the file (you can also use the **bunzip2** command).
-v	Verbose: Display percentage of compression.

The **gzip, xz**, and **bzip2** commands are very similar. The biggest difference is the technique used to compress files. The **gzip** command uses the Lempel-Ziv coding method, whereas the **bzip2** command uses the Burrows-Wheeler block-sorting text-compression algorithm and Huffman coding. The **xz** command uses the LZMA and LZMA2 compression methods.

zip

The **zip** command is used to merge multiple files into a single, compressed file. To create a compressed file named **mail.zip** that contains all the files in the **/etc/mail** directory, use the following format:

```
[student@OCS ~]$ zip mail /etc/mail*
  adding: etc/mail/ (stored 0%)
  adding: etc/mailcap (deflated 53%)
  adding: etc/mailman/ (stored 0%)
  adding: etc/mail.rc (deflated 49%)
```

The following table details some important options:

Option	Description
-d	Decompress the file (you can also use the **unzip** command). Note that the zipped file is not deleted.
-v	Verbose: Display percentage of compression.
-u	Update a **.zip** file with new content.
-r	Zips recursively, meaning you can specify a directory, and all of the contents in that directory (including all subdirectories and their contents) will be zipped.
-x *file(s)*	Specify *file(s)* to be excluded from the **.zip** file.

Backup Types

Many backup tools allow you to specify what to back up by using predetermined types. This section covers these types.

Incremental

An incremental backup will include all files that have changed since the last incremental or full backup.

Incremental backups provide several advantages:

- Each backup takes less time than a full backup and, in most cases, a differential backup.

- Incremental backups are normally smaller than full and differential backups, so they take up less storage space.

However, there are some disadvantages:

- Restoring from incremental backups can be time consuming. First, the full backup must be restored, and then each incremental backup must be restored until the incident that caused the loss of data is reached.

- Finding a specific file from an incremental backup can be difficult because the file can be located in different locations.

Also see the "Full" and "Differential" subsections in this chapter.

Full

With a full backup, everything from the source is backed up. This can include files that haven't changed since previous backups.

Full backups provide several advantages:

- All of the source data is located in one backup, making it easier to find.

- Restoring from a full backup is quicker than other backup methods.

However, there are some disadvantages:

- A full backup can be a very time-consuming process.

- Normally much more storage space is used for full backups than other methods.

- If the backup is performed remotely, a full backup will use much more bandwidth than other methods.

Also see the "Incremental" and "Differential" subsections in this chapter.

Snapshot Clones

With Logical Volume Management (LVM), you can have a snapshot of a logical volume, which is a frozen image of the filesystem. This allows you to safely back up a live file-system, as the snapshot clone will always provide a static view of the filesystem when the snapshot was created.

See the "LVM" section in Chapter 4, "Given a scenario, manage storage in a Linux environment," for more details regarding LVM.

Differential

A differential backup will archive any files since the last full backup. Differential back-ups don't take into account files that were backed up with previous differential or incremental backups.

Differential backups provide several advantages:

- All of the source data is located in two backups (the full and differential), making it easier to find files than with incremental backups.

- Restoring from a differential backup is quicker than with the incremental method.

However, there are some disadvantages:

- Using a differential backup scheme can be a time-consuming process compared to incremental backups.

- Normally, more storage space is used for differential backups than incremental backups.

- If the backup is performed remotely, a differential backup will use more band-width than incremental backups.

Also see the "Incremental" and "Full" subsections in this chapter.

Image

Image is the term used for the format of the backup data. There are several different types of images, including:

- **tar**: The format of a file that is generated by the **tar** command.

- **ISO**: A format that is often used to generate a CD-ROM filesystem.

The image is important because you need to use the right utility to properly work with an image. Sometimes the extension of the filename (**file.tar**, **sample.iso**, and so on) will provide the image type. In cases where the image isn't descriptive, use the **file** command:

```
[student@OCS ~]$ file sample
sample: POSIX tar archive (GNU)
```

Off-Site/Off-System Storage

An objective of the Linux+ exam is to know how to use tools to transfer data to remote storage locations (called "off-site storage"). This section introduces these tools.

SFTP

The **sftp** command uses the SSH (Secure Shell) protocol to securely transfer files across the network. To access a remote system, use the following syntax:

```
sftp user@machine
```

After logging in to the remote system, you are provided with an interface that begins with the following prompt:

```
sftp>
```

At this prompt, several commands can be used to transfer files and perform other operations. The following table describes the more important of these commands:

Command	Description
pwd	Display the current remote directory.
lpwd	Display the current local directory.
cd	Change to a different directory on a remote system.
lcd	Change to a different directory on the local system.
get	Download a file from the current directory on the remote system to the current directory on the local system. Use **-r** to get entire directory structures.
put	Upload a file from the current directory on the local system to the current directory on the remote system. Use **-r** to put entire directory structures.
ls	Display files in the current directory of a remote system.
lls	Display files in the current directory of the local system.
exit	Quit **sftp**.

SCP

See the "scp" subsection in Chapter 9, "Given a scenario, create, modify, and redirect files."

rsync

See the "rsync" subsection in Chapter 9.

Integrity Checks

While a file is transferred from one system, either via the network or some other means, it is possible that the file may be replaced by an imposter or fake. Imagine using data from a remote backup in which a hacker has injected data. This could result in a compromised system.

This section covers techniques that can be used to verify the integrity of a file.

MD5

The **md5sum** command creates a unique "message digest" that can be used to verify a file in the future. The following creates this digest:

```
[student@OCS ~]$ md5sum output
b46d07ef1778eaaabbffca5e1cc94f81   output
```

If the file changes, the output of **md5sum** will also change.

Here are some important options of the **md5sum** command:

Option	Description
-b	Treat the file as a binary.
-c	Read a message digest from a file and check it against an existing file.

SHA

Like the **md5sum** command, another set of commands (**sha224sum**, **sha256sum**, **sha384sum**, and **sha512sum**) creates message digests, but using different algorithms:

```
[student@OCS ~]$ sha256sum output
3c00f1d1b69b5fd901d6ff087d603bb07d272911254926d870c04
   8a69614ae96   output
[student@OCS ~]$ sha512sum output
5da0fb5eba5f8ac5bf9c7a58f3ca6c325294fc94595f386863c41
   f236ea84abf115642667ef16fc5d632466a91410929339e8b80fa8
   351f7cf982f9a20eee738   output
```

Although the algorithm and output are different, these commands share the same options as the **md5sum** command. See the previous subsection, "MD5," for more details.

## CHAPTER 21

Given a scenario, analyze system properties and remediate accordingly

This chapter provides information and commands concerning the following topics:

Network monitoring and configuration

- Latency (bandwidth, throughput)
- Routing
- Saturation
- Packet drop
- Timeouts
- Name resolution
- Localhost vs. Unix socket
- Interface configurations
- Commands
    - **nmap**
    - **netstat**
    - **iftop**
    - **route**
    - **iperf**
    - **tcpdump**
    - **ipset**
    - Wireshark
    - **tshark**
    - **netcat**
    - **traceroute**
    - **mtr**
    - **arp**
    - **nslookup**
    - **dig**
    - **host**
    - **whois**
    - **ping**

- **nmcli**
- **ip**
- **tracepath**

Storage monitoring and configuration

- **iostat**
- **ioping**
- IO scheduling (cfq, noop, deadline)
- **du**
- **df**
- LVM tools
- **fsck**
- **partprobe**

CPU monitoring and configuration

- **/proc/cpuinfo**
- **uptime**
- **loadaverage**
- **sar**
- **sysctl**

Memory monitoring and configuration

- **swapon**
- **swapoff**
- **mkswap**
- **vmstat**
- Out of memory killer
- **free**
- **/proc/meminfo**
- Buffer cache output

Lost root password

- Single user mode

Network Monitoring and Configuration

This section focuses on commands and files related to the monitoring and configuration of the network interfaces.

Latency

Think of latency as any sort of delay in communication (for example, the time it takes for a network packet to travel from one host to another host). Sometimes latency is measured by the roundtrip time of communication (how long to send a network packet and receive a response). Use tools like the **ping** and **traceroute** commands to determine if there are latency issues.

Bandwidth

Bandwidth is the maximum amount of data that can travel through media. The media could be network cables, wireless, or even the network interface itself. A useful tool for determining bandwidth is the **netstat** command.

Throughput

Throughput is the actual amount of data that passes through media. This value is limited by many factors, including bandwidth, latency, and interference. The **netstat** and Wireshark utilities can be useful for determining throughput.

Routing

Routing is the process of sending network data from one Internet Protocol (IP) network to another via a gateway. A gateway is a system that has multiple network interfaces and transfers the data between the networks. Use the **route** or **netstat** command to determine routing on a host.

Saturation

Saturation occurs when throughput often (or constantly) reaches the value of the bandwidth. Saturation is likely in just about every network from time to time, but when it becomes a regular occurrence, the network will appear to be slow or sluggish.

This will increase problems with latency and make users frustrated. Use network-monitoring tools like Wireshark to determine if saturation is occurring too often.

Packet Drop

A packet drop is when a remote system doesn't respond to an inbound network packet. This could be the result of firewall rules, saturation, or a misconfigured network.

Timeouts

A timeout is a software component that is used to determine if a packet drop has occurred. A program will send a network packet to a remote system and wait for a specific period of time for a response. If the response doesn't occur within this period of time, then the software packet considers the response to have "timed out." A timeout can result in error messages from the software. Some software will use a retry value to attempt to send the network packet again in the event that an error or problem (such as saturation) prevents the first network packet from reaching its destination.

Name Resolution

A name resolution is when a hostname is translated into an IP address. A reverse name resolution is when an IP address is translated into a hostname. Tools like the **dig**, **host**, and **nslookup** commands can provide name resolution functionality.

Localhost vs. Unix Socket

The term "localhost" refers to a system communicating via a special localized network interface. Any network traffic sent to localhost (IP address 127.0.0.1) is not sent on the network but rather kept internally. It does, however, act like network traffic, so you can use network-sniffing tools like Wireshark to see this traffic if you are on the local machine.

Using a "Unix socket" is a method to allow processes on the same system to communicate with each other. This information is not sent via any network interface, so it is not possible to use network-sniffing tools to view the network traffic. This makes troubleshooting Unix socket issues much more difficult.

Interface Configurations

Interface configuration involves assigning settings such as IP address, netmask, and router information to a network interface. Use tools like the **ip** and **route** commands to display this information.

Commands

This section focuses on a collection of commands that are useful in troubleshooting networking-based issues.

nmap

The **nmap** command is used to probe a remote system to determine which network ports are reachable from the local system. To use the **nmap** command, provide either the IP address or the hostname of the system that you want to scan. Here is an example:

```
# nmap 192.168.1.1
Starting Nmap 5.51 ( http://nmap.org ) at 2015-10-31 23:22 PDT
Nmap scan report for 192.168.1.1
Host is up (2.9s latency).
Not shown: 987 closed ports
PORT     STATE SERVICE
23/tcp   open  telnet
25/tcp   open  smtp
53/tcp   open  domain
80/tcp   open  http
110/tcp  open  pop3
119/tcp  open  nntp
143/tcp  open  imap
465/tcp  open  smtps
```

```
563/tcp   open   snews
587/tcp   open   submission
993/tcp   open   imaps
995/tcp   open   pop3s
5000/tcp open   upnp
Nmap done: 1 IP address (1 host up) scanned in 4.89 seconds
```

netstat

The **netstat** command is used to display network statistics in order to determine if there is an issue with transmitting or receiving data. See the "netstat" section of Chapter 3, "Given a scenario, configure and verify network connection parameters," for details about this command.

iftop

The **iftop** command provides a good way to display the network connections using the most bandwidth. It is an interactive display that updates every second by default to display the "top" network connections. See Figure 21.1 for an example.

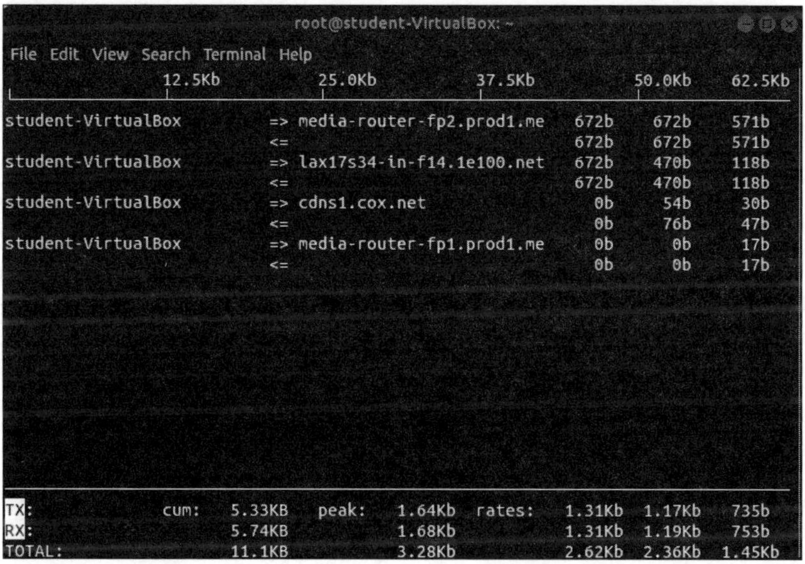

Figure 21.1   The **iftop** Command

route

The **route** command is used to display the routing table in order to determine if a route to another network is correctly configured. See the "route" subsection of Chapter 3 for details about this command.

iperf

The **iperf** command provides a means to create tests of the throughput between two systems. It requires installing and configuring the tool on two systems: a client and a server. Complete coverage of the command is beyond the scope of the exam. You should be aware of the purpose of the tool and the fact that it requires both client and server setup.

tcpdump

When troubleshooting network issues or performing network security audits, it can be helpful to view the network traffic, including traffic that isn't related to the local machine. The **tcpdump** command is a "packet sniffer" that allows you to view local network traffic.

By default, the **tcpdump** command displays all network traffic to standard output until you terminate the command. This could result in a dizzying amount of data flying by on your screen. You can limit the output to a specific number of network packets by using the **-c** options:

```
# tcpdump -c 5
tcpdump: verbose output suppressed, use -v or -vv for full
  protocol decode
listening on eth0, link-type EN10MB (Ethernet), capture size 65535 bytes
11:32:59.630873 IP localhost.43066 > 192.168.1.1.domain:
  16227+ A? onecoursesource.com. (37)
11:32:59.631272 IP localhost.59247 > 192.168.1.1.domain:
  2117+ PTR? 1.1.168.192.in-addr.arpa. (42)
11:32:59.631387 IP localhost.43066 > 192.168.1.1.domain:
  19647+ AAAA? onecoursesource.com. (37)
11:32:59.647932 IP 192.168.1.1.domain > localhost.59247:
  2117 NXDomain* 0/1/0 (97)
11:32:59.717499 IP 192.168.1.1.domain > localhost.43066:
  16227 1/0/0 A 38.89.136.109 (53)
5 packets captured
5 packets received by filter
0 packets dropped by kernel
```

ipset

The IPSet utility is designed to create a "set" of IP addresses and then use this set to apply rules to a collection of systems. For example, the following command will create a set:

```
root@OCS:~#  ipset create test hash:net
```

The next set of rules will add IP addresses to the "test" set:

```
root@OCS:~#  ipset add test 192.168.100.0/24
root@OCS:~#  ipset add test 192.168.110.0/24
root@OCS:~#  ipset add test 192.168.120.0/24
```

And the next command will apply a rule to this set:

```
root@OCS:~# iptables -I INPUT -m set --match-set
  test src -j LOG
```

See Chapter 19, "Given a scenario, implement and configure Linux firewalls," for more details about the **iptables** command and firewall configuration.

Wireshark

Wireshark is an amazing network sniffer that provides both a GUI-based and TUI-based tools. To start the GUI tool, execute the **wireshark** command. The output should be similar to Figure 21.2.

Figure 21.2 The **wireshark** Command

To view network traffic, you need to start a capture. Click **Capture**, **Start**. You can also limit what is captured by setting filters and options (click **Capture**, **Options**).

To use the TUI-based form of Wireshark, execute the **tstark** command as the root user. Here is an example:

```
# tshark
Capturing on 'enp0s3'
    1 0.000000000    10.0.2.15 → 68.105.28.11 DNS
  81 Standard query 0xeec4 A google.com OPT
```

```
    2 0.001031279    10.0.2.15 → 68.105.28.11 DNS
  81 Standard query 0x3469 AAAAgoogle.com OPT
    3 0.017196416 68.105.28.11 → 10.0.2.15      DNS
  109 Standard query response 0x3469 AAAA google.com AAAA
2607:f8b0:4007:800::200e OPT
    4 0.017265061 68.105.28.11 → 10.0.2.15      DNS
  97 Standard query response 0xeec4 A google.com A 172.217.14.110 OPT
    5 0.018482388    10.0.2.15 → 172.217.14.110 ICMP
  98 Echo (ping) request  id=0x122c, seq=1/256, ttl=64
    6 0.036907577 172.217.14.110 → 10.0.2.15     ICMP
  98 Echo (ping) reply    id=0x122c, seq=1/256, ttl=251 (request in 5)
    7 1.021052811    10.0.2.15 → 172.217.14.110 ICMP
  98 Echo (ping) request  id=0x122c, seq=2/512, ttl=64
    8 1.039492225 172.217.14.110 → 10.0.2.15     ICMP
  98 Echo (ping) reply    id=0x122c, seq=2/512, ttl=251 (request in 7)
```

tshark

See the "Wireshark" subsection in this chapter.

netcat

The man page for **nc** (also referred to as the **netcat** command) provides an excellent summary of the **nc** command:

> "The nc (or netcat) utility is used for just about anything under the sun involving TCP or UDP. It can open TCP connections, send UDP packets, listen on arbitrary TCP and UDP ports, do port scanning, and deal with both IPv4 and IPv6. Unlike telnet(1), nc scripts nicely, and separates error messages onto standard error instead of sending them to standard output, as telnet(1) does with some."

You can use the **nc** command to display open ports, similar to the **netstat** command:

```
# nc -z localhost 1000-4000
Connection to localhost 3260 port [tcp/iscsi-target] succeeded!
Connection to localhost 3333 port [tcp/dec-notes] succeeded!
```

The **-z** option can also be used to port-scan a remote host. The following table describes other useful options for this command:

Option	Description
-w	This option is used on the client side to close a connection automatically after a timeout value is reached. For example, **nc -w 30 server 333** closes the connection 30 seconds after it has been established.
-6	Use this option to enable IPv6 connections.
-k	Use this option to keep a server process active, even after the client disconnects. The default behavior is to stop the server process when the client disconnects.

Option	Description
-u	Use UDP connections rather than TCP connections (the default). This is important for correctly testing firewall configurations, as a UDP port might not be blocked while the TCP port is blocked.
-l *port_num*	Enable the **nc** command to act like a server listening to the port number specified by the *port_num* argument.

traceroute

When you send a network packet to a remote system, especially across the Internet, it often needs to go through several gateways before it reaches its destination. You can see the gateways that the packet passes through by executing the **traceroute** command:

```
# traceroute onecoursesource.com
traceroute to onecoursesource.com (38.89.136.109), 30 hops max, 60 byte
packets
 1   10.0.2.2 (10.0.2.2)  0.606 ms   1.132 ms   1.087 ms
 2   b001649-3.jfk01.atlas.cogentco.com (38.104.71.201)
  0.738 ms   0.918 ms   0.838 ms
 3   154.24.42.205 (154.24.42.205)   0.952 ms   0.790 ms 0.906 ms
 4   be2629.ccr41.jfk02.atlas.cogentco.com (154.54.27.66)
  1.699 ms   1.643 ms 1.347 ms
 5   be2148.ccr41.dca01.atlas.cogentco.com (154.54.31.117)
  8.053 ms   7.719 ms   7.639 ms
 6   be2113.ccr42.atl01.atlas.cogentco.com (154.54.24.222)
  18.276 ms 18.418 ms 18.407 ms
 7   be2687.ccr21.iah01.atlas.cogentco.com (154.54.28.70)
  32.861 ms   32.917 ms   32.719 ms
 8   be2291.ccr21.sat01.atlas.cogentco.com (154.54.2.190)
  38.087 ms   38.025 ms   38.076 ms
 9   be2301.ccr21.elp01.atlas.cogentco.com (154.54.5.174)
  48.811 ms   48.952 ms   49.151 ms
10   be2254.ccr21.phx02.atlas.cogentco.com (154.54.7.33)
  57.332 ms 57.281 ms   56.896 ms
11   te2-1.mag02.phx02.atlas.cogentco.com (154.54.1.230)
  56.666 ms 65.279 ms   56.520 ms
12   154.24.18.26 (154.24.18.26)   57.924 ms 58.058 ms   58.032 ms
13   38.122.88.218 (38.122.88.218)   79.306 ms 57.740 ms 57.491 ms
14   onecoursesource.com (38.89.136.109)   58.112 57.884 ms 58.299 ms
```

mtr

If you want a really cool variation of the **traceroute** command (see the "traceroute" subsection in this chapter), install the **mtr** command. This command performs a "**traceroute**-like" operation every second, updating the display with statistics, as demonstrated in Figure 21.3.

```
                        student@student-VirtualBox: ~                    ● ◐ ⊗
 File  Edit  View  Search  Terminal  Help
                        My traceroute  [v0.92]
student-VirtualBox (10.0.2.15)                        2019-01-11T17:08:51-0800
Keys:  Help    Display mode    Restart statistics    Order of fields    quit
                                 Packets                      Pings
 Host                              Loss%   Snt   Last   Avg  Best  Wrst StDev
 1.  _gateway                       0.0%    6     0.3   0.3   0.3   0.4   0.0
 2.  192.168.0.1                    0.0%    6    19.6   6.6   2.9  19.6   6.4
 3.  10.159.0.1                     0.0%    6    11.4  11.8  11.1  12.5   0.5
 4.  68.6.14.98                     0.0%    6   103.1  27.7  12.3 103.1  37.0
 5.  100.120.108.14                 0.0%    6    52.2  40.6  11.5 140.7  51.5
 6.  ae56.bar1.SanDiego1.Level3.net 0.0%    6    73.1  39.0  13.5 102.8  39.1
 7.  4.69.140.102                  83.3%    6    37.2  37.2  37.2  37.2   0.0
 8.  ???
 9.  Cogent-level3-100G.LosAngeles1.L 0.0%  6    17.4  30.8  16.6  97.7  32.8
10.  be3271.ccr41.lax01.atlas.cogentc 0.0%  6   116.0  39.9  18.3 116.0  38.9
11.  be2931.ccr31.phx01.atlas.cogentc 0.0%  6    93.9  56.6  29.3 122.4  41.0
12.  be2929.ccr21.elp01.atlas.cogentc 0.0%  6    43.2  66.0  36.7 200.1  65.8
13.  be2927.ccr41.iah01.atlas.cogentc 0.0%  6    51.3  68.3  51.0 149.5  39.8
14.  be2687.ccr41.atl01.atlas.cogentc 0.0%  6    67.7  84.0  66.7 162.0  38.3
15.  be2112.ccr41.dca01.atlas.cogentc 0.0%  6   150.3  99.4  78.1 150.3  30.3
16.  be2806.ccr41.jfk02.atlas.cogentc 0.0%  6   180.7 116.6  79.9 189.9  53.3
17.  be2896.rcr23.jfk01.atlas.cogentc 0.0%  6   129.6  99.1  80.9 138.9  27.4
18.  be2803.rcr21.b001362-2.jfk01.atl 0.0%  6    82.5 105.8  82.2 221.0  56.4
19.  38.104.71.202                    0.0%  5   120.5  90.0  81.3 120.5  17.1
```

Figure 21.3   The **mtr** Command

arp

The **arp** command is used to view the ARP table or make changes to it. When executed with no arguments, the **arp** command displays the ARP table:

```
# arp
Address          HWtype  HWaddress          Flags Mask      Iface
192.168.1.11     ether   30:3a:64:44:a5:02  C                eth0
```

In the event that a remote system has its network card replaced, it may be necessary to delete an entry from the ARP table. This can be accomplished by using the **-d** option to the **arp** command:

```
# arp -i eth0 -d 192.169.1.11
```

Once the address has been removed from the ARP table, there should be no need to add the new address manually. The next time the local system uses this IP address, it sends a broadcast request on the appropriate network to determine the new MAC address.

nslookup

The **nslookup** command is used to display the results of hostname-to-IP-address lookup (or the reverse). See the "nslookup" section of Chapter 3 for details about this command.

dig

The **dig** command is used to display the results of hostname-to-IP-address lookup (or the reverse). See the "dig" section of Chapter 3 for details about this command.

host

The **host** command is used to display the results of hostname-to-IP-address lookup (or the reverse). See the "host" section of Chapter 3 for details about this command.

whois

The **whois** command is useful for determining which company or person owns a domain. Often the output will also contain information regarding how to contact this organization, although this information might be redacted for privacy reasons:

```
# whois onecoursesource.com | head
    Domain Name: ONECOURSESOURCE.COM
    Registry Domain ID: 116444640_DOMAIN_COM-VRSN
    Registrar WHOIS Server: whois.tucows.com
    Registrar URL: http://www.tucows.com
    Updated Date: 2016-01-15T01:49:45Z
    Creation Date: 2004-04-07T19:45:31Z
    Registry Expiry Date: 2021-04-07T19:45:31Z
    Registrar: Tucows Domains Inc.
    Registrar IANA ID: 69
    Registrar Abuse Contact Email:
```

ping

The **ping** command is used to determine if a remote system can be reached via the network. See the "ping" section of Chapter 3 for details about this command.

nmcli

The **nmcli** command is used to display network settings in order to identify misconfigured interfaces. See the "nmcli" section of Chapter 3 for details about this command.

ip

The **ip** command is used to display network device settings, such as IP address or subnet address, in order to identify misconfigured interfaces. See the "ip" section of Chapter 3 for details about this command.

tracepath

For the exam, you should also be aware of the **tracepath** command—a command very much like the **traceroute** command (see the "traceroute" subsection in this chapter). In fact, the man page for the **tracepath** command does a succinct job of describing the differences:

"It is similar to traceroute, only does not require superuser privileges and has no fancy options."

Storage Monitoring and Configuration

This section focuses on commands and files related to the monitoring and configuration of the storage devices.

iostat

See the "iostat" section of Chapter 4, "Given a scenario, manage storage in a Linux environment," for details regarding using this command.

ioping

The purpose of the **ioping** command is to perform simple latency tests on a disk. Latency is how the delay in data transfer is measured. Typically you want to perform multiple tests on a device, such as the following command, which ends up performing 100 tests on the filesystem for the current directory (the **tail** command was used to limit output):

```
[root@OCS ~]# ioping -c 100 . | tail
4 KiB <<< . (ext4 /dev/sda1): request=96  time=210.6 us
4 KiB <<< . (ext4 /dev/sda1): request=97  time=280.7 us
4 KiB <<< . (ext4 /dev/sda1): request=98  time=249.2 us
4 KiB <<< . (ext4 /dev/sda1): request=99  time=230.1 us
4 KiB <<< . (ext4 /dev/sda1): request=100 time=210.9 us

--- . (ext4 /dev/sda1) ioping statistics ---
99 requests completed in 22.6 ms, 396 KiB read, 4.38 k iops,
   17.1 MiB/s
generated 100 requests in 1.65 min, 400 KiB, 1 iops, 4.04 KiB/s
min/avg/max/mdev = 143.1 us / 228.1 us / 369.1 us / 40.4 us
```

IO Scheduling

Kernel parameters can be used to optimize the IO (Input/Output) scheduler. Several parameters can be set to change the behavior of the scheduler. This section covers the parameters that are important for the Linux+ exam.

To see the current scheduler, view the contents of the **/sys/block/**<*device*>/queue/scheduler file (replace <*device*> with the actual device name). Here's an example:

```
[root@OCS ~]# cat /sys/block/sda/queue/scheduler
[noop] deadline cfq
```

The value within the square brackets is the default. To change this, use the **echo** command, as shown here:

```
[root@OCS ~]# echo "cfq" > /sys/block/sda/queue/scheduler
[root@OCS ~]# cat /sys/block/sda/queue/scheduler
noop deadline [cfq]
```

cfq

The Completely Fair Queuing schedule has a separate queue for each process, and each queue is served in a continuous loop.

noop

This schedule follows the FIFO (First In, First Out) principal.

deadline

This is the standard scheduler. This scheduler creates two queues—a read and a write queue. It also puts a timestamp on each I/O request to ensure that requests are handled in a timely manner.

du

See the "du" section of Chapter 4 for details regarding the use of this command.

df

See the "df" section of Chapter 4 for details regarding the use of this command.

LVM Tools

See the "LVM Tools" section of Chapter 4 for details regarding the use of this command.

fsck

See the "fsck" section of Chapter 4 for details regarding the use of this command.

partprobe

The **partprobe** command is normally only needed in situations where the partition table has changed and the system needs to be informed of these changes. The most common example is when you use the **fdisk** command to change a partition on a device that currently has mounted filesystems. The **fdisk** command attempts to inform the system of changes to the partition table by using a kernel call, which fails because of the "live" filesystem.

To overcome this, just execute the **partprobe** command after exiting the **fdisk** utility.

CPU Monitoring and Configuration

This section focuses on commands and files related to the monitoring and configuration of the CPU.

/proc/cpuinfo

One way of discovering information about CPUs is by viewing the contents of the **/proc/cpuinfo** file. The contents of this file contain detailed information about each CPU, as demonstrated next:

```
[root@OCS ~]# cat /proc/cpuinfo
processor       : 0
vendor_id       : GenuineIntel
cpu family      : 6
model           : 13
```

```
model name      : QEMU Virtual CPU version (cpu64-rhel6)
stepping        : 3
microcode       : 0x1
cpu MHz         : 2666.760
cache size      : 4096 KB
physical id     : 0
siblings        : 1
core id         : 0
cpu cores       : 1
apicid          : 0
initial apicid  : 0
fpu             : yes
fpu_exception   : yes
cpuid level     : 4
wp              : yes
flags           : fpu de pse tsc msr pae mce cx8 apic
   sep mtrr pge mca cmov pse36 clflush mmx fxsr sse sse2
   syscall nx lm nopl pni cx16 hypervisor lahf_lm
bugs            :
bogomips        : 5333.52
clflush size    : 64
cache_alignment : 64
address sizes   : 40 bits physical, 48 bits virtual
power management:

processor       : 1
vendor_id       : GenuineIntel
cpu family      : 6
model           : 13
model name      : QEMU Virtual CPU version (cpu64-rhel6)
stepping        : 3
microcode       : 0x1
cpu MHz         : 2666.760
cache size      : 4096 KB
physical id     : 1
siblings        : 1
core id         : 0
cpu cores       : 1
apicid          : 1
initial apicid  : 1
fpu             : yes
fpu_exception   : yes
```

```
cpuid level     :  4
wp              :  yes
flags           :  fpu de pse tsc msr pae mce cx8 apic sep
  mtrr pge mca cmov pse36 clflush mmx fxsr sse sse2 syscall nx
  lm nopl pni cx16 hypervisor lahf_lm
bugs            :
bogomips        :  5333.52
clflush size    :  64
cache_alignment :  64
address sizes   :  40 bits physical, 48 bits virtual
power management:
```

uptime

The **uptime** command shows how long the system has been running. More importantly
for system monitoring, it provides a quick snapshot of how many users are on the system
and the system load average over the last 1, 5, and 15 minutes:

```
[root@OCS ~]# uptime
 16:16:00 up 1 day,  1:05,  6 users,  load average: 0.60, 0.51, 0.25
```

loadaverage

The **loadaverage** command displays system load average. See the "uptime" subsection
in this chapter.

sar

The **sar** command displays the same information as **iostat**; however, this information is
displayed as it occurs over time (typically at 10 minute intervals). Here's an example:

```
[root@OCS ~]# sar | head
Linux 3.10.0-229.el7.x86_64 (localhost.localdomain)
  09/06/2015      _x86_64_(1 CPU)

12:00:01 AM  CPU    %user   %nic   %syste   %iowai   %stea   %idle
12:10:01 AM  all    0.11    0.00   0.10     0.01     0.00    99.78
12:20:01 AM  all    0.08    0.00   0.07     0.02     0.00    99.84
12:30:01 AM  all    0.10    0.00   0.11     0.01     0.00    99.79
12:40:01 AM  all    0.06    0.00   0.04     0.00     0.00    99.89
12:50:01 AM  all    0.08    0.00   0.04     0.00     0.00    99.88
01:00:02 AM  all    0.10    0.00   0.11     0.01     0.00    99.79
01:10:01 AM  all    0.10    0.00   0.05     0.00     0.00    99.85
```

NOTE: The **sar** utility is not always installed on distributions by default. You may need
to install the sysstat package to have access to this command.

sysctl

See the "IO Scheduling" subsection in this chapter.

Memory Monitoring and Configuration

This section focuses on commands and files related to the monitoring and configuration of RAM (aka, memory).

swapon

To see your currently active swap devices, execute the **swapon** command with the **-s** option:

```
[root@OCS ~]# swapon -s
Filename        Type        Size        Used      Priority
/dev/dm-1       partition   1048568     27100     -1
```

From the output of the **swapon -s** command, you can see the device name (**/dev/dm-1**) that holds the swap filesystem, the size (in bytes) of the swap filesystem, and how much of this space has been used. The priority indicates which swap filesystem should be used first.

If you have an existing swap device, such as a swap file, you can add it to the currently used swap devices by using the **swapon** command. For example, the following command adds the **/var/swap** file:

```
[root@OCS ~]# swapon /var/swap
[root@OCS ~]# swapon -s
Filename        Type        Size        Used      Priority
/dev/dm-1       partition   1048568     27484     -1
/var/swap       file        51192       0         -2
```

To have this swap device enabled each time you boot the system, add a line like the following to the **/etc/fstab** file:

```
/var/swap swap                      swap      defaults        0 0
```

swapoff

If you decide you want to manually remove a device from current swap space, use the **swapoff** command:

```
[root@OCS ~]# swapon -s
Filename        Type        Size        Used      Priority
/dev/dm-1       partition   1048568     27640     -1
/var/swap       file        51192       0         -2
[root@OCS ~]# swapoff /var/swap
[root@OCS ~]# swapon -s
Filename        Type        Size        Used      Priority
/dev/dm-1       partition   048568      27640     -1
```

mkswap

Assuming you have already created a new partition with a tag type of 82 (**/dev/sdb1** in this example), you can format it as a swap device by executing the following command:

```
[root@OCS ~]# mkswap /dev/sdb1
Setting up swapspace version 1, size = 203772 KiB
no label, UUID=039c21dc-c223-43c8-8176-da2f4d508402
```

To create a swap file, you first need to create a large file. This is most easily accomplished by using the **dd** command. The following example demonstrates how to create a 200MB file named **/var/extra_swap** and then enable it as swap space:

```
[root@OCS ~]# dd if=/dev/zero of=/var/extra_swap
  bs=1M count=200
200+0 records in
200+0 records out
209715200 bytes (210 MB) copied, 4.04572 s, 51.8 MB/s
[root@OCS ~]# mkswap /var/extra_swap
mkswap: /var/extra_swap: warning: don't erase bootbits sectors
        on whole disk. Use -f to force.
Setting up swapspace version 1, size = 204796 KiB
no label, UUID=44469984-0a99-45af-94b7-f7e97218d67a
[root@OCS ~]# swapon /var/extra_swap
[root@OCS ~]# swapon -s
```

Filename	Type	Size	Used	Priority
/dev/dm-1	partition	1048568	37664	-1
/dev/sdb1	partition	203768	0	-2
/var/extra_swap	file	204792	0	-3

vmstat

If you need more detail than the **free** command provides, you can execute the **vmstat** command. Consider the output of the following example:

```
[root@OCS ~]# vmstat
procs ----------memory---------- ---swap-- -----io----
  -system-- ------cpu-----
 r  b  swpd  free  buff  cache  si  so  bi  bo  in
  cs us sy id wa st
 2  0     0 776828  1704 2329456   0   0  49  89 115
  120  6  1 93  0  0
```

It is not critical to memorize each line, but you should be familiar with what output the **vmstat** command can provide. For example, in the output of the preceding example is a column labeled "-----io----". Under this column are two subcolumns:

- **bi:** Also called "blocks in," this value represents how many blocks have been received from a block device (like a hard disk).

- **bo:** Also called "blocks out," this value represents how many blocks have been sent to a block device (like a hard disk).

These values can be used to determine whether a performance issue is memory based or disk based. If the **bi** and **bo** values are high, this could mean processes are being blocked on I/O.

Out of Memory Killer

What happens when the system uses too much memory? The Linux kernel has a feature called the OOM Killer (Out of Memory Killer) that will kill processes to clear up memory. Without this feature, the system may grind to a halt and new processes would fail to execute.

The OOM Killer determines which process to kill by assigning a score to each process (called a "badness score") and killing the worst one. Often this is the process using the most memory and, very likely, a key process on a server, like the mail service or the web server.

You can search log files (typically either **/var/log/messages** or **/var/log/kern.log**) to find evidence that the OOM Killer has struck. Error messages will look like the following:

```
host kernel: Out of Memory: Killed process 1466 (httpd).
```

> **NOTE:** There are methods of configurating the OOM Killer (using kernel parameters), but they are beyond the scope of the Linux+ exam. For the exam, you should be aware of the function of the OOM Killer and how you can determine if the OOM Killer has taken action.

free

The **free** command provides a summary of virtual memory (RAM and swap space utilization), as shown next:

```
[root@OCS ~]# free
            total     used    free   shared   buff/cache available
Mem:        3883128  774752  777300  18200    2331076    2784820
Swap:       839676        0  839676
```

The **Mem:** line describes RAM, and the **Swap:** line describes virtual memory. The columns of output are described here:

- **total**: The total amount of memory on the system.
- **used**: The amount of memory currently being used.
- **free**: The amount of memory available.
- **shared**: This is how much memory is used by tmpfs, which is a filesystem that appears to be normal hard disk space but is really storing data in memory.
- **buff/cache**: A buffer or cache is a temporary storage location.
- **available**: How much memory is available for new processes.

The following table describes useful options for this command:

Option	Description
-b or **--bytes**	View information in bytes.
-m or **--mega**	View information in megabytes.
-g or **--giga**	View information in gigabytes.
-h or **--human**	Display in whatever value is appropriate for "human readable sizes."

/proc/meminfo

Most of the data displayed by the **free** and **vmstat** commands actually comes from the **/proc/meminfo** file, which can be viewed directly.

See the "vmstat" and "free" subsections in this chapter for more details regarding these commands.

Buffer Cache Output

The **vmstat** command displays "buffer cache output." The buffer (under the **buff** column) is a value that represents how much RAM is currently in use for disk block caching (especially file metadata). The cache itself contains file contents that are temporarily stored in memory.

See the "vmstat" subsection in this chapter for more details regarding the **vmstat** command.

Lost Root Password

If you forget the root password or come across a system where the root password is unknown, here are the general steps to fixing this problem:

1. Reboot the system to single user mode (see the "Single User Mode" section in this chapter for more details).

2. Mount the root filesystem.

3. Manually edit the **/etc/shadow** file and remove the root password.

4. Reboot the system and log in as the root user (no password required).

5. Set the root password.

NOTE: This step may vary depending on your distribution and other configuration settings. Consult your distro documentation for additional details.

Single User Mode

Single user mode is the operating system level in which only the root user can log in. This level has limited functionality (typically no networking, no graphical user interface, and so on). Administrators use this level to fix system boot problems or to recover the root password.

Details on how to get into single user mode are found in Chapter 4.

## CHAPTER 22

Given a scenario, analyze system processes in order to optimize performance

This chapter provides information and commands concerning the following topics:

Process management

Process states

- Zombie
- Uninterruptible sleep
- Interruptible sleep
- Running
- Priorities

Kill signals

Commands

- **nice**
- **renice**
- **top**
- **time**
- **ps**
- **lsof**
- **pgrep**
- **pkill**
- PIDs

Process Management

A process is a program running on the system. Management tasks include starting, viewing, and pausing processes. This chapter focuses on these topics.

Process States

Each process is assigned a state, depending on the current actions the process is taking (or if it is not taking any actions at all). This section describes the important process states.

Note that the **ps** and **top** commands can display the state a process is currently in. See the "ps" and "top" subsections in this chapter for more details.

Zombie

A zombie process is one that has terminated but still has not been entirely cleared out of memory. Each process is started by another process, creating a "parent-child" relationship. When a child process ends, the parent process is responsible for telling the system that all details about the child process should be removed from memory.

In some rare cases, a child process may end without the parent being aware. This will result in a zombie process. Zombie processes are fairly rare on modern Linux systems and typically indicate a bug that needs to be fixed.

Uninterruptible Sleep

A process that is in an uninterruptible sleep state is one that is performing certain system calls that prevent it from being interrupted (killed). This is fairly rare to see on most modern Linux systems because these system calls are executed very quickly.

If a process stays in uninterruptible sleep for a noticeable period of time, it is likely the result of a bug in the software.

Interruptible Sleep

A process that is in an interruptible sleep state is one that is performing some sort of I/O (Input/Output) operation, such as accessing a hard disk. This is a fairly common state, as I/O operations may take some time.

However, a process that is in interruptible sleep for a long period of time, especially if it is impacting the performance of the system, can indicate a problem. Either the device the process is attempting to access has an error (like a bad data block on a hard disk) or the program has a bug.

Running

A running process is one that currently has operations taking place on the CPU or has operations on the CPU queue.

Priorities

Nice values are used to indicate to the CPU which process has the higher priority for access to the CPU. The values range from –20 (highest priority) to 19 (lowest priority). The default priority of any job created by a user is 0.

See the "nice" subsection in this chapter for details on how to set a different priority when executing a command.

Kill Signals

The **kill** command can be used to change the state of a process, including stopping (killing) it. To stop a process, first determine its process ID or job number and then provide that number as an argument to the **kill** command:

```
[student@OCS ~]$ jobs
 [1]- Running                    sleep 999 &
 [2]+ Running sleep 777 &
[student@OCS ~]$ kill %2
[student@OCS ~]$ jobs
 [1]- Running                    sleep 999 &
 [2]+ Terminated                 sleep 777
[student@OCS ~]$ ps -fe | grep sleep
 student 17846 12540 0 14:30 pts/2            00:00:00 sleep 999
 student 17853 12540 0 14:31 pts/2            00:00:00 grep
  --color=auto sleep
[student@OCS ~]$ kill 17846
[student@OCS ~]$ ps -fe | grep sleep
 student 17856 12540 0 14:31 pts/2            00:00:00 grep
  --color=auto sleep
 [1]+ Terminated                 sleep 999
```

The following table details some important options for the **kill** command:

Option	Description
-9	Force kill. Used when the process doesn't exit when a regular kill command is executed.
-l	Used to provide a list of other numeric values that can be used to send different kill signals to a process.

A signal is a special code to indicate what sort of operation the process should take. Signals are used to pause a process, stop a process, restart a process, or some other operation.

The following table details some important signals for the **kill** command:

Signal	Description
SIGHUP	Also called signal 1; used to simulate a terminal disconnect (like if a remote connection was lost). Typically a SIGHUP will cause a program to terminate, but this can be avoided by using the **nohup** command. See Chapter 12, "Given a scenario, automate and schedule jobs," for details regarding the **nohup** command.
SIGINT	Also called signal 2; used to simulate a **Ctrl-c** operation. See the "Ctrl-c" subsection in Chapter 12 for details regarding the **Ctrl-c** operation.
SIGKILL	Also called signal 9; used to force the termination of a process.

Signal	Description
SIGTERM	Also called signal 15; used to terminate a process normally. This is the default signal of the **kill** command.
SIGTSTP	Also called signal 20; used to stop (pause) a program, similar to the **Ctlr-z** operation. See the "Ctrl-z" subsection in Chapter 12 for details regarding the **Ctrl-z** operation.

Commands

Several Linux commands can be used to control processes. This section covers these commands.

nice

To specify a different nice value than the default, execute the job via the **nice** command:

```
[student@OCS ~]$ nice -n 5 firefox
```

Note that regular users cannot assign a negative nice value. These values can only be used by the root user. There are no additional useful options besides the **-n** option.

To view the nice value of a process, use the **-o** option with the **ps** command and include a value of "nice":

```
[student@OCS ~] ps -o nice,pid,cmd
NI PID CMD
0 23865 -bash
0 27969 ps -o nice,pid,cmd
```

renice

Use the **renice** command to change the nice value of an existing job. Here is an example:

```
[student@OCS ~] ps -o nice,pid,cmd
NI PID CMD
0 23865 -bash
5 28235 sleep 999
0 28261 ps -o nice,pid,cmd
[student@OCS ~] renice -n 10 -p 28235
28235 (process ID) old priority 5, new priority 10
[student@OCS ~] ps -o nice,pid,cmd
NI PID CMD
0 23865 -bash
10 28235 sleep 999
0 28261 ps -o nice,pid,cmd
```

NOTE: Regular (non-root) users can only change the priority of an existing process to a lower priority. Only the root user can alter a process priority to a higher priority.

The following table details some important options for the **renice** command:

Option	Description
-g *group*	Change the priority of all files owned by *group*.
-u *user*	Change the priority of all files owned by *user*.

top

The **top** command displays process information that is updated on a regular basis (by default, every 2 seconds). The first half of the output of the **top** command contains overall information, whereas the second half displays a select list of processes (by default, the processes that are using the CPU the most).

Figure 22.1 shows some typical output of the **top** command.

```
top - 16:09:10 up 2 days,  3:07,  2 users,  load average: 0.00, 0.07, 0.12
Tasks: 119 total,   2 running, 117 sleeping,   0 stopped,   0 zombie
%Cpu(s):  1.3 us,  1.0 sy,  0.0 ni, 97.0 id,  0.3 wa,  0.0 hi,  0.3 si,  0.0 st
KiB Mem:   4048292 total,  3832140 used,   216152 free,   356468 buffers
KiB Swap:        0 total,        0 used,        0 free.  1610568 cached Mem

  PID USER      PR  NI    VIRT    RES    SHR S %CPU %MEM     TIME+ COMMAND
26159 root      20   0 2461400 1.243g  24040 S  2.7 32.2  44:59.94 java
  965 root       0 -20       0      0      0 S  0.3  0.0   0:35.58 loop0
27545 nobody    20   0   87524   3616    892 S  0.3  0.1   0:05.32 nginx
28770 root      20   0   12824    940    776 S  0.3  0.0   0:14.39 ping
    1 root      20   0   33604   2952   1476 S  0.0  0.1   0:00.98 init
    2 root      20   0       0      0      0 S  0.0  0.0   0:00.00 kthreadd
    3 root      20   0       0      0      0 S  0.0  0.0   0:05.72 ksoftirqd/0
    5 root       0 -20       0      0      0 S  0.0  0.0   0:00.00 kworker/0:0H
    7 root      20   0       0      0      0 S  0.0  0.0   1:12.43 rcu_sched
    8 root      20   0       0      0      0 R  0.0  0.0   1:39.49 rcuos/0
    9 root      20   0       0      0      0 S  0.0  0.0   0:00.00 rcu_bh
   10 root      20   0       0      0      0 S  0.0  0.0   0:00.00 rcuob/0
   11 root      rt   0       0      0      0 S  0.0  0.0   0:00.00 migration/0
```

Figure 22.1   The **top** Command Output

The following table describes the output displayed in Figure 22.1:

Output	Description
First line	Output derived from the **uptime** command.
Second line	A summary of processes running on the system.
Third line	CPU statistics since the last time top data was refreshed.
Fourth line	Physical memory statics. (Note: Type **E** while in the **top** command to change the value from kilobytes to another value.)
Fifth line	Virtual memory statics.
Remaining lines	A list of processes and associated information.

While the **top** command is running, you can use interactive commands to perform actions such as change display values, reorder the process list, and kill processes.

These interactive commands are single characters. The more important interactive commands are provided in the following table:

Command	Description
h	Help. Display a summary of interactive commands.
E	Change the default value from kilobytes to another value; values "cycle" around back to kilobytes.
Z	Toggle color highlighting on; use lowercase z to toggle color and non-color.
B	Toggle bold on and off.
< >	Move the sort column to the left (<) or the right (>).
s	Set the update value to a different value than the default of 2 seconds.
k	Kill a process by providing a process ID (PID).
q	Quit the **top** command.

The **top** command also supports several command-line options, including the following:

Option	Description
-d	Set the time between data refresh.
-n *number*	Maximum number of data refreshes until the **top** command exits.
-u *username*	Display only processes owned by *username*.

time

The **time** command is used to determine how long it takes to run a command. Here is an example:

```
[student@OCS ~]$ time wget www.onecoursesource.com/index.php
--2019-05-04 05:17:29--  http://www.onecoursesource.com/index.php
Resolving www.onecoursesource.com (www.onecoursesource.com)
   ... 38.89.136.109
Connecting to www.onecoursesource.com
   (www.onecoursesource.com)|38.89.136.109|:80... connected.
HTTP request sent, awaiting response... 200 OK
Length: unspecified [text/html]
Saving to: 'index.php'


index.php       [ <=>  ]   12.25K  --.-KB/s    in 0s


2019-05-04 05:17:29 (97.0 MB/s) - 'index.php' saved [12548]



real    0m0.404s
user    0m0.000s
sys     0m0.000s
```

The output includes how much overall time elapsed (the "real" value), how much CPU time was taken by user processes (the "user" value), and how much CPU time was taken by system processes (the "sys" value).

ps

The **ps** command is used to list processes that are running on the system. With no arguments, the command will list any child process of the current shell as well as the BASH shell itself, as shown here:

```
[student@OCS ~]$ ps
     PID TTY          TIME CMD
18360 pts/0        00:00:00 bash
18691 pts/0        00:00:00 ps
```

The **ps** command is unusual in that it supports older BSD options that normally don't have a hyphen (-) character in front of them.

The following table details some important options for the **ps** command:

Option	Description
-e	Display all processes running on the system; the BSD method of **ps ax** can also be used.
-f	Display full information (additional information about each process).
-u *username*	Display all processes owned by *username*.
-forest	Provide a process hierarchy tree.

lsof

The **lsof** command is used to list open files. When used with no arguments, it will list all the open files for the OS, as shown next:

```
[root@OCS ~]# lsof | wc -l
25466
```

A more useful technique would be to list all files related to open network connections:

```
[root@OCS ~]# lsof -i
COMMAND    PID    USER      FD    TYPE    DEVICE    SIZE/OFF   NODE    NAME
avahi-dae  674    avahi     13u   IPv4    15730                0t0
                  UDP    *:mdns
avahi-dae  674    avahi     14u   IPv4    15731                0t0
                  UDP    *:49932
sshd       1411   root      3u    IPv4    18771                0t0
                  TCP    *:ssh (LISTEN)
sshd       1411   root      4u    IPv6    18779                0t0
                  TCP    *:ssh (LISTEN)
```

```
master     2632     root      14u     IPv4      20790        0t0
               TCP     localhost:smtp (LISTEN)
master     2632     root      15u     IPv6      20791        0t0
               TCP     localhost:smtp (LISTEN)
dnsmasq    2739     nobody    3u      IPv4      21518        0t0
               UDP       *:bootps
dnsmasq    2739     nobody    5u      IPv4      21525        0t0
               UDP     192.168.122.1:domain
dnsmasq    2739     nobody    6u      IPv4      21526        0t0
               TCP     192.168.122.1:domain (LISTEN)
cupsd      4099     root      12u     IPv6      564510       0t0
               TCP     localhost:ipp (LISTEN)
cupsd      4099     root      13u     IPv4      564511       0t0
               TCP     localhost:ipp (LISTEN)
dhclient   26133    root      6u      IPv4      1151444      0t0
               UDP       *:bootpc
dhclient   26133    root      20u     IPv4      1151433      0t0
               UDP       *:14638
dhclient   26133    root      21u     IPv6      1151434      0t0
               UDP       *:47997
```

The following table describes common options for the **lsof** command:

Option	Description
-i	Match the Internet address; could also be used to display based on IP version (**-i4** or **-i6**) or port (**-i TCP:80**), or to display all open connections.
-u *user*	List files opened by *user*.
-p *pid*	List files opened by the process with a process ID of *pid*.

pgrep

Typically you utilize a combination of the **ps** and **grep** commands to display specific processes, like so:

```
[student@OCS ~]$ ps -e | grep sleep
25194 pts/0 00:00:00 sleep
```

However, the **pgrep** command can provide similar functionality:

```
[student@OCS ~]$ pgrep sleep
25194
```

The following table details some important options for the **pgrep** command:

Option	Description
-G *name*	Match processes by group name.
-l	Display process name and PID.
-n	Display most recently started processes first.
-u *name*	Match processes by user *name*.

pkill

When sending signals to a process using the **kill** command, you indicate which process by providing a process ID (PID). With the **pkill** command, you can provide a process name, a username, or another method to indicate which process or processes to send a signal to. For example, the following will send a kill signal to all processes owned by the user sarah:

```
[student@OCS ~]$ pkill -u sarah
```

The following table details some important options for the **pkill** command:

Option	Description
-G *name*	Match processes by group *name*
-u *name*	Match processes by user *name*

PIDs

A process ID (PID) is a unique number assigned to each process on a system. This number is used to control the process when using commands like **kill**, **nice**, and **renice**.

To view PIDs, use commands like **ps**, **pgrep**, and **top**. See the "ps," "pgrep," and "top" sections in this chapter for more details.

To see examples of PIDs being used to control processes, see the "Kill Signals," "nice," "renice," and "pkill" sections in this chapter.

## CHAPTER 23

Given a scenario, analyze and troubleshoot user issues

This chapter provides information and commands concerning the following topics:

Permissions

- File
- Directory

Access

- Local
- Remote

Authentication

- Local
- External
- Policy violations

File creation

- Quotas
- Storage
- Inode exhaustion
- Immutable files

Insufficient privileges for authorization

- SELinux violations

Environment and shell issues

NOTE: This chapter focuses on tools and techniques to troubleshoot user issues. In many cases, the core knowledge of the content has been covered in other chapters. Therefore, the focus in this chapter will solely be on the troubleshooting techniques, and references will be provided for more details about specific topics.

Permissions

When a user attempts to access a file or directory, the permissions of that object will determine if the access is permitted. This section covers how to handle problems regarding file and directory permissions.

See Chapter 15, "Given a scenario, apply or acquire the appropriate user and/or group permissions and ownership," for additional details about permissions.

File

Sometimes it can be really frustrating to determine why you cannot access a file or directory. For example, consider the following command:

```
bob@OCS:~# cp sample /etc/skel
cp: cannot create regular file '/etc/skel/sample1':
  Permission denied
```

What is the problem? Keep in mind that several permissions are checked, like the read permission on the **sample** file, the execute permissions on the **/**, **etc**, and **skel** directories, as well as the write permissions on the **skel** directory.

To discover the error, first look closely at the output of the error message. In this case, the problem seems to be with creating the file in the **/etc/skel** directory, not with the **sample** file itself (which would have resulted in an error like "cannot open 'sample1' for reading").

Next, determine if you can get into all of the directories by either looking at the permissions for each one or using the **cd** command to move into each directory. Lastly, look for the write permission on the destination directory.

Directory

Directory permissions can be tricky, making it difficult to troubleshoot access to a directory. For example, consider the following situation:

```
[julia@OCS mydata]$ ls -l info
-rwxrwxrwx 1 julia julia 240 Feb  4 22:16 info
[julia@OCS mydata]$ rm info
rm: cannot remove 'info': Permission denied
```

It doesn't seem to make any sense that the julia user isn't able to delete the **info** file. The file is owned by the julia account, and the julia account has all permissions on the file. The problem here is that the permission required to delete a file is the write permission in the directory the file is in, as shown here:

```
[julia@OCS mydata]$ ls -ld .
dr-xrwxr-x 2 julia julia 4096 Feb  4 22:16 .
[julia@OCS mydata]$ chmod u+w .
[julia@OCS mydata]$ ls -ld .
drwxrwxr-x 2 julia julia 4096 Feb  4 22:16 .
[julia@OCS mydata]$ rm info
```

Whenever you deal with permission problems, first ask yourself what permissions you need to complete this task. Consider writing out the command using a full path. For example, in this case, instead of thinking about the **rm info** command, think about the **rm /home/julia/data/info** command. Review the permissions on each directory to determine where the problem might be.

Access

Two components must be considered when a user attempts to access a system, such as when they attempt to log in: the access itself and authentication. This section focuses on issues that may arise when a user attempts to access to system, while the "Authentication" section focuses on issues that arise when a user account is authenticated.

Local

The ability to access a system locally refers to physically sitting down in front of the system and attempting to log in directly. Compared to remote access, relatively few problems can arise with local access:

- Hardware malfunctions.

- Entering incorrect user account information. Consult log files to discover these sorts of errors.

- PAM restrictions (see Chapter 16, "Given a scenario, configure and implement appropriate access and authentication methods," for more information about PAM).

Remote

Remote access is when a user attempts to connect to a system via the network. In addition to the problems described in the previous section, "Local," other problems with remote access can include the following:

- **TCP Wrapper rules**: See Chapter 16 for more information about TCP Wrappers.

- **Misconfiguration of the service**: For example, if the user is connecting via SSH, the SSH server may be misconfigured or not even running.

- **Service-based security restrictions**: Each service typically has its own security features. For example, SSH servers can be configured to not allow the root user to log in directly (see Chapter 16 for more information about SSH service configuration).

- **Network-base issue**: If the remote system isn't accessible via the network, the user won't be able to access it due to this network issue.

- **Firewall restrictions**: Firewalls can block access to remote systems, making it impossible for a user to access the system via the network (see Chapter 19, "Given a scenario, implement and configure Linux firewalls," for more information about firewalls).

Authentication

The process of authentication is related to determining whether a user is permitted to access a system. For example, is the user providing the correct credentials, such as the correct password? Or, is the user logging in during the correct time and day? This section focuses on how to determine whether a problem arises during the authentication process.

Local

Local user authentication typically relies on password information stored in the **/etc/shadow** file. A user could have local authentication issues for the following reason:

- The user forgot the account password.
- The account has passed its expiration date.
- The account has password aging restrictions and the user has violated these restrictions. For example, an account can be configured to require a new password every 60 days. If the user doesn't change the account password within this timeframe, the account can be locked out.
- An administrator may have manually locked a user account.
- A PAM restriction may limit user authentication.

Here are some helpful hints at troubleshooting local authentication issues:

- Check the security log file for error messages.
- Review the user account settings in the **/etc/shadow** file. See Chapter 8, "Given a scenario, manage users and groups," for details about this file.
- Review PAM restrictions. See Chapter 16 for more information about PAM.

External

External authentication is handled by a service like the Lightweight Directory Access Protocol (LDAP). See Chapter 16 for more information about LDAP.

Policy Violations

Policies are typically defined by PAM. See Chapter 16 for more information about PAM.

File Creation

Users may be limited in their ability to create files because of several different issues. This section focuses on the primary reasons users may be blocked from creating files. Note that one of the most common reasons for this problem, permissions, was already covered in the "Permissions" section of this chapter.

Quotas

If quotas are enabled on a filesystem, users may be limited in their ability to create new files. To determine if a quota is the cause of a problem, consider using the following commands:

- System administrators should use the **repquota** command to display quotas for all users on a filesystem.
- Regular users should use the **quota** command to display quota limitations for their own accounts.

See Chapter 8 for more information about quotas.

Storage

If a filesystem is full, users won't be able to create new files in the filesystem. The **df** command is useful for troubleshooting this problem. See Chapter 4, "Given a scenario, manage storage in a Linux environment," for more information about displaying filesystem usage.

Inode Exhaustion

Each file must have a unique inode, which is used to keep track of file metadata. Each filesystem has a limited number of inodes. Normally this limit is very high, and running out of inodes is rare, but if a filesystem has many small files, then it is possible this might pose a problem.

The **--inodes** option to the **df** command is useful in troubleshooting this problem:

```
[student@OCS ~]$ df --inodes | grep /tmp
tmpfs             505992      602    505390     1% /tmp
```

Immutable Files

File attributes affect how users access files and directories. For example, a useful file attribute is one that will make a file "immutable." An immutable file is completely unchangeable; it cannot be deleted or modified by anyone, including the root user. To make a file immutable, use the **chattr** command, as shown next:

```
root@localhost:~# chattr +i /etc/passwd
```

Note that now no user can change the **/etc/passwd** file, which means no new users can be added to the system (and existing users cannot be removed).

To see the attributes for a file, use the **lsattr** command:

```
root@OCS:~# lsattr /etc/passwd
----i--------e-- /etc/passwd
```

The hyphen (-) characters indicate file attributes that are not set. A complete list of attributes can be found in the man page for the **chattr** command. The following table describes the file attributes that are important for system security:

Attribute	Description
a	Append only mode; only allow new data to be placed in the file.
A	Disable modifying the access timestamp. This timestamp can be important for security reasons to determine when key system files have been accessed. However, for noncritical files, disabling the access time can make the system faster because it results in fewer hard drive writes.
e	Extent format, which allows for key features such as SELinux (discussed later in this chapter).
i	Immutable; file cannot be deleted or modified.
u	Undeletable; file cannot be deleted, but contents can be modified.

To remote the immutable file attribute, use the following command:

```
root@OCS:~# chattr -i /etc/passwd
root@OCS:~# lsattr /etc/passwd
-------------e-- /etc/passwd
```

Important options for the **chattr** command include the following:

- **-R**: Recursively apply changes to an entire directory structure.
- **-V**: Verbose. Produce output demonstrating the changes made.

Insufficient Privileges for Authorization

A couple primary facilities can deny authorization to users due to privilege-based restrictions: PAM and SELinux. PAM is covered in Chapter 16. Chapter 15 provides detailed information about SELinux and how to determine if an SELinux violation has occurred.

Environment and Shell Issues

The configuration of a user account can have an impact on how the account functions. One of the primary considerations is how the user's shell variables are configured. See Chapter 25, "Given a scenario, deploy and execute basic BASH scripts," for details about shell variables. Note that you need to pay special attention to the PATH variable, as this affects which commands a user can execute without providing a complete pathname.

## CHAPTER 24

Given a scenario, analyze and troubleshoot application and hardware issues

This chapter provides information and commands concerning the following topics:

SELinux context violations

Storage

- Degraded storage
- Missing devices
- Missing mount point
- Performance issues
- Resource exhaustion
- Adapters
    - SCSI
    - RAID
    - SATA
    - HBA
- Storage integrity (bad blocks)

Firewall

- Restrictive ACLs
- Blocked ports
- Blocked protocols

Permission

- Ownership
- Executables
- Inheritance
- Service accounts
- Group memberships

Dependencies

- Patching
- Update issues
- Versioning

- Libraries
- Repositories

Troubleshooting additional hardware issues

- Memory
- Printers
- Video
- GPU drivers
- Communications ports
- USB
- Keyboard mapping
- Hardware or software compatibility issues
- Commands
    - **dmidecode**
    - **lshw**

SELinux Context Violations

See Chapter 15, "Given a scenario, apply or acquire the appropriate user and/or group permissions and ownership," for details regarding SELinux context violations.

Storage

This section discusses the concepts of troubleshooting storage devices. You will be introduced to common storage issues and learn about where to look for the cause of a problem.

Degraded Storage

Over time, storage devices will degrade and (sometimes suddenly) fail. To determine if there are any problems with a drive before it fails, consider the following proactive measures:

- **Search for bad blocks**: An increase of bad blocks on a device can indicate degraded storage. See the "Bad Blocks" section in this chapter for more details.

- **Use the SMART tool**: Self-Monitoring, Analysis, and Reporting Technology (SMART) is a tool available on hard disks and SSD (solid state drives) that monitors the health of a drive. Not all disks support this utility, but most modern ones do. The **smartctl** command is used to display information about the hard disk. For example, to perform a health check, try the **smartctl -HH** *device_name* command.

Missing Devices

A storage device may be missing for several reasons, such as the following:

- If it is a removable device, it may not be attached (or not attached properly).
- If it is a removable device, it may need to be powered on.
- If it is an internal device, it may have a loose connection. This can often happen if the system is transported.
- It may have just broken.
- Storage devices also need kernel adapters (aka, kernel modules), and the modules might not be loaded into memory.

Missing Mount Point

When you're mounting a partition or volume, the mount point (aka, mount directory) must already exist. If it doesn't, the following error will appear (with **/data** replaced by your mount point):

```
mount: mount point /data does not exist
```

To resolve this, create the mount point:

```
root@OCS:~# mkdir /data
```

Performance Issues

A storage device's performance can be tested by using the **dd** command:

```
root@OCS:~# dd if=/dev/zero of=/var/test bs=1G
  count=1 oflag=direct
1+0 records in
1+0 records out
1073741824 bytes (1.1 GB) copied, 42.474 s, 25.3 MB/s
```

The **dd** command is used to create large files. The advantage of this command is that it displays exactly how long it took to create the file, giving you a good idea of the performance of the storage device. You can run this command at different times (when the system is busy, when it is not, different times of days, and so on) to establish baselines.

Performance can also be related to using the cache. To activate the cache, execute the following command:

```
hdparm -W1 /dev/sda
```

To deactivate the cache, use the following command:

```
hdparm -W0 /dev/sda
```

Consider running the **dd** command in both situations (cache on and off) to see how it affects performance.

Resource Exhaustion

For storage devices, resource exhaustion can mean one of the following:

- The device has no more available space to create more files. The **df** command can determine if this is a problem. See the "df" section in Chapter 4, "Given a scenario, manage storage in a Linux environment," to learn more about this command.

- The device is out of inodes. Every file needs an inode to store metadata. If there are no more inodes left, no new files can be created. The **df** command can determine if this is a problem. See the "df" section in Chapter 4 and the "inodes" subsection in Chapter 9, "Given a scenario, create, modify, and redirect files," to learn more about this command and inodes.

- The user is limited by disk quotas. See the "Quotas" section in Chapter 8, "Given a scenario, manage users and groups," to learn about disk quotas.

Adapters

In Linux terms, an adapter is a kernel module that is used to access a device. To see this information, use the **lspci -v** command (the **tail** command was used in this case because the SATA drive was the last device listed):

```
root@OCS:~# lspci -v | tail -13
00:0d.0 SATA controller: Intel Corporation 82801HM/HEM
  (ICH8M/ICH8
M-E) SATA Controller [AHCI mode] (rev 02) (prog-if 01 [AHCI 1.0])
        Flags: bus master, fast devsel, latency 64, IRQ 21
        I/O ports at d040 [size=8]
        I/O ports at 0000
        I/O ports at d050 [size=8]
        I/O ports at 0000
        I/O ports at d060 [size=16]
        Memory at f080a000 (32-bit, non-prefetchable) [size=8K]
        Capabilities: [70] Power Management version 3
        Capabilities: [a8] SATA HBA v1.0
        Kernel driver in use: ahci
        Kernel modules: ahci
```

Note the line that lists the "Kernel driver" as "ahci." This is the kernel module used for this SATA device. See Chapter 2, "Given a scenario, install, configure, and monitor kernel modules," for more information about kernel modules.

SCSI

Small Computer System Interface (SCSI) is a device type that can be used to attach storage devices to a system. See the "Adapters" subsection in this chapter to learn more about viewing the device driver for SCSI devices.

RAID

Redundant Array of Independent Disks (RAID) is a device type that can be used to attach storage devices to a system. See the "Adapters" subsection in this chapter to learn more about viewing the device driver for RAID devices. To learn more about RAID devices, see the "mdadm" section in Chapter 4.

SATA

Serial AT Attachment (SATA) is a device type that can be used to attach storage devices to a system. See the "Adapters" subsection in this chapter to learn more about viewing the device driver for SATA devices.

HBA

Host Bus Adapter (HBA) is a device type that can be used to attach a variety of devices to a system. The most common storage devices attached to a system via HBA are Fibre Channel (FC) and Serial-Attached SCSI (SAS) See the "Adapters" subsection in this chapter to learn more about viewing the device driver for HBA devices.

Storage Integrity

This section introduces how bad blocks can be scanned for as they can affect the integrity of a storage device.

Bad Blocks

To test for bad blocks, use the **badblocks** command:

```
root@OCS:~# badblocks -v /dev/sdb1
Checking blocks 0 to 1047551
Checking for bad blocks (read-only test): done

Pass completed, 0 bad blocks found. (0/0/0 errors)
```

The SMART tool can also be used to find bad blocks. See the "Degraded Storage" subsection in this chapter for more information on SMART.

Firewall

When you're troubleshooting access to a system that resides behind a firewall, it is important to know how to seek out the rules that block access to the system. This section focuses on some of these rules you may see questions on during the Linux+ exam.

> **NOTE:** A more detailed discussion of firewalls can be found in Chapter 19, "Given a scenario, implement and configure Linux firewalls." The focus of this section is only troubleshooting access issues due to firewall restrictions.

Restrictive ACLs

If access to a remote system is being blocked by a restrictive firewall ACL, it will be an ACL that has one of the following targets:

- drop
- reject

It is important to note that if a "reject" target ACL is blocking access, then some sort of "denied access" response should be returned to the origin of the packet. If a "drop" target ACL is blocking access, no response will be returned at all.

Blocked Ports

To determine if a packet is being blocked based on its protocol, you should first determine which port is being used. Normally, services will use "standard" ports (which are defined in the **/etc/services** file), but both client and server software can be configured to use non-standard ports. Investigate this first, and once you have determined the port number being used, look for a rule that blocks this port number.

In the following example, you can see that any incoming packet destined for port 23 (which is normally for the telnet service) will be dropped:

```
root@OCS:~# iptables -L INPUT
Chain INPUT (policy ACCEPT)
target     prot opt source               destination
DROP       icmp --  anywhere             anywhere
DROP       tcp  --  anywhere             anywhere    tcp dpt:telnet
```

Blocked Protocols

To determine if a packet is being blocked based on its protocol, you should first determine what the protocol is. Firewall rules can be applied to protocols like ICMP, TCP, and UDP, which would include many different network communications (see "/etc/protocols" for a list of all protocols that could be blocked). When you're viewing firewall rules, a ACL that blocks packets using a drop target based on ICMP would look like the following:

```
root@OCS:~# iptables -L INPUT
Chain INPUT (policy ACCEPT)
target     prot opt source               destination
DROP       icmp --  anywhere             anywhere
```

Permission

File and directory permissions often plague users who may struggle to understand how these permissions can affect access to these objects. This section explores some of these concepts. Also see Chapter 15 for more information regarding permissions.

Ownership

File and directory ownership plays a critical role in permissions. Consider the following:

- The user owner of a file or directory has the ability to change permissions. See the "User, Group, Other" section in Chapter 15 for details.

- The user owner also has a set of permissions separate from all other users. See the "User, Group, Other" section in Chapter 15 for details.

- Group owners have a set of permissions that other users don't share. See the "User, Group, Other" section in Chapter 15 for details.

- User and group ownerships can be modified. See the "chown" and "chgrp" sections in Chapter 15 for details.

Executables

An executable is a file that has the execute permission set. This is critical for a file to be run like a program. See the "Directory and File Permissions" section of Chapter 25, "Given a scenario, deploy and execute basic BASH scripts," for more details.

Inheritance

See the "Inheritance" section in Chapter 15 for details.

Service Accounts

See the "Service" section in Chapter 15 for details.

Group Memberships

See the "Ownership" subsection in this chapter for information as to how group memberships affect permission.

Dependencies

One of the biggest issues when dealing with software packages is dependencies. Fortunately, tools such as the **yum** and **apt** commands handle dependency issues. However, in some situations, manual methods must be used that don't allow for taking advantage of these automated tools.

This section focuses on some of the concepts related to package dependencies you should be aware of for the Linux+ exam.

Patching

Patching is the process of updating software. Typically, organizations follow a patching policy, which indicates how often patching should be performed and in what manner. For example, a policy could require nightly patching on all systems. Or, a policy could require monthly patching using a "rolling method" in which some systems (typically non production systems) are patched first and other systems are patched after some initial testing of the newly patched systems.

Update Issues

Several issues may present themselves when you try to update a system or a specific software package, including the following:

- Access to the repository may not be available.

- You may not have the rights to install an update. Normally this requires root access.

- The update may contain bugs that end up breaking the software.

- The update may contain bugs that end up breaking the entire operating system.

- The update may overwrite previous configuration files. Back up all configuration data before upgrading to avoid this issue.

- The update may overwrite existing data files or databases. Back up all data files before upgrading to avoid this issue.

- An update may cause the program to behave differently. Make sure users are made aware of changes that will occur in the program.

Versioning

When you display a software package, the version of the software is included in the package name. Here's an example:

```
libXau-devel-1.0.8-2.fc32.x86_64.rpm
```

The version of the previous package is "1.0.8-2.fc32". The package name is important because you don't want to attempt to install an older package than the one that currently exists on the system.

Libraries

See the "Shared Libraries" section of Chapter 7, "Given a scenario, conduct software installations, configurations, updates, and removals," for information about libraries.

Repositories

See the "Repositories" section of Chapter 7 for information about repositories.

Troubleshooting Additional Hardware Issues

There are a variety of troubleshooting topics related to hardware devices. This section reviews some of the basics you should consider when working with these devices.

Memory

Most of the useful information regarding troubleshooting memory issues is covered earlier in this chapter and in the "Memory Monitoring and Configuration" section of Chapter 21, "Given a scenario, analyze system properties and remediate accordingly." Beyond that information, always consider compatibility issues with any hardware, including memory sticks.

Printers

The printer service (CUPS) was covered in Chapter 13, "Explain the use and operation of Linux devices." Typically, your biggest issue regarding troubleshooting new printers will be related to printer drivers (consult the cups.org website for new drivers).

Other common issues include the following:

- **Paper jams**: Read the user manual for the printer to learn how to clear paper from the printer.

- **Disabled printer queue**: Consult Chapter 16, "Given a scenario, configure and implement appropriate access and authentication methods," to learn how to change the printer state.

- **Invalid print jobs**: Consult Chapter 16 to learn how to remove print jobs from the print queue.

Video

Normally, video hardware issues stem from broken hardware devices (like the monitor, video card, or monitor cables) or compatibility issues, which often arise when newer hardware is used. For compatibility issues, consult the website of your X server for possible new drivers.

GPU Drivers

A graphics processing unit (GPU) is a device used to process data related to the graphics card (aka, video card). Typically, these devices will need a driver in order to work correctly. This is especially true for any newer GPU. Consult the website of the GPU vendor for details.

A complete discussion of GPU management is beyond the scope of the exam. If you want to learn more about this topic, consider the following site:

https://www.kernel.org/doc/html/v4.20/gpu/index.html

(Note: Replace "v4.20" with the current version of the kernel on your system for the more accurate documentation.)

Communications Ports

Often the term *communication ports* refers to network ports used by services, but because this topic is related to hardware troubleshooting, it most likely refers to I/O ports or "comm ports." I/O ports are used for communication with devices like your keyboard and mouse as well as terminal devices.

To display your I/O ports, view the **/proc/ioports** file (in the following example, the **head** command was just used to reduce the large amount of output):

```
[root@OCS ~]# cat /proc/ioports | head
0000-001f : dma1
0020-0021 : pic1
```

```
0040-0043 : timer0
0050-0053 : timer1
0060-0060 : keyboard
0064-0064 : keyboard
0070-0071 : rtc0
0080-008f : dma page reg
00a0-00a1 : pic2
00c0-00df : dma2
```

Another technique to display hardware information is to execute the **lsdev** command (in the following example, the **head** command was just used to reduce the large amount of output):

```
[root@OCS ~]# lsdev | head
Device              DMA   IRQ  I/O Ports
-----------------------------------------------
0000:00:01.1                  0170-0177 01f0-01f7 0376-0376
  03f6-03f6 d000-d00f
0000:00:03.0                  d010-d017
0000:00:04.0                  d020-d03f
0000:00:05.0                  d100-d1ff d200-d23f
0000:00:0d.0                  d240-d247 d250-d257 d260-d26f
ACPI                          4000-4003 4004-4005 4008-400b 4020-4021
acpi                      9
```

The primary focus of the **lsdev** command is to display hardware dma, ioports, and interrupts. This command gathers the information from the **/proc/dma**, **/proc/ioports**, and **/proc/interrupts** files and displays the information in an easy-to-read format.

USB

To view information about USB devices attached to your system, execute the **lsusb** command. If no devices are currently attached, the output should look like the following:

```
[root@OCS ~]# lsusb
Bus 001 Device 001: ID 1d6b:0001 Linux Foundation 1.1 root hub
```

The previous output shows the root hub, which is essentially the USB ports. Even if you have multiple USB ports, you probably will only see one root hub. In some cases, you may see more than one; for example, if you have both USB 2.0 and USB 1.1 ports, each set of ports might show up as a root hub.

If you attached a device to your system, the output of the **lsusb** command would look something like the following:

```
[root@OCS ~]# lsusb
Bus 001 Device 001: ID 1d6b:0001 Linux Foundation 1.1 root hub
Bus 001 Device 005: ID 058f:6387 Alcor Micro Corp. Flash Drive
```

The **-v** option shows verbose information, and the -d option is used to pass the vendor:product numbers as arguments to limit the verbose output to just a single USB device (in the following example, the **head** command was just used to reduce the large amount of output):

```
[root@OCS ~]# lsusb -v -d 058f:6387


Bus 001 Device 005: ID 058f:6387 Alcor Micro Corp. Flash Drive
Device Descriptor:
    bLength                 18
    bDescriptorType          1
    bcdUSB                1.10
    bDeviceClass             0 (Defined at Interface level)
    bDeviceSubClass          0
    bDeviceProtocol          0
    bMaxPacketSize0         64
```

Whenever you add any hardware device to the system, it can be helpful to view the contents of the **/var/log/messages** file on Red Hat–based systems (or the **/var/log/syslog** file on Debian-based systems), as this file shows you how this device was recognized by the kernel. For example, the following messages appeared when a USB thumb drive was added to the system:

```
[root@OCS ~]# tail /var/log/messages
Nov 10 12:50:15 localhost kernel: scsi10 : SCSI emulation
   for USB Mass Storage devices
Nov 10 12:50:16 localhost kernel: scsi 10:0:0:0: Direct-Access
   Generic  Flash Disk      8.07 PQ: 0 ANSI: 2
Nov 10 12:50:16 localhost kernel: sd 10:0:0:0: Attached
   scsi generic sg8 type 0
Nov 10 12:50:16 localhost kernel: sd 10:0:0:0: [sdg]
   7831552 512-byte logical blocks: (4.00 GB/3.73 GiB)
Nov 10 12:50:16 localhost kernel: sd 10:0:0:0: [sdg]
   Write Protect is off
Nov 10 12:50:16 localhost kernel: sd 10:0:0:0: [sdg]
   Assuming drive cache: write through
Nov 10 12:50:16 localhost kernel: sd 10:0:0:0: [sdg]
   Assuming drive cache: write through
Nov 10 12:50:16 localhost kernel: sdg: sdg1
Nov 10 12:50:16 localhost kernel: sd 10:0:0:0: [sdg]
   Assuming drive cache: write through
Nov 10 12:50:16 localhost kernel: sd 10:0:0:0: [sdg]
   Attached SCSI removable disk
```

By looking at this output, you can determine what type of device was attached (Generic Flash Disk) and what device name it was given ("[sdg]"). So, you can now mount the **/dev/sdg** device and access the data on the USB drive.

Keyboard Mapping

Keyboard mapping is the process of making sure the keys on the keyboard match with the actions you want the keys to take. Use the **xev** command to perform keyboard-mapping operations.

Hardware or Software Compatibility Issues

One question you will often need to answer is whether the current hardware error is a result of an actual hardware issue or is an issue with the software used to access the hardware. There is no hard-and-fast rule to determine the answer, but there are some things you can try to determine the source of the problem, including the following:

- Move the device to another system to see if the problem persists.
- Try another, similar hardware device.
- Reinstall the software.
- Upgrade the hardware drivers.

Commands

This section covers some of the commands that display hardware information.

dmidecode

The **dmidecode** command is used to display a description of hardware components (in the following example, the **head** command was just used to reduce the large amount of output):

```
[root@OCS ~]# dmidecode | head
# dmidecode 3.1
Getting SMBIOS data from sysfs.
SMBIOS 2.5 present.
10 structures occupying 450 bytes.
Table at 0x000E1000.

Handle 0x0000, DMI type 0, 20 bytes
BIOS Information
        Vendor: innotek GmbH
        Version: VirtualBox
```

lshw

The **lshw** command produces a vast amount of information regarding the system hardware, so the output for the following command is limited to just the first ten lines:

```
[root@OCS ~]# lshw | head
student-virtualbox
    description: Computer
    product: VirtualBox
    vendor: innotek GmbH
    version: 1.2
    serial: 0
    width: 64 bits
    capabilities: smbios-2.5 dmi-2.5 vsyscall32
    configuration: family=Virtual Machine
   uuid=DB8F323E-EFB2-4815-880C-86C6E52E5C09
     *-core
```

## CHAPTER 25

Given a scenario, deploy and execute basic BASH scripts

This chapter provides information and commands concerning the following topics:

Shell environments and shell variables

- PATH
- Global
- Local
- export
- env
- set
- printenv
- echo

#!/ bin/bash

Sourcing scripts

Directory and file permissions (chmod)

Extensions

Commenting (#)

File globbing

Shell expansions

- ${}
- $()
- ` `

Redirection and piping

Exit codes

- stderr
- stdin
- stdout

Metacharacters

Positional parameters

Looping constructs

- while
- for
- until

Conditional statements

- if
- case

Escaping characters

Shell Environments and Shell Variables

Shell variables are used to store information. This information is used to modify the behavior of the shell itself or external commands. The following table details some common useful shell variables:

Variable	Description
HOME	The current user's home directory.
ID	The current user's ID.
LOGNAME	The username of the user who logged in to the current session.
OLDPWD	The previous directory location (before the last **cd** command).
PATH	The location where commands are found; see the "PATH" section for more details.
PS1	The primary prompt.
PWD	The current directory.

The **PS1** variable, for example, defines the primary prompt, often using special character sequences (**\u** = current user's name, **\h** = hostname, **\W** = current directory):

```
[student@OCS ~]$ echo $PS1
[\u@\h \W]\$
```

Note that variables are defined without a dollar sign character but are referenced using the dollar sign character:

```
[student@OCS ~]$ PS1="[\u@\h \W \!]\$ "
[student@OCS ~ 93]$ echo $PS1
[\u@\h \W \!]$
```

To see all shell variables, use the **set** command, as demonstrated here:

```
[student@OCS ~ 95]$ set | head -5
ABRT_DEBUG_LOG=/dev/null
AGE=25
BASH=/bin/bash
BASHOPTS=checkwinsize:cmdhist:expand_aliases:extglob:
  extquote:force_fignore:
histappend:interactive_comments:progcomp:promptvars:sourcepath
BASH_ALIASES=()
```

When a variable is initially created, it is only available in the shell where it was created. This variable is referred to as a *local variable*. In some cases, you need to pass a variable into a subprocess. This is done by using the **export** command. See the "export" section in this chapter for additional details.

Note that all variables created in the shell are temporary. To make shell variables permanent (that is, persistent across logins), see the "Profiles" section in Chapter 8, "Given a scenario, manage users and groups."

PATH

Scripts should be located in one of the directories defined by the **$PATH** variable:

```
[root@OCS ~]$ echo $PATH
/usr/local/sbin:/usr/local/bin:/usr/sbin:/usr/bin:/sbin:/bin:
/usr/games:/usr/local/games
```

Often, only the root user will be able to place a file in one of these directories, so regular users can make their own directory and add it to the **$PATH** variable:

```
[bob@OCS ~]$ mkdir /home/bob/bin
[bob@OCS ~]$ PATH="$PATH:/home/bob/bin"
```

Global

See the "Shell Environments and Shell Variables" and "export" sections in this chapter.

Local

See the "Shell Environments and Shell Variables" and "set" sections in this chapter.

export

To convert an existing local variable to an environment variable, use the **export** command:

```
[student@OCS ~]$ echo $NAME
Sarah
[student@OCS ~]$ export NAME
```

If the variable doesn't already exist, the **export** command can create it directly as an environment variable:

```
[student@OCS ~]$ export AGE=25
```

When a variable is converted into an environment variable, all subprocesses will have this variable set. This is useful when you want to change the behavior of a process by modifying a key variable.

For example, the **crontab -e** command allows you to edit your crontab file. To choose the editor that the **crontab** command will use, create and export the **EDITOR** variable: **export EDITOR=gedit**. See Figure 25.1 for a visual example of local versus environment variables.

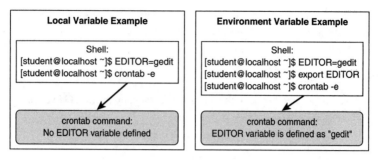

Figure 25.1   Local Versus Environment Variables

The **export** command can also be used to display all environment variables:

```
export -p
```

env

The **env** command displays environment variables in the current shell. Local variables are not displayed when the **env** command is executed.

Another use of the **env** command is to temporarily set a variable for the execution of a command.

Example:

```
[student@OCS ~]# echo $TZ

[student@OCS ~]# date
Thu Dec 1 18:48:26 PST 2016
[student@OCS ~]# env TZ=MST7MDT date
Thu Dec 1 19:48:31 MST 2016
[student@OCS ~]# echo $TZ

[student@OCS ~]#
```

To unset a variable when executing a command, use the **--unset=VAR** option (for example, **env --unset=TZ date**).

set

The **set** command displays all shell variables and values when executed with no arguments. The output also includes any functions that have been declared within the shell.

The **set** command can also be used to modify the behavior of the shell. For example, using an **unset** variable normally results in returning a "null string." Executing the command **set -u** will result in an error message when undefined variables are used, as shown next:

```
[student@OCS ~]$ echo $NOPE

[student@OCS ~]$ set -u
[student@OCS ~]$ echo $NOPE
bash: NOPE: unbound variable
```

The following table provides some additional useful **set** options:

Option	Description
-b	When a background job terminates, report this immediately to the shell. Use **+b** (the default) to have this report occur before the next primary prompt is displayed.
-n	A shell programming feature that reads commands in the script but does not execute the commands. Useful for syntax-error-checking a script.
-u	Issue an error message when an **unset** variable is used.
-C	Does not allow overwriting an existing file when using redirection operators, such as **cmd > file**.

Use the **unset** command to remove a variable from the shell (for example, **unset VAR**).

printenv

Like the **env** command, the **printenv** command is used to display environment variables; however, the **env** command has additional features, whereas the **printenv** command is used solely to display environment variables.

echo

The **echo** command is used to display information. Typically, it is used to display the value of variables.

Example:

```
[student@OCS ~]$ echo $HISTSIZE
1000
```

The **echo** command has only a few options. The most useful one is the **-n** option, which doesn't print a newline character at the end of the output.

There are some special character sequences that can be incorporated within an argument to the **echo** command. For example, the command **echo "hello\nthere"** will send the following output:

```
hello
there
```

The following table describes some useful character sequences for the **echo** command:

Sequence	Description
\a	Ring terminal bell.
\n	Newline character.
\t	Tab character.
\\	A single backslash character.

#!/ bin/bash

The first line of a script should include the path to the interpreter. For BASH shell scripts, this should be the path to the executable **bash** command. This path can be discovered by executing the following command:

```
[root@OCS ~]$ which bash
/bin/bash
```

Add this path to the first line of the script using the following syntax:

```
#!/bin/bash
```

The combination of # (the hash character) and ! (the bang character) forms the shebang sequence. (Say "hash bang" quickly to discover where the term *shebang* comes from; often it will be said with a silent *e*).

Sourcing Scripts

Most commands are executed as separate processes that have their own environment. The **source** command allows you to execute a bash script as if the commands within the script were executed directly on the command line.

Example:

```
[root@OCS ~]$ source ./functions.sh
```

Use the . command to perform the same function as the **source** command, as shown next:

```
[root@OCS ~]$ . ./functions.sh
```

This technique is often used within shell scripts to source code from other shell scripts. For example, a script might need some variables that are declared in another script.

Directory and File Permissions

Scripts should be owned by regular users, not the root user. Running scripts owned by root can result in security issues. If a script is owned by root, it should never have the suid permission set on it because this results in a serious security risk (most modern Linux distributions don't permit suid, root-owned scripts).

After creating a script, you need to add execute permission to run it like a program:

```
chmod a+x script_name
```

chmod

See the "chmod" section in Chapter 15, "Given a scenario, apply or acquire the appropriate user and/or group permissions and ownership."

Extensions

BASH shell scripts should end with a **.sh** extension to indicate the contents of the file contains a BASH shell script. The **.bash** extension is also used, but not as widely.

Other scripting languages should have extensions to indicate the language type:

- Use **.pl** for Perl scripts.
- Use **.py** for Python scripts.
- Use **.tcsh** for TC shell scripts.
- Use **.csh** for C shell scripts.

Commenting

Creating comments in your BASH shell script is important because they help others understand the purpose of the code in the script. This section focuses on how to create comments.

#

Comments are created by starting with a pound sign (#) character and extend to the end of the line. The following demonstrates a comment for an entire line:

```
#Set the count variable:
count = 100
```

The following demonstrates a comment on a line that also contains code:

```
count = 100    #Set the count variable
```

File Globbing

A file glob (also called a *wildcard*) is any character provided on the command line that represents a portion of a filename. The following globs are supported:

Glob	Description
*	Matches zero or more characters in a filename.
?	Matches any single character in a filename.
[ ]	Matches a single character in a filename as long as that character is represented within the [ ] characters.

This example copies all files that end in **.txt**:

```
[student@OCS ~]$ cp *.txt ~
```

The next example will remove all files that are four characters long:

```
[student@OCS ~]$ rm ????
```

To view the file type for all files in the current directory that begin with **a**, **b**, or **c**, execute the following command:

```
[student@OCS ~]$ file [abc]*
```

The preceding command could also be executed as

```
[student@OCS ~]$ file [a-c]*
```

where **a-c** represents a range of characters. This must be a valid range within the ASCII text table. To view this table, execute the following command:

```
[student@OCS ~]$ man ascii
```

Multiple ranges or lists of values are permitted:

```
[student@OCS ~]$ file [a-cg-jz]*
```

By placing a **!** character at the beginning of the range, you specify what characters cannot match. For example, the following command will copy all files in the current directory that don't begin with an **a**, **b**, or **c**:

```
[student@OCS ~]$ cp [!abc]* ~
```

The preceding example also demonstrates that complex patterns can be created using multiple glob characters.

Shell Expansions

The BASH shell treats many characters as "special" and expands them to a different meaning. One example of shell expansion is file globbing (see the "File Globbing" section in this chapter). This section also provides details on other file expansion features.

${}

With the variable expansion BASH feature, you can return a different value. For example, the following will return "Bob" if the **$name** variable isn't set:

```
$ echo "Hello, ${name:-Bob}"
Hello, Bob$
echo "Hello, $name"
Hello,
```

Note that using the preceding syntax doesn't set the variable, but rather uses the provided value for this one situation. To return a value and also set the variable, use the following syntax:

```
$ echo "Hello, ${name:=Bob}"
Hello, Bob
$ echo "Hello, $name"
Hello, Bob
```

There are other variable expansion features. For example, the following syntax will only return the first 24 characters of the variable, resulting in a more "uplifting" statement:

```
$ times="It was the best of times, it was the worst of times."
$ echo ${times: 0:24}
It was the best of times
```

Note that in the preceding example, 0 represents the first character to return and 24 represents the total number of characters to return (starting with character 0).

$()

Command substitution is the process of executing a subcommand within a larger command. This is typically used to gather data and store it in a variable. For example, the following command stores the output of the **date** command in the **$today** variable:

```
today=$(date)
```

Command substitution can be performed by using one of two methods:

- **$(cmd)**
- **'cmd'**

Note that the second method uses backquote characters (also called *backtick* characters), not single-quote characters.

` `

See the "$()" section in this chapter.

Redirection and Piping

See the "Output Redirection" section in Chapter 9, "Given a scenario, create, modify, and redirect files."

Exit Codes

When a command executes, it returns a value of success (0) or failure (>1) to the shell or script from which it was executed. This status is stored in the **$?** variable. Here's an example:

```
[root@OCS ~]$ ls /etc/skel
[root@OCS ~]$ echo $?
0
[root@OCS ~]$ ls /junk
ls: cannot access /junk: No such file or directory
[root@OCS ~]$ echo $?
2
```

This return value can be used in conditional statements to determine if a command exited successfully:

```
some_command
if [ $? -eq 0 ]
then
      echo "command executed successfully"
else
      echo "command failed"
fi
```

See the section in this chapter for additional details.

stderr

See the "stderr" section in Chapter 9.

stdin

See the "stdin" section in Chapter 9.

stdout

See the "stdout" section in Chapter 9.

Metacharacters

Metacharacters are special characters to the BASH shell. For example, file globbing characters (*, [ ], and ?) are considered metacharacters. Additional metacharacters covered in this book include redirection characters (see the "Output Redirection" section in Chapter 9) and the $ character (for variable substitutions).

Positional Parameters

Your script can be run with arguments, like so:

```
./example.sh arg1 arg2 arg3
```

Each of the arguments is stored in $1, $2, $3, and so forth. $0 is the name of the script itself.

The special BASH variable **$#** contains the number of arguments passed to the script.

Looping Constructs

A looping construct is code within a BASH script that performs a set of operations, potentially multiple times. This section exams three commonly used loop constructs: the **while**, **until**, and **for** loops.

while

A **while** loop is designed to perform a set of tasks (commands) as long as a conditional statement returns a value of true. For example, the following code can be used to check user input to verify the correct value is provided:

```
read -p "Enter a zip code: "
while echo $zip | egrep -v "^[0-9]{5}$"
do
    echo "$zip is not a valid ZIP code, try again"
    read -p "Enter a zip code" zip
done
```

Sample output:

```
Enter a zip code: 8888
8888 is not a valid ZIP code, try again
Enter a zip code: huh?
huh? is not a valid ZIP code, try again
Enter a zip code: 92020
```

> **NOTE:** The **read** command reads input from stdin, which is typically the user's keyboard input.

for

A **for** loop is used to iterate over a list of values. For example, the following will execute the **wc -l** command on a list of files:

```
for file in "/etc/r*.conf"
do
    wc -l $file
done
```

Sample output:

```
43 /etc/request-key.conf
 3 /etc/resolv.conf
61 /etc/rsyslog.conf
```

until

The **until** statement works like the **while** statement, but it executes its code set if the conditional statement is false. Compare the pseudocode for the **while** statement to the **until** statement:

```
while conditional_check
do
    #executes if conditional_check returns true
done


until conditional_check
do
    #executes if conditional_check returns false
done
```

Conditional Statements

The **test** statement is used to perform conditional tests. These conditional tests are used to compare values and perform file-testing operations.

A common method of running the **test** statement is to place the operation within square brackets. For example, the following two statements perform the same action:

```
test $name1 = $name2
[ $name1 = $name2 ]
```

The following table describes the common **test** operations:

Operation	Description
str1 = str2	Returns true if two strings are equal to each other.
str1 != str2	Returns true if two strings are not equal to each other.
-z *str*	Returns true if *str* size is zero; for example, [-z $name].
-n *str*	Returns true if *str* size is not zero; for example, [-n $name].
int1 -eq int2	Returns true if two integers are equal to each other.
int1 -ne int2	Returns true if two integers are not equal to each other.
int1 -gt int2	Returns true if the first integer is greater than the second integer.
int1 -ge int2	Returns true if the first integer is greater than or equal to the second integer.

Operation	Description
int1 -lt int2	Returns true if the first integer is less than the second integer.
int1 -le int2	Returns true if the first integer is less than or equal to the second integer.
-d file	Returns true if the file is a directory.
-f file	Returns true if the file is a plain file.
-e file	Returns true if the file exists (regardless of what type of file or directory it is).
-r file	Returns true if the file is readable.
-w file	Returns true if the file is writable.
-x file	Returns true if the file is executable.

if

An **if** statement is used to execute one or more commands based on the outcome of a conditional statement. For example, the following will display "hi" if the **$name** variable is set to "Bob":

```
if [ $name = "Bob" ]
then
    echo "hi"
fi
```

Note that to end the commands executed within an **if** statement, use the **fi** statement ("if" spelled backwards).

An **else** statement is used with an **if** statement to provide an alternative in the event that the condition returns false. Here's an example:

```
if [ $name = "Bob" ]
then
    echo "hi"
else
    echo "I don't know you"
fi
```

Multiple conditional checks can be performed, like so:

```
if [ $name = "Bob" ]
then
    echo "hi, Bob"
elif [ $name = "Sue" ]
then
    echo "hi, Sue"
```

```
else
    echo "I don't know you"
fi
```

See the "Conditional Statements" section in this chapter for additional information on conditional expressions.

case

The **case** statement compares a variable's value to globbing patterns.

Syntax:

```
case $var in
glob 1)
    #statements
    #statements;;
glob 2)
    #statements
    #statements;;
esac
```

Two semicolons (;;) are used to end a set of statements and must be used before the next glob. To end a **case** statement, use **esac** ("case" spelled backward).

Example:

```
case $1 in
 start)
 echo "Starting the process"
 ;;
 stop)
 echo "Stopping the process"
 ;;
 *)
 echo "I need to hear start or stop"
esac
```

Escaping Characters

To escape a character is to have a special character (aka, a metacharacter) treated as a plain character. For example, the following disables the special meaning of the redirection character, using double quotes:

```
$ echo "this | that"
this | that
```

Here are some escaping character essentials:

- Double quotes disable the special meaning of redirection characters (<, >, and |) and globbing characters (*, ?, [, and]).

- Use single quotes to disable all metacharacters, including redirection, globbing, command substitution (the ' ' and $() characters), and variable substitution (the $ character).

- Place a \ character (backslash character) before any metacharacter to make it a plain character for the BASH shell.

## CHAPTER 26

Given a scenario, carry out version control using Git

This chapter provides information and commands concerning the following topics:

Arguments

- clone
- push
- pull
- commit
- merge
- branch
- log
- init
- config

Files

- **.gitignore**
- **.git/**

Arguments

The Linux+ exam will include some questions regarding arguments to the **git** command. This section covers these exam-testable arguments.

clone

The **git clone** command creates a local repository from the contents of a remote repository. The argument provided is the location of the remote repository.

Example:

```
$ git clone https://gitlab.com/borothwell/ocs.git
Cloning into 'ocs'...
Username for 'https://gitlab.com': borothwell
Password for 'https://borothwell@gitlab.com':
remote: Counting objects: 3, done.
remote: Total 3 (delta 0), reused 0 (delta 0)
Unpacking objects: 100% (3/3), done.
Checking connectivity... done.
```

Here are some important options of the **git clone** command:

Option	Description
-v	Be verbose
--single-branch	Only clone a single branch, not the entire repository.

push

The **git commit** command only updates the local repository. To have changes from the local repository sent to the remote repository, use the **git push** command:

```
$ git push -u origin master
Username for 'https://gitlab.com': borothwell
Password for 'https://borothwell@gitlab.com':
Counting objects: 4, done.
Compressing objects: 100% (3/3), done.
Writing objects: 100% (3/3), 370 bytes | 0 bytes/s, done.
Total 3 (delta 0), reused 0 (delta 0)
To https://gitlab.com/borothwell/ocs.git
   12424f5..3b36054  master -> master
Branch master set up to track remote branch master from origin.
```

Note that the last message in the preceding output explains the terms "origin" and "master." "Origin" refers to the remote repository, while "master" refers to the branch that should be updated.

> **NOTE:** The **git push** command will attempt to merge changes into existing files. If this can't be handled automatically, you may have to perform a manual merge operation. See the "merge" section in this chapter for more details.

pull

If changes have been made to remote repository and you want to download these changes into the local repository, use the **git pull** command:

```
$ git pull origin master
```

origin refers to the remote repository, while **master** refers to the branch that should be updated.

> **NOTE:** The **git pull** command will attempt to merge changes into existing files. If this can't be handled automatically, you may have to perform a manual merge operation. See the "merge" section in this chapter for more details.

commit

To have changes made to the working directory placed in the local repository, you first have to add it to the staging area and then you need to commit it to the repository, like so:

```
$ git add first.sh
$ git commit -m "added first.sh"
[master 3b36054] added first.sh
 1 file changed, 5 insertions(+)
 create mode 100644 first.sh
```

The **git add** command will place the file in the staging area. The **git commit** command will take all of the new files in the staging area and commit them to the local repository. The **-m** option is used to add a message (in this case, the reason for the commit was given).

merge

Suppose you create a new branch to add a new feature to a file. After testing out this new feature, you are ready to implement it in the master branch. To do this, you will need to merge the content from the new branch (feature127 branch in the following example) into the master branch. Start by committing all changes in the feature127 branch and then switch back to the master branch:

```
$ git commit -a -m "feature added to showmine.sh"
[feature127 2e5defa] feature added to showmine.sh
 1 file changed, 5 insertions(+), 2 deletions(-)
$ git checkout master
Switched to branch 'master'
Your branch is ahead of 'origin/master' by 3 commits.
  (use "git push" to publish your local commits)
```

You must be in the branch that you want to merge into in order to correctly run the next command. The following **git merge** command will merge the changes from the feature127 branch into the master branch:

```
$ git merge feature127
Updating 4810ca8..2e5defa
Fast-forward
 showmine.sh | 7 +++++--
 1 file changed, 5 insertions(+), 2 deletions(-)
```

This merge process can be more complex. For example, consider the following command's output:

```
$ git merge master
Auto-merging showmine.sh
CONFLICT (content): Merge conflict in showmine.sh
Auto-merging hidden.sh
CONFLICT (content): Merge conflict in hidden.sh
Automatic merge failed; fix conflicts and then commit the result.
```

You can see that the merge was not completed because the automated merge process ran into some conflicts. You can also see these conflicts by executing the **git status** command:

```
$ git status
On branch test
Your branch is ahead of 'origin/test' by 1 commit.
  (use "git push" to publish your local commits)

You have unmerged paths.
  (fix conflicts and run "git commit")

Unmerged paths:
  (use "git add <file>..." to mark resolution)

        both modified:      hidden.sh
        both modified:      showmine.sh

no changes added to commit (use "git add" and/or "git commit -a")
```

One way to handle these conflicts is to use the **git mergetool** command (note that you need to install the git-all package if you want to use the **git mergetool** command):

```
$ git mergetool showmine.sh

This message is displayed because 'merge.tool' is not configured.
See 'git mergetool --tool-help' or 'git help config' for more details.
'git mergetool' will now attempt to use one of the following tools:
opendiff kdiff3 tkdiff xxdiff meld tortoisemerge gvimdiff diffuse
  diffmerge ecmerge p4merge araxis bc3 codecompare emerge vimdiff
Merging:
showmine.sh

Normal merge conflict for 'showmine.sh':
  {local}: modified file
  {remote}: modified file
Hit return to start merge resolution tool (vimdiff):
```

This tool will open the **vimdiff** utility to allow you to make the necessary changes to the file in order to resolve the conflicts.

branch

When you first create a project, the code is associated with a branch called "master." If you want to create a new branch, execute the **git branch** command:

```
$ git branch test
```

This doesn't mean you are suddenly working in the new branch. As you can see from the output of the **git status** command, the **git branch** command doesn't change your current branch:

```
$ git status
On branch master
Your branch is ahead of 'origin/master' by 2 commits.
  (use "git push" to publish your local commits)

nothing to commit, working directory clean
```

The first line of the output of the preceding command, "On branch master," denotes that you are still working in the master branch. To switch to the new branch, execute the **git checkout** command:

```
$ git checkout test
Switched to branch 'test'
```

> **NOTE:**   You can create a branch and switch to it by using the **-b** option to the **git checkout** command: **git checkout -b test**.

Switching actually does two things:

- Makes it so any future commits occur on the test branch
- Makes it so the working directory reflects the test branch

The second item makes more sense with a demonstration. First, observe the following commands, which will end up with a new version of the **hidden.sh** file being placed in the test branch repository:

```
$ git add hidden.sh
$ git commit -m "changed hidden.sh"
[test ef2d7d5] changed hidden.sh
 1 file changed, 1 insertion(+)
```

Note what the file looks like in the current working directory:

```
$ more hidden.sh
#!/bin/bash
#hidden.sh

echo "Listing only hidden files:"
ls -ld .* $1
```

If the project was switched back to the master branch, you can see how the **hidden.sh** file in the working directory is different (note the missing **echo** line, which was added for the test branch only):

```
$ git checkout master
Switched to branch 'master'
Your branch is ahead of 'origin/master' by 2 commits.
  (use "git push" to publish your local commits)
$ more hidden.sh
#!/bin/bash
#hidden.sh

ls -ld .* $1
```

log

You can see the changes made on different branches, along with the comments you provided for each change, by using the **git log** command:

```
$ git log --oneline --decorate --all
ef2d7d5 (test) changed hidden.sh
2b44792 (HEAD, master) deleting test.sh file
19198d7 update 27
07bb91c (origin/master, origin/HEAD) adding showmine.sh
  and hidden.sh
75d717b added first.sh
9eb721e demonstrating status
3b36054 added first.sh
12424f5 add README
```

The **--oneline** option has the **git log** command provide a one-line summary of each change. The **--decorate** option requests additional information such as the branch name. The **--all** option asks to see the log for all branches, not just the current branch.

init

To create a new repository in the current local directory, use the **git init** command:

```
$ git init test
Initialized empty Git repository in /tmp/test/.git/
```

config

The **git config** command is used to configure the **git** utility. Here are some commonly used options:

```
$ git config --global user.name "Bo Rothwell"
$ git config --global user.email bo@onecoursesource.com
```

The **--global** option results in configuration options being stored in a configuration file in the user's home directory, as shown here:

```
$ more ~/.gitconfig
[user]
        name = Bo Rothwell
        email = bo@onecoursesource.com
```

The **git** command will use the settings in this file by default. You can also store these settings in the current repository directory (the **.git** directory under the current directory) by using the **--local** option. Local settings override global settings.

There are dozens of additional settings, but most users of the **git** command will just set **user.name** and **user.email**.

Files

The Linux+ exam will include some questions regarding files that affect the behavior of the **git** command. This section covers these exam-testable files.

.gitignore

To have **git** commands ignore a file, create a file named **.gitignore** in the working directory and place the filename to ignore inside of this file. Here is an example:

```
$ touch notes
~/ocs$ git status -s
?? notes
$ vi .gitignore        #added notes as shown below:
$ cat .gitignore
notes
$ git status -s
?? .gitignore
```

Notice that the **.gitignore** file itself must also be placed in the **.gitignore** file:

```
$ git status -s
?? .gitignore
$ vi .gitignore        #added .gitignore as shown below:
$ cat .gitignore
notes
.gitignore
$ git status -s
```

NOTE: You can also use wildcard characters (*, ?, and [*range*]) in the **.gitignore** file to match a collection of files.

.git/

Local repository data is stored under the **.git** directory under the directory the **git** command created. For example, consider the following command:

```
$ git init test
Initialized empty Git repository in /tmp/test/.git/
```

This command was executed in the **/tmp** directory and created a local repository directory of **/tmp/test**. The repository data is actually stored in the **/tmp/test/.git** directory:

```
$ ls /tmp/test/.git
branches   config   description   HEAD   hooks   info   objects   refs
```

The **.git** directory should not be modified directly. This directory contains a collection of databases that contain all the files and versions for the git repository.

CHAPTER 27

Summarize orchestration processes and concepts

This chapter provides information and commands concerning the following topics:

- **Agent**
- **Agentless**
- **Procedures**
- **Attributes**
- **Infrastructure automation**
- **Infrastructure as code**
- **Inventory**
- **Automated configuration management**
- **Build automation**

NOTE: For the Linux+ certification exam, it is important to note that for the topics listed as objectives, you are supposed to be able to "**summarize** orchestration processes and concepts." In other words, you aren't expected to know details regarding setting up, configuring, and administering orchestration processes; rather, you should understand what the function of the orchestration is.

Agent

The purpose of orchestration is to simplify complex setup tasks. Often, setting up software or a service requires multiple steps, and sometimes these steps need to be performed on multiple systems. With orchestration, these steps are planned out in advance and performed automatically, either by running a single command or pressing a button on a GUI or web-based interface.

Often a component of orchestration is *monitoring*. Monitoring is used to determine if an action needs to take place due to something that has happened on a system. There are two types of monitoring: agent and agentless.

An *agent* monitoring solution means that some software piece has been installed on the system or component that is being monitored. This agent actively probes the system, determining based on these probes if changes have been made that require an action.

An *agentless* monitoring solution means that no software has been installed on the system. An agentless system may either receive data from the system or conduct remote queries to determine if a change has taken place.

Agentless

See "Agent" in this chapter.

Procedures

A *procedure* for orchestration is the collection of steps that need to take place to complete the action. A procedure can be a fairly straightforward collection of steps, or it can be very complex and tied to the values of attributes.

Attributes

An *attribute* is used to define parameters that are used to customize the automation procedure. These attributes contain data that can (and likely will) be different for each orchestration process. For example, suppose the procedure is designed to set up a system that requires access to the network. Attributes would need to be defined for things like the system's IP address, subnet mask, gateway, and router.

Infrastructure Automation

Infrastructure automation is a component of orchestration. While many people use the terms *orchestration* and *automation* interchangeably, there is a difference between the two. You can certainly have orchestration without automation, but often a primary goal of orchestration is to automate the process.

Consider the following orchestration scenario: A user fills in fields of data in a web-based form. The data is used to populate attributes (see "Attributes" in this chapter). The user then clicks an "OK" button, and a procedure (see "Procedures" in this chapter) is performed to orchestrate a service. This is orchestration without automation.

Now consider this scenario: An agent is monitoring a system when a threshold is reached (say, maximum CPU usage in an hour). This triggers a procedure using attributes that are populated automatically from a database to spawn a second instance of the services. No human interaction took place; the orchestration process handed everything automatically. This is orchestration with automation.

Infrastructure as Code

Infrastructure as Code (also referred to as IaC) is the heart of the orchestration process. Instead of manually configuring or provisioning systems, IaC makes use of software tools (orchestration products) to perform these tasks.

Inventory

When something is orchestrated, the orchestration software needs to keep track of it. Often the "something" is referred to as an *instance*, and the information regarding this instance is stored in a database called an *inventory*.

Automated Configuration Management

Configuration management has long been a standard process that system administrators have manually handled. Because it was not automated, this process was often time-consuming and resulted in misconfigured systems.

The purpose of automated configuration management is to ensure that software, services, and systems are maintained in a consistent, predictable state. By using automated configuration management tools, a large amount of the workload is handled by automated processes. This also results in fewer errors when compared to manual configuration management operations.

Common configuration management tools include the following:

- Chef
- Puppet
- Ansible

Build Automation

A build (also called a software build) is when new source code is built into executable code, typically through a process called compiling. This can be a tedious process and subject to errors when performed manually, as there can be many complex steps in building large programs.

Build automation makes use of a utility that follows a set of rules to automate the software build process. When configured correctly, build automation can speed up the build process as well as reduce errors that occur when this process is performed manually.

Here are some common build automation tools:

- Make
- Ant
- Gradle
- Rake
- Cake

Create Your Own Journal

Index

E

G

H

W

X

Y

Z

To receive your 10% off Exam Voucher, register your product at:

www.pearsonitcertification.com/register

and follow the instructions.